The Philosophy of Forgiveness - Volume II
New Dimensions of Forgiveness

Edited by
Court D. Lewis
Owensboro Community & Technical College

Authors

Mariano Crespo
Instituto Cultura y Sociedad, Universidad de Navarra

Elisabetta Bertolino
Private International Law, University of Palermo

Kathleen Poorman Dougherty
Mount Mary University

Joshua M. Hall
Emory University, Oxford College

A.G. Holdier
Colorado Technical University

Leonard Kahn
Loyola University New Orleans

Frederik Kaufman
Ithaca College

Jeff Lambert
Duquesne University

John McClellan
Carson-Newman University

Ryan Michael Murphy
Southwest Colorado Community College

Zachary Thomas Settle
Vanderbilt University

Adrian Switzer
University of Missouri Kansas City

Vernon Series in Philosophy of Forgiveness

Copyright © 2017 Vernon Press, an imprint of Vernon Art and Science Inc, on behalf of the author.

All rights reserved. No part of this publication may be reproduced, stored in a retrieval system, or transmitted in any form or by any means, electronic, mechanical, photocopying, recording, or otherwise, without the prior permission of Vernon Art and Ascience Inc.

www.vernonpress.com

In the Americas:
Vernon Press
1000 N West Street,
Suite 1200, Wilmington,
Delaware 19801
United States

In the rest of the world:
Vernon Press
C/Sancti Espiritu 17,
Malaga, 29006
Spain

Vernon Series in Philosophy of Forgiveness

Library of Congress Control Number: 2016947127

ISBN: 978-1-62273-212-8

Product and company names mentioned in this work are the trademarks of their respective owners. While every care has been taken in preparing this work, neither the authors nor Vernon Art and Science Inc. may be held responsible for any loss or damage caused or alleged to be caused directly or indirectly by the information contained in it.

Table of Contents

Contributors   *vii*

Introduction New Dimensions of Forgiveness   *ix*
Court D. Lewis

Chapter 1   Third-Party Forgiveness   15
Leonard Kahn

Chapter 2   The Heart of the Matter: Forgiveness as an Aesthetic Process   47
A.G. Holdier

Chapter 3   Forgiveness and Warranted Resentment   71
Frederik Kaufman

Chapter 4   Responsibility and Self-Forgiveness in *The Story of Lucy Gault*   87
Kathleen Poorman Dougherty

Chapter 5   Forgiveness and Time: Attitudes, Dispositions, and Philosophical Charity   109
Ryan Michael Murphy

Chapter 6   Betrayal, Forgiveness, and Trusting Again   141
John McClellan

Chapter 7   The Asymmetry of Forgiveness   161
Mariano Crespo

Chapter 8   Forgiveness, One's Voice, and the Law   187
Elisabetta Bertolino

Chapter 9   Twixt Mages and Monsters: Arendt on the Dark Art of Forgiveness   215
Joshua M. Hall

Chapter 10   Im/possible Forgiveness: Derrida on Cosmopolitan Hospitality   241
Adrian Switzer

Chapter 11   Indeterminable Forgiveness: Economic Madness and The Possibility of an Impossible Task   267
Zachary Thomas Settle

Chapter 12   Absolute Forgiveness: Material Intimacy and Recognition in Hegel   289
Jeff Lambert

Index   *317*

Contributors

Mariano Crespo obtained his Ph.D. in Philosophy at the Complutense University in Madrid (Spain). He has been Professor at the San Damaso University and at he Francisco de Vitoria University, both in Madrid. From 1995 to 2004 he was Assistant and then Associated Professor at the International Academy of Philosophy in the Principality of Liechtenstein. From 2005 till 2013 he was Associated Professor at the Philosophy Department of Catholic University from Chile. Since 2013 he is Research Fellow of the Group "Emotional Culture and Identity" of the Institute Culture and Societ (ICS) of the University of Navarra. He has also been Visiting Scholar at the Husserl Archives of the Catholic University of Leuven (Belgium) and at the Phenomenology Research Center of the Southern Illinois University (USA). He is the author of the books *Das Verzeihen. Eine philosophische Untersuchung* (2002), *El valor ético de la afectividad. Estudios de ética fenomenológica* (2012) and with U. Ferrer, *Die Person im Kontext von Moral und Sozialität. Studien zur frühen phänomenologischen Ethik* (2016). He has also edited the fourth edition of Alexander Pfänder's *Logik* and the volume *Menschenwürde. Metaphysik und Ethik*. He has published several papers on ontological, epistemological and ethical topics, most of them from a phenomenological standpoint.

Elisabetta Bertolino holds a Doctorate of Philosophy in Law/Legal Theory from Birkbeck College—University of London. She has also completed other studies in Human Rights, English Common Law, and Philosophy and Literature. Her research focuses on one's voice and its potentiality for resistance against constituted and sovereign forms of power. She has published in particular an interview with Adriana Cavarero (*differences* 2008) and is currently working on a book on one's voice in relation to law and politics. Elisabetta currently teaches at DEMS - Interdisciplinary Department, University of Palermo, Italy.

Kathleen Poorman Dougherty has a Ph.D. in Philosophy from the University of Oklahoma. She has held numerous faculty positions, and currently serves as Dean of the School of Humanities, Social Sciences & Education at Mount Mary University. Her scholarly work focuses on the development of moral character, the role of self-knowledge in good character, and the role of personal relationships both for increasing self-knowledge and for fostering the development of good character. In addressing these issues she frequently considers literary texts hand in hand with traditional philosophical texts, because literature allows us the privilege of seeing not only the external life but also the internal life of a character.

Joshua M. Hall is currently Visiting Assistant Professor of Philosophy at Emory University, Oxford College. His research focuses various historical and geographical lenses on philosophy's boundaries, particularly the intersection of aesthetics, psychology and social justice. This includes a critically-acclaimed coedited anthology (*Philosophy Imprisoned*), over two dozen peer-reviewed journal articles (including in *Philosophy and Literature* and *Journal of Aesthetic Education*), and eight anthology chapters (including *Philosophical Perspectives on the Devil*). His related work in the arts includes one chapbook collection and sixty-five individual poems in literary journals internationally (including multiple Pushcart Prize-winners *Ibbetson St. Magazine*, *Main Street Rag*, and *Shampoo*), as well as over twenty years' experience as a dancer and choreographer.

A.G. Holdier is teacher and Program Director for Southern Idaho's Minidoka Christian Education Association, as well as an ethics instructor for Colorado Technical University. His work on the intersection of aesthetics, ethics, and religion has been published in *The Journal of Agricultural and Environmental Ethics*, *The Journal for Cultural and Religious Theory*, and volumes from publishers such as Lexington

Press and Palgrave Macmillan. The development of his *phronesis* is still undergoing considerable emplotment.

Leonard Kahn is an Assistant Professor in the Department of Philosophy at Loyola University New Orleans. He is the editor of *Mill on Justice* (Palgrave 2012) and of *John Stuart Mill's "On Liberty"* (Broadview 2015). He is also the co-editor of *Consequentialism and Environmental Ethics* (Routledge 2013). He has published articles in *Philosophical Studies*, *The Journal of Moral Philosophy*, *Ethical Theory & Moral Practice*, and *Ethics, Policy, & Environment*, as well as chapters in books published by Brill, Oxford University Press, Palgrave, and Routledge.

Frederik Kaufman is Professor in the Department of Philosophy and Religion at Ithaca College. He works primarily in moral philosophy and has published on war, death, animals, and environmental philosophy.

Jeff Lambert is a Ph.D. candidate at Duquesne University. His philosophical interests are primarily centered on Modern Philosophy (particularly late Leibniz) but he is also interested in Contemporary Continental Philosophy, Feminist Philosophy, and Critical Race Theory. His research is particularly focused on exploring and developing questions regarding the Philosophy of Intimacy. His dissertation investigates a form of intimacy within Leibniz's system of monads, by examining Leibniz's concept of the "vinculum substantiale."

John McClellan is currently Assistant Professor of Philosophy at Carson-Newman University in Jefferson City, TN. He received his Ph.D. in philosophy from the University of Tennessee, Knoxville in 2013 and a B.A. in philosophy from the University of North Carolina at Greensboro in 2004. His primary scholarly interests are in Philosophy of Religion.

Ryan Michael Murphy teaches philosophy at Southwest Colorado Community College and works in the Registrar's Office at Fort Lewis College, both in Durango, Colorado. He completed his M.A. in Philosophy at San Francisco State University. His primary philosophical interests include ethics; social and political philosophy; Buddhist philosophy; and questions concerning agency, action, and responsibility. His past works address desire-satisfaction and wellbeing, Plato's *Phaedrus* and the rhetoric of writing, and the distribution of higher education as a social good. In his free time, Ryan enjoys running, cooking with family and friends, and gardening.

Zachary Thomas Settle is currently a Ph.D. student in the Graduate Department of Religion at Vanderbilt, where he works in the areas of theology and political economy. He is the theology editor of *The Other Journal,* and has written for numerous publications, including the *Journal of Cultural and Religious Theory* and *The Other Journal.* He is also the co-editor, alongside Dr. Taylor Worley, of a volume on theology, phenomenology, and film, entitled *Dreams, Doubt, and Dread: The Spiritual in Film* (Cascade, 2016).

Adrian Switzer, Ph.D. is an Associate Professor in the Department of Philosophy at the University of Missouri Kansas City (UMKC) where he specializes in Kant and post-Kantian Continental Philosophy. Co-translator of books on Parmenides and Kant, and author of numerous journal articles and book chapters on such figures as Kant, Nietzsche, Foucault, Deleuze, Merleau-Ponty, Jean-Luc Nancy and Luce Irigaray, Dr. Switzer is currently completing a manuscript on the aesthetics and politics of the student protests in Paris in May 1968.

Introduction
New Dimensions of Forgiveness

Court D. Lewis

Volume II of Vernon Press's series on the Philosophy of Forgiveness is named *New Dimensions of Forgiveness* for a specific reason—each chapter contained within seeks either to develop and explain a conception of forgiveness in a new way, or to offer a unique explanation of how to conceptualize and make sense of forgiveness. Together, they break new ground, support new conclusions and understandings, and illuminate new conceptual spheres of forgiveness.

Like Volume I's *Explorations of Forgiveness*, my goal with Volume II is to stay out of the way and let each author make the strongest case possible for her or his respective position. To reiterate, it is my hope that this series will create dialogue, both within philosophy but also between philosophy and other fields of study. Specialization is valuable because it allows researchers the opportunity to become experts in a particular field, offering insights that might otherwise go unnoticed by novices. However, specialization can also create barriers that hinder dialogue, which then prevent the full-understanding of an issue or topic. It is sometimes good to push the boundaries of research, especially if one is motivated to both create a rich intra- and inter-disciplinary dialogue and foster a more complete understand of the topic. For, it is only by stepping back and looking at a problem from new and different perspectives that we are sometimes able to see the previously unnoticed solution.

With that said, this is a book of philosophical writings that range from contemporary forgiveness research and literature, to Jacques Derrida, Emmanuel Levinas, and G.W.F. Hegel. So, no matter the reader's research interests, there is a contribution that she or he will find valuable. In terms of organization, instead of breaking the volume into several sections, chapters are organized in such a way as to create a series of dialogues, with some level of overlap between each chapter. The following will provide a brief overview of each chapter, detailing key features of each.

The book opens with Leonard Kahn's chapter "Third-Party Forgiveness," in which he presents a case against the possibility of third-party forgiveness. Using two recent terror attacks as focal points of discussion, Kahn examines the "standard account" of forgiveness, the relationship between acts of forgiveness and speech-acts, and delineates the limits of a legitimate standing to forgive. More specifically, Kahn investigates the moral standing of a third-party bystander, who has no close moral connection to the victim(s), yet attempts to forgive the wrongdoer. Kahn puts forward a series of compelling arguments to show that not only would such an example not meet the requirements of forgiveness, but neither would examples involving more intimate relationships. He ends his chapter by showing how accepting third-party forgiveness as a legitimate type of forgiveness only serves to devalue 'forgiveness' as a moral term.

One of the interesting features of Kahn's chapter is the role of emotional feelings within the act and speech-acts of forgiveness, and Chapter 2 focuses specifically on these emotional states. In "The Heart of the Matter: Forgiveness as an Aesthetic Process," A.G. Holdier explores the aesthetic components of forgiveness, and argues that in order to fully-understand "real-world" forgiveness, we must understand the emotional affective states that inform the "phenomenological process that negotiates our cognitive judgments regarding forgiveness." So, instead of focusing on epistemic or moral concerns, he expands the scope of the discussion into the periphery of the philosophical conversation, in order to build a philosophical structure around the everyday experience of forgiveness as a peace-seeking enterprise.

Unlike Holdier's emphasis on the aesthetic process of forgiveness, in "Forgiveness and Warranted Resentment," Frederik Kaufman stress the epistemic concerns of forgiveness regarding the nature of reason-giving and warranted resentment. Kaufman worries that if apology makes warranted resentment unwarranted (as he suggests many contemporary writers maintain), then forgiveness loses its elective nature. Opposed to such a conclusion, Kaufman examines the nature of moral deliberation and reason-giving to argue that forgiveness should remain elective and be marked by victims relinquishing *warranted* resentment, not unwarranted resentment.

Tying together the emotional and epistemic themes of the previous two chapters, Kathleen Poorman Dougherty's "Responsibility and Self-Forgiveness in *The Story of Lucy Gault*" inspects William Trevor's novel *The Story of Lucy Gault* for insights into the nature of self-forgiveness. Dougherty argues that the novel prompts us to reconsider the kinds of actions thought to make self-forgiveness morally challenging, showing that self-forgiveness can be extremely difficult, even in morally neutral cases. Second, it encourages us to reflect upon the dependence of self-forgiveness on interpersonal forgiveness, demonstrating that self-forgiveness must sometimes function independently of other-forgiveness. Finally, it challenges our understanding of the relationship between responsibility and forgiveness. Dougherty's inspection of the novel raises some intriguing and difficult questions about responsibility, ignorance, personal identity, and how these influence the nature of self-forgiveness in tragic ways that are sometimes inconsistent with human flourishing.

Chapter 6 features Ryan Michael Murphy's "Forgiveness and Time: Attitudes, Dispositions, and Philosophical Charity." Murphy investigates the possibility of future-oriented *forgivingness*—attitudinal dispositions that make it more likely for agents to forgive in cases of wrongdoing that *might* occur in the future. Moving beyond mere attitudinal dispositions, in this thought-provoking chapter Murphy provides valuable insights into the temporal nature of forgiveness and its role in illuminating a new way to consider the moral dimensions of philosophical methodology.

Though conceptual in nature, Murphy's chapter is concerned with the pragmatic outcomes of forgiveness, which is also the focus of John McClellan's "Trusting Again." McClellan examines the nature of forgiveness and how it relates to trust. By examining cases of infidelity, and the common desire of victims to forgive their betrayers, McClellan argues that trusting again can be epistemically justifiable, even if a victim's trust is not based on a well-grounded set of reasons that support the betrayer's *future* trustworthiness. Realizing the difficulty of such a position, McClellan's underlying goal is to illustrate a possible irreconcilable tension between epistemic norms and an admirable form of relational forgiveness.

In "The Asymmetry of Forgiveness," Mariano Crespo examines the asymmetrical relationship between forgiveness's "settling of debts" and its resulting postivie attitudes toward the wrongdoer, in order to offer insights into both the metaphysics of being a person and a general theory of action. By examining the metaphysical nature of the forgiver's and wrongdoer's moral life as it relates to forgiveness, Crespo emphasizes the voice of the victim. This shift in emphasis paves the way for Elisabetta Bertolino's chapter, "Forgiveness, One's Voice and the Law."

Bertolino analyzes two different voices of forgiveness: the voice of individuals and the voice of institutionalized legal systems. The former illustrates the uniqueness and vulnerability of individuals, while the latter illustrates an institutionalized logic of exchange. Bertolino argues that the legal voice creates a logic of exchange where resentful institutions are only interested in the conditions associated with wrongdoing, such as punishment. For Bertolino, the voice of individuals resist this legal approach to forgiveness, and by foster the individual voice, we foster the creation of a space for an inner-forgiveness that transcends the voice of legal institutions and retribution.

Continuing the focus on how forgiveness affects and manifests within individuals, Joshua M. Hall's "Twixt Mages and Monsters: Arendt on the Dark Art of Forgiveness" discusses the "magical" nature of forgiveness. Couched in Hannah Arendt's understanding of personal subjectivity and forgiveness, Hall offers a strategic new interpretation of Arendt, one that maintains we should understand seemingly unforgivable acts as merely a failure of imagination. Hall argues that we should interpret Arendt as suggesting we expand our imaginative powers to see "unforgivable" wrongdoers as insufficiently unimaginative, which allows us to reimagine them as beings whom we are willing and able to forgive. To support this conclusion, Hall provides a provocative reading of Arendt that couches her use of "mental imagery" in terms of a type of mental "magic." In the end, the inability to forgive is an inability to use one's mind to "magically" reimagine the world.

Since the focus of Hall's chapter is on the unforgivable, it is appropriate to be followed by Adrian Switzer's "Im/possible Forgiveness: Derrida on Cosmopolitan Hospitality." Switzer's chapter focuses on Jacques Derrida's *On Cosmopolitanism and Forgiveness*, and examines the relationship between im/possible forgiveness and current global cosmopolitan issues. More specifically, he uses a narrative-style approach centered on the real-life death of Aylan Kurdi, a three-year-old Syrian refugee found dead on the shore of Bodrum, Turkey, to show that the sovereign right of forgiveness illustrates that we are all refugees deserving of moral respect. According to Switzer, Kant's Cosmopolitanism shows that we are all citizens of the Earth, and when coupled with the im/possibility of forgiveness, there is an unconditional demand to extend hospitality (i.e. forgiveness) to all those in need.

Zachary Thomas Settle's "Indeterminable Forgiveness: Economic Madness and The Possibility of an Impossible

Task" continues our examination of Derrida by providing an in-depth analysis of Derrida's position that "pure" forgiveness is the possibility of the impossible. Settle brings clarity to Derrida's examination of the required absolute encounter between the Self and the Other, showing that Derrida's "forgiveness" is marked by hospitality and justice, which opens itself up to an unforeseen possibility of the impossible (i.e. forgiveness), a process perpetually underway and never complete.

The volume concludes with Jeff Lambert's examination of forgiveness in G.W.F. Hegel's *Phenomenology of Spirit*. Lambert's "Absolute Forgiveness, Material Intimacy and Recognition in Hegel" provides a detailed argument for how best to understand the crucial moment of forgiveness in Hegel's text. According to Lambert, the initial moment of forgiveness is deficient because it lacks recognition of the intimacy between Substance and Subject, which runs counter to the interpretations offered by Catherine Malabou and John Russon. Since the initial moment of forgiveness only involves Subject, the Spirit's journey towards the recognition of Substance must continue. By providing a careful analysis of Hegel's *Phenomenology of Spirit*, Lambert shows that the moment of Substantial recognition associated with forgiveness does not occur until the final section, "Absolute Knowing."

As you can tell from this brief summary, there is a lot of conceptual ground to be covered. It has been a pleasure to work on this volume, and I would like to thank the contributing authors for their willingness to push themselves and readers in new directions. With that said, I will leave you to your explorations.

Chapter 1

Third-Party Forgiveness

Leonard Kahn

It is surely better to pardon too much, than to condemn too much.

—George Eliot, *Middlemarch*

She dare not forgive him! Let her forgive him for herself, if she will, let her forgive the torturer for the immeasurable suffering of her mother's heart. But the sufferings of her tortured child she has no right to forgive; she dare not forgive the torturer, even if the child were to forgive him! And if that is so, if they dare not forgive, what becomes of harmony? Is there in the whole world a being who would have the right to forgive and could forgive?

—Fyodor Dostoevsky, *The Brothers Karamazov*

I. Introduction

On Friday, November 13, 2015 a sequence of coordinated terrorist attacks were carried out in Paris, France. The terrorists killed 130 victims and injured over 350 more. One of those killed was Anne-Laure Arruebo, a thirty-six year-old customs inspector who was sitting at one of the cafés that came under assault. Fabien Clain immediately claimed responsibility for the attacks on behalf of the Islamic State of Iraq and Syria (ISIS). It had been less than a year since ISIS had taken credit for the 17 killings at the office of *Charlie Hebdo* in Paris.

I vividly remember learning of the November 13 attack. I had spent the day driving, without the benefit of a radio, across Louisiana and Texas. When I stopped for dinner I was given a full accounting of what had happened. I felt sympathy for the victims, but more importantly for the purposes of this chapter, I also felt a series of closely related emotions toward the terrorists: blame, disgust, indignation, resentment, and even hatred. I was hardly alone. International organizations from the African Union, through NATO, to the United Nations were quick to condemn the terrorists and their deeds. The governments of nations from Afghanistan to Zimbabwe issued statements denouncing both the attack and the attackers. Similar reactions from private individuals and public figures were overwhelmingly on display on social media sites such as Facebook and Twitter.

Yet suppose that, after initially reacting in this way to the November 13 attackers, I reflected for a few moments and then told my dinner companions in Texas that I forgave the terrorists. I forgave, for example, Mr. Clain, who claimed to rejoice in the killing of unarmed and helpless civilians, and that I forgave whichever of the terrorists killed Ms. Arruebo as she was quietly enjoying herself at a café. Let us call the general type of action in question "third-party forgiveness," and let us say that:

> *Agent A engages in third-party forgiveness toward Agent B for doing action F to agent C if and only if (1) A forgives B for doing F to C and (2) A is an unrelated third-party with regard to B and C.*

The purpose of this chapter is to make progress with the question of whether third-party forgiveness is possible. Many thoughtful people have suggested to me that it is not, and a number of philosophers have sided with them.[1] With appropriate qualifications, I side with these skeptics of third-party forgiveness. But before explaining why I do so, however, it will be necessary to lay some groundwork. In Section 2, I outline the standard account of forgiveness. In Section 3, I describe the relationship between the act of forgiveness and speech acts. In Sections 4, 5, and 6 I delineate the limits of standing to forgive. I conclude in Section 7 by raising some general questions about the importance of forgiveness.

II. Forgiveness—the standard account

What is forgiveness? We owe the most influential answer of the past few decades to Joseph Butler, by way of Jeffrie Murphy:

> *Forgiveness, Bishop Butler teaches, is the forswearing of resentment—the resolute overcoming of the anger and hatred that are naturally directed toward a person who has done an unjustified and non-excused moral injury. (Murphy and Hampton 1988, 15)*

I shall call this "the standard account of forgiveness." There is, of course, much to unpack here, and I shall get to that task in a moment. But let me first make clear that my intention in this chapter is to advance and to use a philosophically profitable understanding of forgiveness. I will not attempt to offer a scholarly exegesis of either Butler's or Murphy's thought,

---

[1] See, Swinburne (1989).

though I happily borrow from them when they say something helpful—as they often do. Moreover, I will not offer a detailed defense of the standard account of forgiveness. Such a defense would be worth making, but it is a task for another time. In the rest of this section, I focus on three major expository points about the standard account.

First, let me disambiguate two senses of the word 'resentment' and explain which of these is most relevant for the purposes of this chapter. On the one hand, it is possible to speak of resentment in a quite narrow sense in which this emotion is distinct from other attitudes such as indignation, schadenfreude, outrage, and blame.[2] On the other hand, one can speak of resentment as denoting an entire range of emotions, including not only indignation, outrage, and blame but also anger, hatred, and even the narrow sense of resentment just mentioned.[3] It seems clear enough that the standard account is best understood as the forswearing and overcoming of resentment in the broad sense, rather than merely in the narrow sense of the term. Hence, one can forgive another, on the standard account, by forswearing and overcoming, e.g., anger or outrage, not just resentment in the narrow sense. Of course, using the term "resentment" to refer to a somewhat indeterminate grouping of emotions introduces some problems. In particular, doing so makes difficult—if not impossible—to say of at least some purported cases of forgiveness that they are actual cases of forgiveness or not.

---

[2] See, Feather and Sherman (2002) and Kahn (2011a).

[3] See Gibbard (1990, 42). Murphy (2002, 16) sometimes calls these "the vindictive passions," though he appears to be the only one who uses this terminology, with the exception of Jeremy Bentham (1838, 512). Call them what you will, these emotions fall into the category that Peter Strawson (1962) famously called the "participant reactive attitudes," our attitudinal reactions to other persons *qua* persons. On the centrality of these emotions to forgiveness, see Enright, et al. (1998) and Kahn (2011b).

However, folk psychological terms are often quite vague,[4] as is the term "forgiveness" itself. The standard account would appear somewhat artificial if it did not reflect these facts. So this problem need not detain us.

Second, let me address another point regarding the standard account—namely, its blurring of the distinction between attempting to forgive and completing acts of forgiveness. Attempting to forgive most closely corresponds to "the forswearing of resentment," while the latter more resembles the "overcoming of the anger and hatred" of which Murphy speaks. While attempting to forgive is for the most part under our direct control, what follows this forswearing need not be. One can forswear chocolate for Lent or sex for Ramadan, but it does not follow that one will, in fact, abstain from eating chocolate or from having sex, since the human will is far from perfect. Likewise, one might try to forgive but be unable to do so. That is to say, one might forswear resentment against a student who cheated on her midterm or a referee who rejected one's article because of a misplaced comma and yet be unable to overcome resentment toward these individuals.

In fact, these phenomena are well explained by the standard account of forgiveness, provided that the emotions that fall under the heading "resentment" are judgment-sensitive attitudes. As T.M. Scanlon puts the matter:

> *These are attitudes that an ideally rational person would come to have whenever that person judged there to be sufficient reasons for them and that would, in an ideally rational person, 'extinguish' when that person*

---

[4] On the vagueness of the terms of folk psychology, see, e.g., Stich (1993, 98).

> *judged them not to be supported by reasons of the appropriate kind. (1988, 18)*[5]

For an ideally rational agent, in Scanlon's sense of the expression, to judge that one has sufficient reason to feel admiration toward another and to feel admiration toward that person are *almost* the same thing. One's admiration simply tracks one's judgments about one's reasons to admire. In a similar vein, for an ideally rational agent forswearing resentment and overcoming resentment would be all but indistinguishable. Yet those of us who fall short of the rational ideal can forswear resentment (i.e., attempt to forgive) but fail to overcome resentment (i.e., completing the act of forgiveness). Indeed, as Marietta Jaeger cheekily put it, "forgiveness is not for wimps…it is hard work" (12). And, since most of us are far from ideally rational agents, it makes sense to distinguish carefully between trying to forgive and completing an act of forgiveness. A final point about fleshing out the standard account of forgiveness with reference to judgment-sensitive attitudes needs to be made here. Something counts as a judgment-sensitive attitude because, as Scanlon puts the matter, it is sensitive to judgments about reasons for having that attitude. So a proponent of the standard account must understand attempting to forgive as not only forswearing resentment but also as judging that he/she has sufficient reason to do so. This complication raises a host of intriguing questions, but they are not germane to the topic at hand, so I leave them for another time. Moreover, in order to avoid prolixity in what follows I only tease apart the judgment that there is sufficient reason to forswear resentment and the actual forswearing of resentment only when doing so is necessary.

---

[5] See also Smith (2005), Levy (2005), and Kahn (2011b).

Third, successful forgiveness involves not just the conjunction of forswearing resentment and overcoming resentment; it involves a causal connection between these two events. In other words, in order to count as having forgiven, say, the person who burgled my home, I must overcome my feeling of resentment toward him/her precisely *because* I have forsworn these feelings. So that we can see clearly why there needs to be this causal connection, let us imagine two cases in which it is lacking. First, suppose that on Monday I forswear resentment toward the burglar, but my feelings of resentment toward him/her remain. Then on Tuesday a stranger gives me, without my knowledge, a drug that makes it permanently impossible for me to feel resentment. I have forsworn resentment, and I have overcome resentment, but I have *not* successfully forgiven the burglar.[6] None of this is to say that in order to forgive, one's attempt to forgive needs to be the *only* cause of overcoming resentment. I might forgive someone with help in the form of spiritual guidance or psychotherapy. I might take medication that prevents me from being as anxious as I currently am in order to get a better perspective on the wrong done to me. I might even consult a philosopher, if I were sufficiently desperate. Perhaps the best that we can say is that in order to count as successfully forgiving the burglar, my forswearing resentment toward the burglar must be a direct cause of my overcoming resentment toward the burglar. To go any farther than that generalization is unnecessary here.

---

[6] Does the term 'overcome' in the phrase "overcome resentment" already presuppose a causal connection with one's agency? It's not unreasonable to think so, but I think the weight of the evidence suggests otherwise. One can, after all, correctly be said to overcome cancer even when it is one's doctors, nurses, lab technicians, etc. who are the cause of one's recovery. Other examples are relatively easy to produce.

Now imagine a second case of failure to forgive. Let us suppose that I attempt to forgive my burglar, but the effort of doing so causes me to have a minor stroke. Moreover, the stroke causes me to forget that I have been burgled. It even, rather conveniently for the purpose of this thought experiment, keeps me from forming new memories about this specific event. Here I have forsworn resentment toward the burglar, and I have overcome my feeling of resentment toward him/her, and I have even done so in such a way that my forswearing resentment is a direct cause of my overcoming resentment. Yet I have surely *not* forgiven him/her. This second case introduces another complexity, that of the possibility of deviant causal chains. This possibility is not unique to considerations of forgiveness, of course. As Donald Davidson pointed out:

> *[N]ot just any causal connection between rationalizing attitudes and a wanted effect suffices to guarantee that producing the wanted effect was intentional. (1973, 78)*

Attempts to spell out the ways in which causal chains are deviant in order to avoid apparent counterexamples to an analysis of a concept or phenomenon are common but have met with mixed success. Yet since my goal is downstream of a full analysis I shall simply acknowledge the need for a principled treatment of deviant causal chains here and move on.[7]

Let me make two more points in passing. First, the standard account focuses squarely on what we might call *moral* forgiveness, as is clear from Murphy's characterization of it

---

[7] There is good reason to think that a general criterion for identifying deviant causal chains is neither possible nor required. See, Tännsjö (2009).

as "directed toward a person who has done an unjustified and non-excused *moral* injury" (my emphasis). But it is a mistake to think, as some do,[8] that forgiveness is only pertinent to actions that are morally salient. There are, of course, non-moral forms of forgiveness as well. To take but two examples, I might be able to forgive one of my teammates for striking out with the bases loaded, and I might be unable to forgive one of my publishers for misspelling my name. Both striking out and misspelling a name are actions over which agents have at least some control and about which we rightly assign praise or blame. They are even actions in which we might take umbrage or feel anger. In short, they are actions in virtue of which we can resent their agents, and, if we wish, we can forswear this resentment. But they are not, in and of themselves, either moral or immoral actions. These actions are simply non-moral.[9] However, the relationship between moral forgiveness and non-moral forgiveness is not my subject here, and I shall concern myself solely with moral forgiveness in this chapter.

Second, the nature of the emotions involved in forgiveness does nothing to speak to the possibility or impossibility of third-party forgiveness, as some have thought. Murphy, e.g., claims, "Resentment is a response not to general wrongs but to wrong against oneself," and for this reason he once held that third-party forgiveness was impossible (Murphy and Hampton 1988, 16). However, he later came around to the view, in my terminology, that he had confused resentment in

---

[8] See, Yandall (1998, 35) and Vetlesen (2011, 143).

[9] Some philosophers—e.g., Frye (1983) and Solomon (1993)—maintain that *every* instance of anger is charged with moral content. Obviously, it is a consequence of the conjunction of the standard account of forgiveness and the distinction between moral and non-moral forgiveness that one must reject this view, though I do not have a novel argument to offer here for that conclusion.

the narrow sense with resentment in the broad sense (Murphy 2012, 185).[10] To the extent that we are interested in whether third-party forgiveness is possible, we must look elsewhere.

III. Forgiveness and speech acts

Let me begin this section by quickly reminding the reader both of what a speech act is and how a speech act is shaped by questions of standing. Loosely speaking, X is a speech act just in case X is action that is performed by the very act of saying that one is performing the action (Searle 1996). For example, the act of saying "I promise to play drums in your band" is, under the right circumstances, the action of promising to play drums in your band. There are, of course, other ways to promise to play drums in your band. Obviously, I might use a locution that doesn't use the word "promise," such as "I will play drums in your band." More importantly, one might promise by raising one's hand if asked, "Who promises to play drums in my band" or one might even remain silent when told, "Please say something if you do not promise to play drums in my band." But, paradigmatically, promises are speech acts. So too are other actions such as marrying, betting, bequeathing, bidding, joining, quitting, christening, and many others as well.

I mentioned a moment ago that the act of saying "I promise to play drums in your band" is, *under the right circumstances*, promising to play drums in your band. But what are those circumstances? As J.L. Austin first pointed out:

> *Besides the uttering of the words of the so-called performative, a good many other things have as a general rule to be right and*

---

[10] On this point, see also Radzick (2010).

> *to go right if we are said to have happily brought off our action....And for this reason we call the doctrine of the things that can be and go wrong on the occasion of such utterances, the doctrine of infelicities. (1962, 14)*

Crudely put, the circumstances that must be met in order for my saying "I promise" to be my making of a promise are the felicity conditions of the speech act. Attempted speech acts that fail to meet their relevant felicity conditions are, in John Searle's phrase "defective" (1969, 54). Consider marrying. One person might say to two others, "I now pronounce you married," but it does not follow from this fact alone that the two silent individuals are now married. Rather, the two count as married only if the felicity conditions are met. We can divide these felicity conditions into two rough-and-ready categories. The first category concerns the speaker, who at a minimum must have the authority to marry others, i.e., be a solemniser. Let's call this condition *having standing to marry*. As it so happens, I lack standing to marry. As a result, I can say "I now pronounce you married" as much as I like without managing to marry anyone. My speech act would be defective, to use Searle's term. However, I know many people—priests, rabbis, imams, and judges—who are solemnisers and thus do have standing to marry. I am even told that I could join them in having standing to marry by becoming a solemniser; all I need is a few dollars and an Internet connection, though the prospect does not move me.[11] The second category concerns our silent pair, who at a minimum must be possible subjects of marriage. Let's call this condi-

---

[11] Other conditions fit into this first category, such as saying "I now pronounce you married" as part of an actual marriage ceremony, not, e.g., while performing in a play. But these conditions aren't central to the point I am making here.

tion *having standing to be married*. Right now and around here, humans generally have standing to be married,[12] though the young do not, those who are already married do not, and, in many places, those of the same sex do not. Furthermore, non-human animals, plants, rocks, baseball stadiums, sewage treatment plants, and any number of other things do not either. No amount of saying, "I now pronounce you married" to the thigh bone of a woolly mammoth and the Large Hadron Collider will cause the two of them to be married. My attempt to marry these marvels of nature and humanity would, again, be defective.

Let me return now make the connection between the foregoing and forgiveness explicit. I have already pointed out that, at least on the standard account, forgiveness is partially constituted by forswearing resentment. Moreover, forswearing is paradigmatically a speech act. We forswear or renounce something in most cases by announcing that we are doing so, as we might say aloud or to ourselves, "That's it: I quit smoking" or "I'll never try to write a term paper the night before it's due again." Forgiving is just a special case of this phenomenon in which we forswear resentment toward someone by using a locution such as "I forgive you" or "All is forgiven."[13] Hence, there are felicity conditions on forgiving, and an attempt to forgive that does not meet these conditions is, to use Searle's term once again, defective.[14]

---

[12] I am ignoring relatively minor issues here such as the possession of a marriage license.

[13] More generally, forgiveness is a form of speech act known as an avowal. On avowals as speech acts, see, e.g., Warnock (1989, 108) and Snowdon (2012, 253).

[14] Obviously, standing to marry and standing to be married are, in the context of this discussion, conventional. Our conventions change over time, and perhaps there will come a time in which more than two people have standing to be married to one another, etc. But it is wise to separate the question of whether convention does, in fact, provide one with standing in these cases from the

We are now in a position to offer a working version of the standard account of forgiveness. Let us say that A forgives B if and only if the following conditions are jointly satisfied:

1. A judges that he/she has sufficient reason to forswear resentment toward B;
2. A forswears resentment toward B;
3. A overcomes resentment toward B;
4. A's forswearing of his/her resentment toward B is a cause of A's overcoming her resentment toward B that is both
    a. direct,
    b. non-deviant;
5. B has standing to be forgiven.[15]
6. A has standing to forgive.

IV. Harms and the standing to forgive

We are now in a position to throw some light on our original question about the possibility of third-party forgiveness. There is, to be sure, no doubt about whether I can *say*, "I forgive Mr. Mr. Clain for his actions on November 13th" or "I forgive the terrorist who killed Ms. Arruebo." I can even successfully forswear feeling resentment both toward Mr. Clain and toward the man who murdered Ms. Arruebo. But what

---

question of whether it morally ought to be the case that convention provides one with standing.

[15] I won't be discussing standing to be forgiven much in this paper. However, it does seem like a topic worth investigating further. It is obvious enough that at a minimum, only agents have standing to be forgiven, but it is not clear that all agents do. Some actions might be unforgivable (Flannigan 1998). Somewhat less dramatically, it might be the case that only those who seek forgiveness have standing to be forgiven.

remains to be seen is whether I have standing to forgive these individuals.

In order to make some progress, let us consider several hypotheses about standing to forgive. In this and the next two sections, I shall be primarily concerned with two questions. One of these is whether the hypothesis in question allows for the possibility of third-party forgiveness. The second question is whether the hypothesis is inherently sensible as a characterization of standing to forgive. Let's start by considering:

Hypothesis-1: A has standing to forgive B for B's doing F only if B's doing F harmed A.

If Hypothesis-1 is correct, then I lack standing to forgive Mr. Clain. Why? While I was offended, and even disgusted, by Mr. Clain and his actions, it does not follow that I was harmed by them.[16] On the contrary, I was several thousand miles away when the attacks on Paris occurred, and I am no worse for wear as a result of them. It would be absurd, for example, for me to file a lawsuit against ISIS because of the damage done to me in the November 13th attacks, not only because ISIS is unlikely to recognize the legitimacy of such legal proceedings but also (and more importantly) because nothing that we would think of as a relevant harm has occurred to me because of the attacks in Paris.

But let us move on to the credibility of Hypothesis-1 as an account of standing to forgive. Initially, Hypothesis-1 looks plausible. It is often the case that we are in a position to forgive those who have harmed us, precisely because they have done so. Moreover, in articulating the standard account Murphy himself speaks of "unjustified and non-excused moral *injury*" (my emphasis), and talk of injury puts one in

---

[16] See, e.g., Mill ([1859] 2015) and Feinberg (1984).

mind of harms. However, it does not require much reflection to see that Hypothesis-1 is too restrictive. For it is often reasonable for me to forgive others for actions that do not harm me. Suppose, e.g., that a student promises to meet me during my office hours. I know that the student wants to talk about her poor grade in one of my classes, and I anticipate a difficult discussion. Suppose further that the student does not show up, as she promised to do. Given the fact that I have been spared what was likely to be an uncomfortable quarter of an hour explaining to another human being the myriad ways in which she has failed to meet basic academic standards, I haven't been harmed by her failure; I've been benefited.[17] Nevertheless, it makes perfect sense for me to resent the student for her failure to keep her promise. While it might seem over the top to tell the student that I *forgive* her for her moral lapse, I might forgive her nonetheless by using a deflationary locution such as "Don't worry about it." The upshot of all of this is that Hypothesis-1 fails as a theory of standing to forgive.

V. Wrongs and the standing to forgive

Let us consider another possibility:

Hypothesis-2: A has standing to forgive B for B's doing F only if B's doing F wronged A.

Unlike Hypothesis-1, Hypothesis-2 is not overly narrow. Hypothesis-2 can, e.g., make sense of my ability to forgive my student for breaking her promise to see me during my office hours. Though my student did not harm me, she certainly did wrong me, though not in an especially grave sense. One can be excused for thinking that Hypothesis-2 does not

---

[17] I clarify the distinction between being harmed and being wronged below.

allow any room at all for me to forgive Mr. Clain for his actions in Paris. For one might think that just as I have not been *harmed* by the attacks of November 13, so too I have not been *wronged* by them either. Nevertheless, matters are a little bit more complicated. In the rest of this section I'll consider two examples of phenomena that count as forgiveness according to Hypothesis-2 and which initially look like examples of third-party forgiveness, though on closer examination fail to do so.

First, let me acknowledge the obvious truth: a person can be wronged through the violation of one or more of her rights, as Ms. Arruebo was wronged when she was killed. But let me also suggest that the moral community whose norms have been violated can also be wronged. Explaining precisely how the moral community can be wronged in this way is difficult without presupposing more in the way of a normative ethical theory than is appropriate for this chapter. However, as an illustration one can frame the issue in terms of contractualism. According to a contractualist:

> *An act is wrong if its performance under the circumstances would be disallowed by any set of principles for the general regulation of behavior that no one could reasonably reject as a basis for informed, unforced, general agreement. (Scanlon, 153)*[18]

Hence, the moral community in question is formed by those many of us who seek to live together under principles that no one could reasonably reject. Whenever someone undertakes an action such that every principle that permits it could be

---

[18] See also Darwall (2006: 314) and Parfit (2011: 360).

reasonably rejected by those concerned to live together under principles that no one could reasonably reject, that person wrongs the moral community as a whole. This is true in part because of the disrespect that the action shows for the valid moral norms that hold the community together.[19]

While I think that there is much to be said for the idea that a moral community can be wronged, I do not think that it settles the question of whether or not third-party forgiveness is possible. There are two main reasons for reaching this conclusion. First, it would be an example of the fallacy of decomposition to infer from the fact that the moral community is wronged the further fact that each—or any—of the members of the community is wronged. Hence, Mr. Clain might well have wronged the moral community by the part he played in the attacks on Paris. Yet it does not follow that he wronged *me* by doing so. And if he did not wrong me, then Hypothesis-2 does not provide standing for me to forgive him. Second, even my role in whatever forgiveness the moral community can extend to Mr. Clain is limited. I cannot unilaterally forgive Mr. Clain for the wrong done to the moral community, since my place within this community is no more (and no less) important than anyone else's place. I might sensibly say, "The moral community ought to forgive Mr. Clain," but I can no more extend forgiveness in this way for the entire community than I can extend an offer of the presidency of the United States to my favored candidate.[20]

---

[19] The moral community counts as having shared agency in virtue of its individual agents sharing the intention to live together under valid moral norms. These agents have what Searle (1990) and others call a "we-intention."

[20] This point can be made in another way by looking at how forgiveness is often sought in Christian contexts, where God establishes and maintains the moral order. Mistress Quickly says to Sir Falstaff, "Lord Lord! Your worship's a wanton! Well, heaven forgive you

However, let's consider another angle on the question of third-party forgiveness. I do not know whether Ms. Arruebo had a partner, a family, or a group of close friends, and out of respect for her privacy I have not tried to find out. But let us imagine what the position of Ms. Arruebo's parents would be. After the death of their daughter, it would seem natural for them to say, "We can never forgive the people who took Anne-Laure from us," and we might think them to be some kind of moral saints if they were to say, "We are distraught over Anne-Laure's death, but as deeply religious people we offer our forgiveness to her killers." In other words, Ms. Arruebo's parents certainly seem to have standing to forgive the terrorists.

But does the forgiveness of Ms. Arruebo's parents count as third-party forgiveness? The process of answering this question will shed light on two important issues. First, we need to pay especially close attention to the kind of wrong that Ms. Arruebo's parents have suffered. Ms. Arruebo's parents did not have a right not to have their daughter killed, except in as much as they were the moral beneficiaries of Ms. Arruebo's own right not to be killed. As far as I can tell, none of Ms. Arruebo's parents' rights were violated when Ms. Arruebo's was killed. Nevertheless, Ms. Arruebo's parents did suffer an unjustified serious harm. They were deprived of one of the most important relationships that human beings can have and are likely to suffer greatly as a result. As a result of this

---

and all of us, I pray!" Falstaff's wantonness wrongs Quickly and the other merry wives of Windsor, but the ultimate standing to forgive is in the hands of the creator of the moral order that is violated by Falstaff's actions. While non-divine agents can forgive or fail to forgive the wrongs of others, it is largely their own fortunes that are at stake since their failure to forgive is a wrong done to others that might not in turn be forgiven by God. But, in contrast, I assume in this chapter an entirely secular moral community in my discussion of forgiveness.

unjustified serious harm, it appears reasonable to conclude that Ms. Arruebo's parents were wronged. And it is this very fact that explains why, according to Hypothesis-2, they are in a position to forgive the terrorists, should they wish to do so. Yet note that they are in a position to forgive because of the harm done *to them*. They have standing to forgive because they have been wronged, not because their daughter has been wronged.

In order to see this fact a little more clearly, suppose that Ms. Arruebo had not been killed on November 13th. Suppose that, instead, she had been partially paralyzed. In this second scenario, Ms. Arruebo has been wronged as a result of the violation of her right not to be deprived of the use of her legs.[21] And Ms. Arruebo's parents have also been wronged as a result of the unjustified harm they have undergone. Though her parents have not been deprived of their daughter's company, they must endure Ms. Arruebo's suffering as she tries to overcome her newfound impairment, they must withstand Ms. Arruebo's diminished life-prospects, and so on. Hence, both Ms. Arruebo and Ms. Arruebo's parents have standing to forgive. And suppose that in this second scenario, Ms. Arruebo's parents forgive the terrorists. How should we understand her parents' action? If we understand their action as forgiving the terrorists for the unjustified harm that has been done to them, then I think there is no reason to think that anything is amiss. However, the action so understood is clearly not a case of third-party forgiveness since it is forgiveness for an unjustified serious harm done to the parents themselves. Yet if we understand the parents as forgiving the terrorists for violating Ms. Arruebo's right, then matters seem rather different. Certainly, this would be a case of third-party forgiveness. But the right

---

[21] More generally speaking, this right is an instance of her right not to have her body violated and not to have its functioning impaired.

that has been violated *belongs* to Ms. Arruebo, and those who do not posses this right seem ill placed to forgive with respect to it. At best, it seems presumptuous for Ms. Arruebo's parents to forgive the terrorists for violating Ms. Arruebo's right; at worst, it seems downright incoherent.[22] Perhaps at first it seems difficult to tease apart these considerations because the rights violation and the unjustified serious harm are tokened in the very same event, viz., the killing of Ms. Arruebo. But reflection on this second scenario strongly suggests that either Ms. Arruebo's parents forgiveness is either not an example of third-party forgiveness or it is a case of attempting to forgive without the standing to do so, i.e., a defective example of forgiving.

I want to pause here momentarily in order to look more closely at the idea of an unjustified serious harm. It seems to me perfectly clear that both in the original scenario and in the second scenario that Ms. Arruebo's parents suffer a harm of this kind. Yet I would be hard-pressed to provide necessary and sufficient conditions for what constitutes an unjustified serious harm. I am sure that *I* did not suffer an unjustified serious harm as the result of Ms. Arruebo's death, since I did not even know of her existence until after she had died. And I am reasonably sure that the harm that Ms. Arruebo's casual acquaintances (the woman who worked in another department but often passed her in the hallway, the man with whom she sometimes shared an elevator ride in her apartment building) suffered as a result of her death was not serious enough to provide standing to forgive. But there are possible cases between Ms. Arruebo's casual acquaintances and her parents about which I have no reliable intuitions. As

---

[22] It is worth noting that there is evidence that parties other than those whose rights have been violated are often slower to forgive (if they forgive at all) than the parties whose right has been violated. See, Green et al. (2008).

I warned above, the concept of forgiveness is somewhat vague, and there might well be a range of borderline cases in which we are simply left unable to offer a principled answer to the question, "Does this person have standing to forgive Ms. Arruebo's killers?" I am not sure that this outcome is a reason for despair since it is true to the phenomenon.

A final point: The standing to forgive does not just depend in cases like these on how painful the harm is. For example, suppose that unbeknownst to her, Ms. Arruebo has a stalker; let us call him Mr. Harceleur. We might imagine that Mr. Harceleur gets tremendous pleasure from illicitly watching Ms. Arruebo's daily routine, and he is left at his wit's end by Ms. Arruebo's death. Nevertheless, I do not believe that Mr. Harceleur has standing to forgive the terrorists, even though he certainly has suffered a serious loss. Standing to forgive is, in part, a moral category, and Mr. Harceleur not only lacks any special claim to the pleasure he received from Ms. Arruebo, she most likely would have been offended to learn that he took such pleasure. There is, in short, no special relationship between Ms. Arruebo and Mr. Harceleur to ground the claim of an unjustified serious loss.

VI. Forgiveness by proxy

Let me turn to the second of the two important issues I mentioned a moment ago. Though it seems clear enough that Ms. Arruebo's parents do not have standing to forgive the terrorists for the violation of Ms. Arruebo's right in the second scenario (in which Ms. Arruebo survives the rights violation), the situation might appear different in the original scenario in which Ms. Arruebo is killed. In the original scenario, Ms. Arruebo cannot forgive anyone because she is dead. Does anyone have standing to forgive Ms. Arruebo's killer for violating her right not to be killed? I believe that the answer "yes." The appropriate model in this case appears to be that of a semi-transferable right to forgive.[23] Since Ms. Arruebo cannot exercise her right to forgive her killer, the right naturally devolves to others. To whom? The most credible response is to those with whom she was closest.[24] Marietta Jaeger speaks movingly about trying to forgive her daughter's murderer in just such a situation:

> *Though [Jaeger's daughter's killer] was liable for the death penalty, I felt it would violate and profane the goodness, sweetness, and beauty of Susie's life by killing the kidnapper in her name. She was deserving of a more noble and beautiful memorial than a cold-blooded, premeditated, state-sanctioned killing of a restrained defenseless man, however deserving of death he may be deemed to be. (Tutu 1999, 13)*

It seems to me that Jaeger is describing precisely what it looks like when standing to forgive devolves into the hands of a person who takes seriously their obligations to the person who is no longer in a position to forgive or to abstain from forgiving.

Cases like these are common enough to inspire despair. Desmond Tutu tells the story of a man (whom he does not

---

[23] I call this a "semi-transferable right" because it can only be transferred under a fairly limited set of conditions. One could not, e.g., sell one's right to forgive on eBay! Likewise, one could not give it to a stranger. The right is transferable along lines of special relations only.

[24] Under the right conditions, standing to forgive can plausibly be passed down through generations. See, Scarre (2011).

name) whose brother was abducted during by the final days of the Apartheid regime in South Africa. Years later, the man learned that his brother had been tortured for months before being executed. He was able to recognize his brother's corpse only by the shoes that he himself had bought for him. This man was faced with a decision that is probably harder than any I shall ever have to make, viz., whether or not to forgive his brother's murderer, Andy Taylor a former policeman in the South African Security Service, who had applied for amnesty (Tutu 1999, 192). I can see no good reason to deny that the man whose brother was killed had standing to forgive Taylor, or to decide not to do so.

Yet now we must ask, "Are these really examples of third-party forgiveness?" Some philosophers have thought so,[25] but they are mistaken. Recall from section 1, that I defined third-party forgiveness as follows:

A engages in third-party forgiveness toward B for doing F to C if and only if (1) A forgives B for doing F to C and (2) A is an unrelated third-party with regard to B and C.

But surely Jaeger does not count as an unrelated third-party with regard to the man who murdered her daughter. Likewise, Ms. Arruebo's parents do not count as an unrelated third-parties with regard to the man who murdered theirs. Simply lumping cases like these under the heading of third-party forgiveness obscures the important but distinct category: forgiveness by proxy, in which a closely related individual (or individuals) gain standing to forgive because the party that was wronged no longer has the capacity. Forgiveness by

---

[25] For example, Griswold (2007, 118).

proxy is a wholly different phenomenon than the one at stake when I consider over dinner whether to forgive Mr. Clain for his role in the attacks of November 13th.

In virtue of the forgoing considerations, it should also be clear that we need to expand our conception of standing to forgive as follows:

> Hypothesis-3: A has standing to forgive B for B's doing F only if:
>
> (1) B's doing F wronged A or
>
> (2) B's doing F wronged C, and A is C's proxy for forgiveness.

VII. Forgiveness, shmorgiveness

I can see no reason to extend standing to forgive beyond Hypothesis-3. As a result, attempts by the likes of me to forgive Mr. Clain or the murderers of Ms. Arruebo are unsuccessful and bootless. I can say the words, "I forgive them," but they are part of a defective speech act, the success of which is a necessary condition for forgiveness. The same is true of other attempts at third-party forgiveness, as far as I can see.

But how significant is this state of affairs? As a matter of fact, our practice of forgiveness requires that the forgiver have standing of a certain type. But this fact is thoroughly contingent since forgiveness is, to use a term that is no longer as popular as it once was, socially constructed.[26] We could quite easily have had a different practice, a practice that we can call *shmorgiveness*. Let us say that A shmorgives B if and only if the following conditions are jointly satisfied:

---

[26] See, e.g., Hacking (1999) and Haslanger (2012).

1. A judges that he/she has sufficient reason to forswear resentment toward B;
2. A forswears resentment toward B;
3. A overcomes resentment toward B;
4. A's forswearing of his/her resentment toward B is a cause of A's overcoming her resentment toward B that is both
   a. direct,
   b. non-deviant;
5. B has standing to be forgiven.

Unlike forgiveness, shmorgiveness has no sixth condition, i.e., no restrictions of standing to forgive. While I cannot forgive Mr. Clain, I can shmorgive him to my heart's contentment. In general, though there is no such thing as third-party forgiveness, there is as much third-party shmorgiveness as anyone could want—and perhaps more. So we must ask, "Is there any reason to continue with the concept of forgiveness, or should we consider switching to shmorgiveness, with its less uptight view of the world?"

It has to be said that shmorgiveness might well accomplish many of the valuable social functions that forgiveness does. Why? The sentence "A forgives B for doing F" entails the sentence "A shmoregives B for doing F," since shmorgiveness is just forgiveness without the sixth necessary condition. So every instance of forgiveness is also an instance of shmorgiveness. Hence, if forgiveness makes restorative justice more likely (Dickey 1998), then so would shmorgiveness. And if forgiveness provides opportunities for psychotherapeutic healing (Fitzgibbons 1998), then so would shmorgiveness. And, again, if self-forgiving allows one to successfully rewrite one's self (Hagberg 2011), so too would self-shmorgiveness. In fact, one might think that shmorgiveness can accomplish all of these good things to an even greater degree since there are fewer restrictions on the shmorgiver than on the forgiver.

However, I do not think that we should to be too quick to give up of forgiveness in favor of shmorgiveness. To begin with, shmorgiveness obscures the importance of the relationship between the person who wrongs and the person who is wronged. Moral wrongs often consist of something more than mere harm or injury, as we have seen. Wrongs consist of one person violating the moral boundaries of another. The result is that the moral relationship between these persons is damaged. Talk of repairing this damage is hopelessly metaphorical but not, I think, entirely misleading. Now, it seems a commonplace that if I wrong another person, I cannot repair my relationship with that person by having someone else either successfully forswear resentment toward me. Rather, the damage can only be rectified with the aid of the person who has been wronged.[27] The concept of forgiveness seems tailor made for this task. Replacing forgiveness with schmorgiveness would leave us with a less perspicuous appreciation of this fact.

Furthermore, replacing forgiveness with shmorgiveness would blur the boundaries in an unhelpful way between what is traditionally thought of as forgiveness and distinct but related practices. As Jacques Derrida pointed out, it is already difficult to track these distinctions.\:

> *Forgiveness is often confounded, sometimes in a calculated fashion, with related themes: excuse, regret, amnesty, prescription, etc. (2002: 27).*

Derrida might have added condonation and atonement to this list as well as the occasionally necessary practice of

---

[27] The unusual exception is forgiveness by proxy, discussed above.

simply giving up on agents as morally incorrigible. These distinctions tend to be especially conspicuous for one who is considering the possibility of forgiving someone else. For instance, if someone has wronged me, then it makes all the difference whether I forgive him or whether I condone his actions. For if I condone when I should only forgive, I act in a servile manner and I add a further wrong done to myself to the wrong already done to me.[28] In contrast, if I am considering shmorgiving Mr. Clain for his role in the attacks of November 13th, I run no such risk to myself. At worst, I act in a manner that is insensitive to the Parisians, which is a wrong to them but not to me.

Finally, as any economist will be happy to point out, the quickest way to decrease the value of anything is to increase its quantity. If Fabergé eggs and first editions of *Moby Dick* were available on every street corner, we would value them far less than we actually do. Likewise, if we had a practice of shmorgiveness that allowed anyone to shmorgive anyone else from a wrong that he or she had done, then it is likely that we would find it to be less valuable than a practice of forgiveness that is discriminating. Perhaps something like this is what those who oppose same-sex marriage have in mind when they complain that allowing men to marry other men and women to marry other women devalues traditional marriages. While I certainly disagree with this particular point, it is not hard to imagine how a conception of marriage run riot—shmarriage, if you will—would threaten to devalue marriage. If we really did allow a wooly mammoth bone to be married to the Large Hadron Collider, many of us would likely consider another practice that distinguished the commitment that adult humans can make to one another from

---

[28] Hill (1973), Murphy and Hampton (1988: 18), and Griswold (2007: 32).

this practice. We would, as it were, have to reinvent marriage. I suspect that much the same is true if we tried to replace forgiveness with shmorgiveness. If I have wronged another, what I want is for the person that I have wronged to successfully forswear resentment against me. I cannot get that for a third party, however well intentioned he or she might be.[29]

---

[29] I am grateful to my colleagues Ben Bayer, Drew Chastain, and Joel MacClellan for helpful comments, questions, and criticisms. I also thank the students in both sections of my honors ethics course at Loyola University New Orleans during the spring 2016 term for valuable discussions of the subject of this paper. Finally, my thanks to Court Lewis for his valuable input.

References

Austin, J.L. 1962. *How To Do Things with Words.* Cambridge, Massachusetts: Harvard University Press.

Bentham, Jeremy. 1838. "The Principles of Penal Law." *The Works of Jeremy Bentham*, Part II. Edinburgh, UK: William Tait.

Darwall, Steven. 2006. "Contractualism, Root and Branch." *Philosophy & Public Affairs* 34.2: 193–214.

Davidson, Donald. 1973. "Freedom to Act." *Essays on Freedom of Action.* Edited by Ted Honderich. London: Routledge. Reprinted in Donald Davidson. 1980. *Essays on Actions and Events.* Oxford, UK: Oxford: Oxford University Press: 63-82.

Derrida, Jacques. 2002. *On Cosmopolitanism and Forgiveness.* Translated by Mark Dooley and Michael Hughes. London: Routledge.

Dickey, Walter J. 1998. "Forgiveness and Crime: The Possibilities of Restorative Justice." *Exploring Forgiveness.* Edited by Robert D. Enright and Joanna North. Madison, WI: University of Wisconsin Press.

Dostoevsky, Fyodor. [1880] 2002. *The Brothers Karamazov.* 12th edition. Translated by Richard Pevear and Larissa Volokhonsky. New York, NY: Farrar, Straus and Giroux.

Eliot, George. [1871] 2003. *Middlemarch: A Study of Provincial Life.* London: Penguin Classics.

Enright, Robert D., Suzanne Freedman, and Julio Rique. 1998. "The Psychology of Interpersonal Forgiveness." *Exploring Forgiveness.*

Feather, N.T. and Rebecca Sherman. 2002. "Envy, Resentment, Schadenfreude, and Sympathy: Reactions to Deserved and Undeserved Achievement and Subsequent Failure." *Personality and Social Psychology Bulletin* 28.7: 953-961.

Feinberg, Joel. 1984. *Harm to Others: The Moral Limits of the Criminal Law.* Oxford: Oxford University Press.

Fitzgibbons, Richard. 1998. "Anger and the Healing Power of Forgiveness: A Psychiatrist's Point of View." *Exploring Forgiveness.*

Flannigan, Beverly. 1998. "Forgivers and the Unforgiveable." *Exploring Forgiveness.*

Frye, Marilyn. 1983. "A Note on Anger." *The Politics of Reality: Essays on Feminist Theory.* Berkeley, CA: Crossing Press.

Hill, Thomas E. Jr. 1973. "Servility and Self-Respect." *Monist* 57.1: 87-104.

Jaeger, Marietta. 1998. "The Power and Reality of Forgiveness: Forgiving the Murderer of One's Own Child." *Exploring Forgiveness.*

Gibbard, Allan. 1990. *Wise Choices, Apt Feelings: A Theory of Normative Judgment.* Cambridge: Harvard University Press.

Green, Jeffrey D., Jennie L. Burnette, and Jody L. Davis. 2008. "Third-Party Forgiveness: (Not) Forgiving Your Close Other's Betrayer." *Personality and Social Psychology Bulletin* 34.3: 407-418.

Griswold, Charles L. 2007. *Forgiveness: A Philosophical Exploration.* Cambridge: Cambridge University Press.

Hacking, Ian. 1999. *The Social Construction of What?* Cambridge: Harvard University Press.

Hagberg, Garry L. 2011. "The Self Rewritten: The Case of Self-Forgiveness." *The Ethics of Forgiveness.* Edited by Charles Fricke. London: Routledge.

Haslanger, Sally. 2012. Resisting Reality: Social Construction and Social Critique. Oxford: Oxford University Press

Kahn, Leonard. 2011a. "Conflict, Regret, and Modern Moral Philosophy." *New Waves in Ethics.* Edited by Thom Brooks. New York: Palgrave Macmillan.

———. 2011b. "Moral Blameworthiness and the Reactive Attitudes." *Ethical Theory and Moral Practice* 14.2: 131-142.

Levy, Neil. 2005. "The Good, the Bad, and the Blameworthy." *Journal of Ethics and Social Philosophy* 1.2: 2-16.

Mill, John Stuart. [1859] 2015. "On Liberty." *"On Liberty" and Other Writings.* Edited by Leonard Kahn. Calgary, Alberta: Broadview Press.

Murphy, Jeffrie G. 2012. Punishment and the Moral Emotions: Essays in Law, Morality, and Religion. Oxford: Oxford University Press.

———. 2002. *Getting Even: Forgiveness and Its Limits.* Oxford: Oxford University Press.

Murphy, Jeffrie G. and Jean Hampton. 1988. *Forgiveness and Mercy.* Cambridge: Cambridge University Press.

Parfit, Derek. 2011. *On What Matters.* Volume 1. Oxford: Oxford University Press.

Radzick, Linda. 2010. "Moral Bystanders and the Virtue of Forgiveness." *Forgiveness in Perspective.* Edited by Christopher R. Allers and Marieke Smit. Amsterdam: Rodopi Press, 69–89.

Scanlon, T.M. 1998. *What We Owe to Each Other.* Cambridge: Harvard Belknap Press.

Scarre, Geoffrey. 2011. "Apologizing for Historical Injustices." *The Ethics of Forgiveness.* Edited by Charles Fricke. London: Routledge.

Searle, John R. 1996. "What Is a Speech Act?" Unpublished but available at
<https://faculty.unlv.edu/jwood/unlv/Articles/SearleWhatIsASpeechAct.pdf>.

_____. 1990. "Collective Intentions and Actions." *Intentions in Communication*. Edited by P. Cohen, J. Morgan and M. Pollack. Cambridge: MIT Press.

_____. 1969. *Speech Acts: Essays in the Philosophy of Language*. Cambridge: Cambridge University Press.

Shakespeare, William. [1602] 2004. *The Merry Wives of Windsor*. New York, NY: Simon & Schuster.

Smith, Angela M. 2005. "Responsibility for Attitudes: Activity and Passivity in Mental Life." *Ethics* 115.2: 236-271.

Swondon, Paul. 2012. "How to Think about Phenomenal Self-Knowledge." *The Self and Self-Knowledge*. Edited by Annalisa Coliva. Oxford: Oxford University Press.

Solomon, Robert. 1993. *The Passions: Emotions and the Meaning of Life*. Second Edition. Indianapolis, IN: Hackett.

Stich, Stephen. 1993. "Will the Concepts of Folk Psychology Find a Place in Cognitive Science?" *Folk Psychology and the Philosophy of Mind*. Edited by Scott Christensen and Dale R. Turner. Hillsdale, New Jersey: Lawrence Earlbaum and Associates Publishers.

Strawson, Peter. 1962. "Freedom and Resentment." *Proceedings of the British Academy* 48: 1–25.

Swinburne, Richard. 1989. *Responsibility and Atonement*. Oxford: Oxford University Press.

Tännsjö, Torbjörn. 2009. "On Deviant Causal Chains – No Need for a General Criterion." *Analysis* 69.3: 469-473.

Tutu, Desmond. 1999. No *Future without Forgiveness*. New York, NY: Image.

Vetlesen, Arne Johan. 2011. "Can Forgiveness Be Morally Wrong?" *The Ethics of Forgiveness*.

Warnock, G.J. 1989. *J.L. Austin*. London: Routledge.

Yandall, Keith E. 1998. "The Metaphysics and Morality of Forgiveness." *Exploring Forgiveness*

Chapter 2

The Heart of the Matter: Forgiveness as an Aesthetic Process

A.G. Holdier

In Joseph Butler's second sermon on resentment and forgiveness, the good bishop stresses the importance of proper judgment for sensible living, arguing that although the experience of ill-will towards another can be provoked by all manner of wrongs and confusions, the first necessary step to forgive requires the recognition that the "false light" of self-prejudice is indeed a false way of seeing the world (Butler 1792, 141). By defining forgiveness relative to resentment grounded in self-love, Butler argues that both virtuous and vicious people can forgive others, for the process equates to a cognitive reorientation of attitudes dependent on the volitional choice of the agent to perceive reality properly, regardless of his or her character (1792, 141). Following a common misreading of Butler that defines forgiveness simply as the "overcoming of resentment,"[30] much of the literature in the philosophy of forgiveness has therefore focused on either epistemic questions (surrounding the possibility, effectiveness, and process of forgiving another, as well as its connection to forgetfulness) or on related moral concerns (such as

---

[30] As Griswold (2007, 20) explains, a trend in the Butler-tradition mistakenly defines Butler's view of forgiveness as the "overcoming of resentment," though, as will be explained below, this is far from Butler's intention.

forgiveness' potential status as a virtue and its possible obligatoriness in given situations).

Rembrandt's 1668 oil painting *Return of the Prodigal Son* begins a case for a different focus in the philosophy of forgiveness: one grounded on procedural aesthetic concerns and virtue-based emotional states—and one that Butler himself would likely appreciate. No stranger to bringing together both light and darkness on his canvases, Rembrandt wields both in his adaptation of the biblical parable of the Prodigal to create a dyadic focus circulating around the contrasted forgiving spirit of the penitent's father and the oppositional disbelief of the returned son's brother.[31] By highlighting both the tender father-son embrace on the left of the scene and the disapproving gaze of the figure on the right, Rembrandt communicates the complicated mess of emotions displayed in Luke 15:11-32, thereby demonstrating the difficulty of recognizing Butler's "false light" for what it is (Proimos 2011, 297). Despite seeing the change in his brother's character that might warrant the generous forgiveness extended by their father, the brother's emotions prevent him from being able—at the point depicted by Rembrandt—to achieve Butler's cognitive reorientation and see through his resentment to forgive. Therefore, rather than demonstrating a triumphal conquering of resentment in his display of forgiveness, Rembrandt indicates that such a painful emotion often will, instead, exist in tension with the choice to forgive.

---

[31] Proimos (2011, 295-296) makes a convincing case for the identity of the right-most figure as such.

The Heart of the Matter 49

The Return of the Prodigal Son, Rembrandt van Rijn

Indeed, by equally portraying both a forgiving father and unforgiving brother responding to the same experience, Rembrandt's painting subtly comments on the nature of reconciliation judgments and their disconnect from the reconciled individuals' emotional states. *Return of the Prodigal Son* is a powerful scene of forgiveness, despite its conflicting set of emotions—including the strongly resentful figure—that it contains. Contra the Butler-tradition, Rembrandt's painting demonstrates the aesthetic component of the experience of forgiveness itself—that is to say, the phenomenological process that accompanies an agent's cognitive judgments and understanding with the forgiver's emotional affective states; this has been largely resigned to the periphery of the philosophical conversation, despite its locus at the core of any real-world impulse for forgiveness. In short, Rembrandt's painting comments on how it *feels* to forgive.

For the forgiver, the cathartic relief that accompanies the release of grudges and associated tensions is a powerful motivation for engaging in the process of forgiveness altogether, but the simple definition of forgiveness as resentment-overcoming hamstrings a philosopher's ability to consider this key affective product. If forgiveness does not obtain unless emotional states are squashed, then genuine forgiveness will be a bird so rare as to defy counting as a relevant element of conversation. The real experience of forgiveness is far more messy and, I contend (following thinkers like Marilyn McCord Adams [1991, 297] and Aurel Kolnai [1973-1974, 95]), something which precedes emotional catharsis as its prerequisite, not as its definition. In short, a choice to forgive *results* in the peacefulness of overcome resentment; it is not identical with that emotional state. Consequently, forgiveness is a virtue insofar as it contributes to the creation of a more beautiful world than that which would obtain in its absence.

Therefore, following in Joram Haber's "common-sense" footsteps in this field, I aim to build a philosophical structure around the every-day experience of forgiveness as a peace-seeking enterprise by reintroducing an underrepresented concern in contemporary philosophy of forgiveness: the aesthetic process of forgiveness and the related role of the forgiver's experienced emotions. Rather than viewing the experience of forgiveness as a chiefly epistemic process (which can lead to paradoxical conclusions related to deservingness and memory),[32] I adapt the long-standing binary model of aesthetic judgment and emotion put forth by Leder et al. to the process of forgiveness so as to better retain an

---

[32] See, Kolnai (1973-1974, 95-99) for such examples.

appreciation of the phenomenology of forgiveness throughout the analytic process.

The beauty of virtue

Although the notion of applying an aesthetic framework to a process frequently defined in terms of normative properties might now appear strange, this approach finds its roots in Aristotelian virtue ethics that predate the aesthetic-ethical split of the European Enlightenment. Aristotle consistently structures his theory of ethical action in terms of the pursuit of the *kalon*: a word that has been translated variably as "beautiful," "noble," and "fine"—in each case, evoking a sense of completion as with a work of art to which nothing can either be added or removed without diminishing its beauty (Kraut 2014).[33] This sense of fitness or appropriateness to a given situation grounds the identification of Aristotelian virtues as features which contribute to the overall pursuit of *eudaimonia* in an agent's life; features which, as John Milliken has pointed out, are assessed primarily in aesthetic categories when "the virtuous agent steps back and sees, not the embodiment of a principle of reason, but an instance of aesthetic perfection. He is moved not by the reasonableness of an act, but by its beauty" (Milliken 2006, 327). Rather than analyze virtues simply in terms of functionality or rationality, Aristotle identifies them via their contribution to the beautiful *eudaimonia*, therefore "The noble [*kalon*] is fundamentally an aesthetic concept…it is a matter of perception and not one of calculation" (Milliken 2006, 327).[34]

---

[33] See, also Aristotle, *Nicomachean Ethics* 1106b5-14 and 1120a23-4.

[34] As Aristotle says in *NE* 1109b20 that the right thing to do "is not easy to determine by reasoning, any more than anything else that is perceived by the senses; such things depend on particular facts, and the decision rests with perception."

Notably, Aristotle did not see forgiveness as such a virtue. As Charles Griswold explains, Aristotle's characterization of the great-souled man (*megalopsuchos*) disqualifies any such virtuous person from the field of forgiveness-based exchanges altogether, both as the penitent (for the *megalopsuchos* would never wrong someone to consequently seek forgiveness) and as the forgiver (for the absolute self-sufficiency of the *megalopsuchos* would require nothing from "inferior" people—not even penance) (2007, 8-9). The truly magnanimous individual, instead, transcends the imperfect relationships of more common men and women—relationships that include wrongdoing and, therefore, forgiveness. Being magnanimous is not easy, for as Aristotle himself says, "it is difficult to be truly magnanimous, since it is not possible without being fine and good" (*NE* 1124a3-5). Griswold's comments on this passage may understate the matter when he observes that Aristotle's "paradigm of moral virtue sets a *very* high standard" (2007, 9).

In describing the *megalopsuchos* as "fine and good," Aristotle relies on another important Greek concept that spans the post-Kantian gap between aesthetics and ethics: *kalokagathia*. Comprised of the terms *kalos* and *agathos*—harmoniously beautiful and morally good, respectively—this rare word in antiquity was normally reserved for either deities or especially exemplary models of human beings who were, as Plato puts it in the *Lysis* (207a), "worthy to be called not just beautiful, but imbued with *kalokagathia*" (Weiler 2002, 11). These supreme exemplars of human behavior exhibit *kalokagathia* naturally, having cultivated every intellectual, moral, social, and economic virtue in their pursuit of the *kalon*. Therefore *kalokagathia* is simply "the character and conduct of *kalos kagathos*, that is, of the perfect and just man" (Petrochilos 2002, 604). So, the truly well-lived life of the perfect person (in the sense of *eudaimonia* achieved interchangeably by the *kalos kagathos* or the *megalopsuchos*)[35] is one where aesthetic and ethical concepts are inextricably intertwined; something Aristotle underlines in the *Politics* when he equates *kalokagathia* with *arête*, using this aesthetic-ethical notion of nobility interchangeably with virtue (Dover 1974, 44).[36]

However, perfectionistic ethical theories like Aristotle's, based on heroic moral exemplars standing as objectively superior human beings over the common rabble of the less-perfect *hoi polloi*, necessitate a focus on the process of developing such perfect character (and not, as in calculative models, a formulaic application of a moral principle like the categorical imperative or the utilitarian calculus to a specific situation). Consider Aristotle's famous definition of virtue as "a state issuing in decisions, consisting in a mean relative to us, determined by *logos* and by that by which the *phronimos* would determine it" (*NE* 1106b36-1107a2), where virtues are identifiable by the expert *phronimos* who possesses the practical wisdom to understand the right thing to do in a given scenario. If this "situational appreciation" is indeed as "anti-codifiable" as Rosalind Hursthouse (2011, 51) has dubbed it, then it would only be through many hours of practice that

---

[35] Given that both of these titles describe similarly excellent individuals at the pinnacle of the human experience, it seems a small leap to conclude that Aristotle had the same paragon of humanity in mind when employing each term. (For example, see Aristotle's identification of the beautiful nature of the *megalopsuchos* in *NE* 1125a 11-12). See also, in Hutchinson (1995, 203) an identification of Aristotle's "gentleman" (his translation of Aristotle's "noble-and-good"—*kalokagathia*) as the only person who "can be 'magnanimous' (Aristotle's highest term of moral praise), a man who is confident in his possession of all the moral virtues, and confident of deserving what he deserves."

[36] See also Aristotle, *Politics* 1259b34-1260a4.

such skills would be developed (conversely, as Jessica Moss [2011, 205] puts it, we will come to pursue *eudaimonia* "through the non-rational habituation of the non-rational part of the soul" that is crafted through *phronesis*). Admittedly, morality is not often considered a skill—at least, not since Ancient Greece. Picking up on Aristotle's consistent focus on the repetitive habituation of the virtues, Julie Annas (1995, 236-239) not only argues that "a virtue has an intellectual structure, and that it is at many points like the intellectual structure of a skill," but that this structure is what allows us to articulate anything about specific virtues whatsoever (as in the case of bravery, where it is identifiable only through the practices of the agent). All this is to say that if the nobility of the *kalos-kagathos* or the wisdom of *phronimos* is primarily performative,[37] then it is the virtues being demonstrated by those individuals in performance which ground their identities as performers.[38]

In regards to forgiveness' status as a virtue, then, this sense of beautiful-nobility developing from artistic cultivation is well-demonstrated by Butler's actual perspective on forgiveness functioning not as the replacement of emotions, but as their proper refinement through the lens of both the particular situation and the overall project of human flourishing. Rather than suggest that forgiveness requires the foreswearing of resentment itself (as if such an emotion could simply be volitionally jettisoned from an agent's phenomenological stage), Butler recognizes that:

---

[37] For the identification of the *kalos-kagathos* with the achievement of *phronesis*, see Moss (2011, 219) as well as Wood (1999, 262).

[38] Because of the repetitive feedback-loop of the aesthetic process, this means that virtues will function both as prerequisites and as consequences of the continued practice of morality as *techne*. This will be explained more below.

> *Resentment is of two kinds: Hasty and sudden, or settled and deliberate. The former is called anger, and often passion; which, though a general word, is frequently appropriated and confined to the particular feeling, sudden anger, as distinct from deliberate resentment, malice, and revenge. In all these words is usually implied somewhat vicious: somewhat unreasonable as to the occasion of the passion, or immoderate as to the degree or duration of it. But that the natural passion itself is indifferent, St Paul has asserted in that precept, "Be ye angry and sin not;" [Ephes. iv. 26.] which, though it is by no means to be understood as an encouragement to indulge ourselves in anger, the sense being certainly this, "Though ye be angry, sin not;" yet here is evidently a distinction made, between anger and sin, between the natural passion and sinful anger. (1792, 115)*

He therefore calls for a moderated experience of resentment that is appropriately tuned to avoid "both its excess (malice and revenge) and its deficiency (insufficient regard for our well-being)"—in other words, he expects the virtuous agent to first exercise the appropriate skill of knowing how to respond, regardless of the agent's emotional state (Garcia 2011, 10). Insofar as this is accomplished, Butler describes a resultant "forgiving spirit" developing in the agent—a state of mind still possible while feeling the emotional weight of the hurtful experience. Ultimately, it is only that forgiving spirit which can offer, among other things, "hope for peace of mind in our dying moments" (Butler 1792, 145), for this practiced attitude of forgiveness leads to the cathartic release of emotional pain. Importantly, the skill of forgiveness is not identified with the emotional catharsis itself.

The emotion of forgiveness

Apart from the perfectionistic nature of his ethical system, Aristotle also deigned to recognize forgiveness' status as a virtue because of an unusual feature inherent to his conception of solicitude and the proper conditions under which the *megalopsuchos* would actually desire the good for another person. As such, Paul Ricoeur's development of Aristotelian concepts into a characterization of charitable alterity more strongly grounds Butler's view of forgiveness as a preferable character trait that positively contributes to a life well-lived. This not only resonates with the social characterization of aesthetic forgiveness seen in Rembrandt's painting, but is also along the lines of common sense that forgivers themselves typically assume.

To Aristotle, goodwill towards others (*eunoia*) is a natural element of human interaction that comes about when one recognizes and appreciates the value of another person. When expressed reciprocally by two or more people, *eunoia* lays the groundwork for friendship (*NE* 1155b15-1156a6), but it "is not identical with friendship; for one may have goodwill both towards people whom one does not know, and without their knowing it" (*NE* 1166b29-1167a17). Kostas Kalimtzis (2000, 77) argues that *eunoia* is primarily a cognitive property, consisting of "intellectual admiration or the good regard that is aroused [that] is based on the judgment that some excellence has been observed" and that, therefore, it is a passive trait contributing to rational analysis, but not practical action. Kalimtzis (2000, 83) is right to differentiate between *eunoia* and the more engaged principle of *homonoia* that actually motivates public action for the common good, but Aristotle never seems to imply that *eunoia* (in this regard) is anything but a foundational principle on which the practical skills of *phronesis* and *arête* operate. Goodwill, Aristotle says, is "a beginning of friendship, as the pleasure of the eye is the beginning of love" (*NE* 1166b29-1167a17), but that goodwill must be activated through intentional (skillful) choices to develop into something deeper. Consequently, Aristotle sees *eunoia* not only as a necessary condition for friendship, but as one part of the general basis for public engagement *tout court*—a necessary, but not sufficient, condition for public interaction.[39] Given his perfect development of each skill set, the *megalopsuchos* will necessarily exemplify perfect *eunoia* as well.

At this point, Bishop Butler agrees with Aristotle: arguing that "mankind, i.e. a creature defective and faulty, is the proper object of good will, whatever his faults are." Butler (1792, 137) contends that solicitude for others is divinely obligated—even for one's enemies. Therefore, to Butler, forgiveness is "absolutely necessary, as ever we hope for pardon of our own sins, as ever we hope for peace of mind in our dying moments, or for the divine mercy at that day when we shall most stand in need of it"—virtuous character, properly developed, will not neglect to foreswear revenge once given the opportunity to do so (1792, 145). Given the proper perspective, Butler insists that all persons would recognize similar faults in their own lives as in the life of their enemies; whether on pain of irrationality, unfairness, or inconsistency, forgiveness therefore cannot be avoided (regardless of the emotional pain one must endure while practicing it). This leads Butler (1792, 140) to conclude that self-love, the ultimate ground of any excuse to avoid forgiveness, "is a medium of a peculiar kind: in these cases it magnifies everything which is amiss in others, at the same time that it lessens everything amiss in ourselves."

---

[39] As Aristotle explains in book IV of the *Politics*, "Community depends on friendship; and where there is enmity instead of friendship, men will not even share the same path." Aristotle, *Politics* 1295a25-b29.

However, here Aristotle's perfectionism diverges from Butler to argue that human beings, insofar as they are "defective and faulty," do *not* warrant comprehensive expressions of *eunoia*. To Aristotle, self-love is no vice at all, if the agent does indeed deserve to be loved, that is, if the person in question is truly imbued with *kalokagathia*. And when the magnanimous man is focused on the continuous expression of his own virtue, he attains the state of absolute self-sufficiency wherein he "excels his subjects in all good things; and such a man needs nothing further; therefore he will not look to his own interests but to those of his subjects; for a king who is not like that would be a mere titular king" (*NE* 1160a30-1161a8). The optimal form of Aristotelian solicitude, expressed by the perfect example of a virtuous person, is therefore purely paternalistic (Petrochilos 2002, 607).

This characterization of *eunoia* runs contrary to many common-sense interpretations of goodwill's moral obligatoriness being grounded in equality and love, not condescension, with moral agents continually deferring to others out of the recognition of the value of the other, not that of the agent themselves. With his consistent focus on the nature of the truly magnanimous human being, Aristotle passes over any significant consideration of lower-order interpersonal relationships between people who do not exemplify *kalokagathia*—relationships that will frequently be plagued by mistakes and require the exercise of forgiveness to continue. Instead, Aristotle spends a significant amount of ink analyzing the nature of the political obligations of individuals in community (through the *polis*)—but not on private expressions of *eunoia* between specific citizens. Moreover, Aristotle's description of the *megalopsuchos* indicates that such a state is only achievable by the select few who are already ontologically predisposed to being better individuals in the first place.[40] Consequently, *eunoia* is only obligatory towards those select few who genuinely deserve it and forgiveness, therefore, simply falls out of any meaningful conversation.

Contra Aristotle (but in line with Butler), Paul Ricoeur's hermeneutical existentialism maintains a powerful space for forgiveness-as-virtue when it locates personal identity (selfhood) as inextricable from social networks and relationships with others. Arguing that selfhood and alterity are necessary opposites, Ricoeur (1992, 190) insists that an agent cannot come to understand the former without likewise considering the latter, and that, therefore, any endeavor towards self-knowledge will require solicitude's "benevolent spontaneity, intimately related to self-esteem within the framework of the aim of the "good" life."[41] Whereas Aristotle could only discuss social relationships for the perfectly virtuous in terms of civic or political engagement, Ricoeur's assumption of *eunoia* as the simple recognition of another human being's value is basic to Ricoeur's definition of *eudaimonia* as incoherent apart from a communal context.[42] Therefore, despite basing his ethical theory on Aristotle's *eudaimonia*, Ricoeur's notion of alterity fundamentally alters how the skillful practice of Aristotelian virtues plays out.

On that basis, understanding forgiveness as an Aristotelian virtue (or disposition for behavior) becomes easier to devel-

---

[40] Consequently, there is little need for Aristotle to practically explain how one might achieve *kalokagathia* — ethics, instead, is a matter of explaining the beautiful virtues for what they are and trusting that they shall attract the proper people who perceive them appropriately.

[41] Indeed, the very name of the book indicates Ricoeur's position on the ontology of this matter.

[42] Notably, Ricoeur's perspective borrows heavily from the biblical conception of unconditional love (*agape*) that likewise grounds Butler's Christian worldview (1992, 25).

op; overall, the impetus for engaging in the process of forgiveness is best understood narratively as the pursuit of a life well-lived in community.[43] To Ricoeur, a narrative perspective is always to be preferred for temporally-bound agents like human beings, who cannot help but view events individually and then later make sense of them in a process Ricoeur dubbed "emplotment." As he says, emplotment consists of "eliciting a pattern from a succession," creating a structured and coherent picture of one's experience through reflection and analysis (Ricoeur 1983, 153). This is particularly important for an agent in the process of analyzing her own actions, for this "emplotment of [one's own] character" is what allows someone to comprehend her own identity (Ricoeur 1995, 309).[44] Crucial to his conception of this "configurational act of emplotment" is its ability to explain a weakness Ricoeur identified in Aristotle's system: "*Phronesis* tells us that happiness is the coronation of excellence in life and in praxis, but it does not tell us in which ways this state of affairs can be made to reign…it is through our acquaintance with types of emplotment that we *learn* how to link excellence and happiness [*eudaimonia*]" (Ricoeur 1995, 239-240). And forgiveness, insofar as it positively reconfigures a person's relationship with others in his community, is precisely one of the tools that allows an agent to decisively re-work his emplotted narrative to better connect *phronesis* with *eudaimonia* in his own experience.

---

[43] For an extended model of forgiveness based specifically on a narratively-developed view (as opposed to the virtue-based aesthetic model developed here), see Griswold (2007, 98-110).

[44] See also Vanhoozer (1991, 41): "Though narrative aesthetically presents what is beyond the grasp of concepts, the narrative schema is not beyond the means of investigation and explanation." This is simply to say that a narrative perspective can be analyzed for propositional truth, even as it delivers experiential or affective, non-propositional knowledge.

Consequently, because forgiveness contributes to the personal development of the forgiver and, in some cases, the forgiven (when it promotes a general peacefulness among the group), and because it is unavoidably grounded in self-giving Butlerian-love or Ricoeurian-solicitude, forgiveness is therefore revealed as a technique for developing both an optimal personal and public character (in both moral and aesthetic terms insofar as it creates peace). Therefore, the cathartic emotional release that comes as a product of the forgiveness process cannot be identified with forgiveness itself. Instead, rationally desiring the good for another, via a *eunoia*-motivated cognitive recognition that the other simply should be forgiven, is sufficient to motivate the process. Forgiveness can lead to the beautiful emotional release of "overcoming resentment" in the life of the forgiver, but it in no way requires this feeling as a precondition.

Indeed, when Ricoeur justifies his use of the term solicitude on the grounds of the "intimate union between the ethical aim of solicitude and the affective flesh of feelings" he concurs with Aristotle's connection of *eunoia* and different emotional states (Ricoeur 1992, 192).[45] The categorization of forgiveness as a virtue, then, becomes a way to maintain a heuristic emphasis on the subjective emotional state of the forgiver when still considering forgiveness as a cognitive process.

The adapted aesthetic model of forgiveness

In order to map this view of forgiveness-as-judgment alongside the equally important process of forgiveness-towards-emotional-catharsis, the danger of confusing one for the other must first be made clear. In the existing literature on the philosophy of forgiveness, emotions tend to be considered primarily negatively in terms of their distracting ca-

---

[45] See also Konstan (2006, 164) for a related historical assessment.

pacity to irrationally affect cognitive decisions (such as the locutionary act of forgiving).[46] While variant interpretations of Butler's definition have provoked a flurry of debate, both his supporters and detractors tend to agree (along with Aristotle) that emotions must be conquered in order to forgive.

Instead, to maintain a neutral attitude towards emotional states throughout the experience of the forgiveness process, a foundational model of aesthetic appreciation *tout court* developed by Leder et al. can be adapted to map the phenomenon of forgiveness; thereby allowing a simultaneous assessment of forgiveness-as-judgment and forgiveness-towards-emotional-catharsis that both unite under the helm of forgiveness-as-virtue.

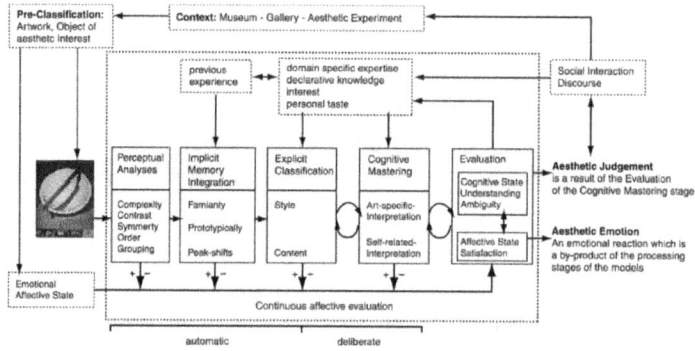

A Model of Aesthetic Appreciation and Judgments (Leder et al. 2004, 492)

---

[46] As exemplified by Murphy (1982, 504), a confusion in the Butler-tradition has, for many years, equated surpassing the painfulness of resentment with the experience of forgiveness itself in varying ways; Haber (1992, 7) agrees, though he qualifies his agreement to allow for agents who have not yet managed to throw off their emotions but plan to do so in the future; and Kolnai (1973-1974, 103) posits that the hardening of one's resentment and hatred might "encourage him to persist in his line of wrongdoing"; little significant consideration of other emotional facets of the experience of forgiveness as it appears to us seem to have been undertaken.

In brief, the model of aesthetic appreciation put forth by Helmut Leder, Benno Belke, Andries Oeberst, and Dorothee Augustin seeks to provide a psychological explanation for an observer's aesthetic experience of a work of art by analyzing the stages of cognitive processing that result in both an aesthetic judgment and an aesthetic emotional response to the piece in question (2004, 491). Because it seeks to consider both cognitive and affective processes as related, though distinct, elements of aesthetic experiences, this model broke new ground in the field of psychological aesthetics and has motivated neuroscientific research into aesthetics since its initial publication in 2004 (Leder and Nadal 2014, 446). Importantly, the Leder model situates an aesthetic experience within a particular context such that "aesthetic experience begins before the actual perception: with the social discourse that configures expectations, anticipations, and an aesthetic orientation, and in the context, which shapes those expectations and orientation, and creates an environment that can contribute to heightening the artistic status of an object" (Leder and Nadal 2014, 445).

For an observer in the proper context (such as a museum gallery), the Leder model takes a work of art as its input and processes it through five distinct cognitive stages that eventually lead to a pair of outputs: a cognitive judgment about the aesthetic merits of the work of art and a subjective emotional response to that artwork. Firstly, the artwork is Analyzed Perceptually for how it appears to the observer (based particularly on several key features of artistic method like contrast and symmetry). This appearance is affected by the observer's past experiences with similar works of art in the second stage of Memory Integration—a stage which often functions implicitly, "because the results of this processing do not have to become conscious in order to affect aesthetic processing" (Leder et al. 2004, 495). Following this initial perception, Explicit Classification labels the experience of the artwork based on the observer's level of knowledge about the subject matter: greater expertise will naturally lead to a more nuanced and informed product of this stage, though even amateurs will be able to accomplish some form of classification based on their limited experience. Importantly, this sort of Classification is grounded firmly on matters of the style evident in the artwork (Ibid. 2004, 498).

With this groundwork laid, the observer then moves into the final two stages which are closely related and deliberately considered: Cognitive Mastering and Evaluation. Functioning in a feedback-loop, the intellectual understanding garnered in the fourth stage is continually and intentionally re-evaluated in the fifth stage to ensure that the overall processing method of the artwork in question has succeeded. As Leder et al. (Ibid., 499) explain, "when the evaluation is not subjectively experienced as successful, the information processing can be redirected to the previous stages," allowing the observer to continue to ponder the artwork until she reaches a satisfactory conclusion about it in her own mind; in short, aesthetic experience is not a single-shot gambit, but can be continued for as long as is necessary to achieve the desired results.

Notable here is the role of the observer's affective state throughout the five cognitive stages; not only do Leder et al. (Ibid., 501-2) "propose that the result of every processing stage in our model can increase or decrease the affective state" of the observer, but also that it is this fluctuating emotional state that regulates the overall aesthetic processing experience such that "the perceiver somehow evaluates his affective state and uses this information to stop the processing once a satisfactory state is achieved." Consequently, the Leder model produces two "relatively independent" outputs: aesthetic emotion (grounded in the subjective pleasure felt as a consequence of the aesthetic experience) and an aesthetic judgment (a cognitive appraisal of the artwork) (Ibid.).

And since the process of forgiveness is similarly involved with both cognitive appraisals and subjective emotional states, this model is not only fruitful for questions of aesthetic experience, but can be adapted to describe the interpersonal experience of forgiveness.

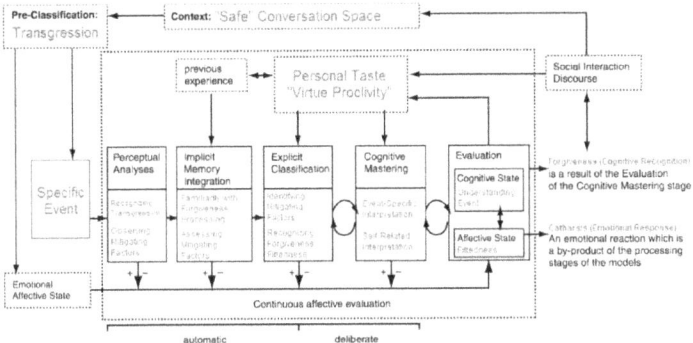

The Adapted Aesthetic Model of Forgiveness

Like the Leder model's assumption of an observer's location in a gallery, the overall context of the forgiveness process is a crucial prerequisite for a genuine experience to unfold. Following both Griswold (2007, 51) and Haber (1991, 40-41), real forgiveness is possible once the wrong in question has ceased.[47] Rather than a work of art, this adapted model takes a transgression as its input; without a wrong to be forgiven, forgiveness is unnecessary. Notably, the input is not an act of contrition from the guilty party, although the offender's repudiation of their actions and some expression of regret can help to further justify the forgiveness process once it is undertaken.[48]

---

[47] Griswold (2007, 49-50) argues that this is largely to maintain the dignity of the victim and to avoid retroactively condoning the wrong behavior in the first place. However, this is not to say that a forgiven wrong might not be repeated and thereby begin the process over again.

[48] This is to say, contra Griswold (2007, 49-50) that a variation of the so-called "unconditional forgiveness" defended by Garrard and

Just as in the original model, the input must be analyzed from within the proper context; it is within this "Safe" Conversation Space that both the cessation of the transgression and the consideration of the transgressor's penitence can obtain so that they can be Analyzed Perceptually in the first step of the adapted model.[49] This initial perception is where what David Konstan (2010, 3) calls the "wrongdoing" (as opposed to the "harm"), which will be identified and whatever mitigating factors of the wrongdoing (such as apologies or acts of contrition on the part of the wrongdoer) will be noticed. Secondly, the forgiver automatically moves to recognize these elements of the transgressive event as relevant through the implicit application of her personal facility with the process of forgiveness and her assessment of the mitigating factors; if the agent determines that forgiveness is indeed warranted, based on the Integration of her Memory into the specifics of the event, then the situation will be Explicitly Classified as a transgression that befits forgiveness.

Following this, the most important element of the model is reached: the repetitive feedback loop where the forgiver repeatedly re-assesses her Evaluation of her continually shifting emotional experience to deliberately Cognitively Master both her thoughts and feelings on the matter—what Griswold (2007, 57) dubs "seeing the offender in a new light." This requires the forgiver to not only continually process the difficult emotional states that inevitably fluctuate through-

---

McNaughton (2003, 39-60) is possible on this model, provided that the context for the process is still appropriately safe for the forgiver and that she continually aims at the proper cognitive mastering of the experience.

[49] Johansson (2009, 545) breaks down four basic conditions that might precipitate a justifiable act of forgiveness: in addition to the two already listed here (that correspond to options (ii) and (iv) in Johansson's paper), a change in the wronged person's perspective might also properly ground forgiveness.

out the cognitive assessment of the penitent's deserving forgiveness in the previous stages (in order to make the shift from automatic to deliberate evaluation), but will simultaneously require the forgiver to navigate his or her proclivity for cultivating the life of virtue. Whereas the original model considered this facet as something involving one's "personal taste," the aesthetic model of forgiveness will return to Aristotle's concept of *kalokagathia* to argue that the proper kind of person will make overall better judgments about the interpersonal situations that warrant forgiveness versus those that do not.

In the end, unlike the models of Haber,[50] Jeffrie Murphy,[51] or others, the adapted aesthetic model of forgiveness continually tracks the emotional experience of the forgiver as she considers the whole of the situation from transgression to cessation to apology and beyond, all the while calibrating the painful emotional fluctuations that shift as the process continues. And like the Leder model, it is precisely the emotional state of the forgiver that delimits the end of the process (once the forgiver is not only cognitively but emotionally satisfied that forgiveness does befit the situation) to allow for two simultaneous outputs: the intellectual result of the Evaluative and Cognitive Mastering that comes to recognize the propriety of forgiveness' extension, as well as the final emotional reaction to the overall process that manifests as some form of catharsis. Again, just as Bishop Butler argued nearly

---

[50] Although Haber (1991, 51) is willing to consider emotional catharsis as a feature of the overall forgiveness experience, his model is not able to either track or describe such an experience beyond the requirement that the forgiver commit to making an attempt at overcoming spiteful emotions at some point in the future.

[51] Adams (1991, 284) summarizes Murphy's definitions of forgiveness and resentment in a manner that helpfully indicates Murphy's failure to engage with the emotions of the question. See also, Murphy (1982, 504).

three centuries ago, this peaceful product comes only as a result of the cognitive-affective processing method as explained here—it is not a prerequisite.

The heart of the matter

Consequently, rather than require the forgiver to jettison his emotional experience in order to cognitively process the situation in question, this model allows those affective states to "ride along" throughout the intellectual analysis of the situation itself. As the forgiver comes to perceive an apology from within the "Safe" context of a ceased transgression and as this penance is implicitly recognized and then explicitly categorized as genuine, the tagged emotional states will be in continual flux, but will consistently interact with the cognitive elements of the process as a whole. Whatever the end result of the mastery-evaluative feedback loop, the twin outputs of a rational determination and an emotional response to that description will have been considered and affected at each step of the process.

And this difficult tension between the rational desert of forgiveness and the emotional difficulty of baring one's heart by extending said forgiveness is not only what Rembrandt captured in his masterful scene of the Prodigal, but is also a familiar experience to anyone who has had cause to forgive another. As Ernesto Garcia (August 2011, 7) observes about Butler's repeated choice of an epigram for his sermons on the topic, forgiving our enemies is not easy precisely because, at the time our forgiveness process engages, our enemies they remain.[52] Forgiveness is, however, a key process that can

---

[52] Butler repeatedly selected Matthew 5:33-34, "You have heard that it was said, 'You shall love your neighbor and hate your enemy.' But I say to you, Love your enemies and pray for those who persecute you..." (ESV).

allow us to move beyond such resentment, promote Ricoeurian solicitude, achieve Aristotelian *kalokagathia*, and thereby contribute to an overall more beautiful world.

References

Adams, Marilyn McCord. July 1991. "Forgiveness: A Christian Model." *Faith and Philosophy* 8.3: 277-304.

Annas, Julia. 1995. "Virtue as a Skill." *International Journal of Philosophical Studies* 3.2: 227-243.

Aristotle. 1980. *The Nicomachean Ethics.* Edited and translated by W.D. Ross and J.O. Urmson. Oxford: Oxford University Press.

Aristotle. 1966. *The Politics.* Edited and translated by Ernest Barker. Oxford: Oxford University Press.

Butler, Joseph. 1792. *Fifteen Sermons Preached at the Rolls Chapel*, 6th ed. London: Rivington and Hayes.

Dover, K. J. 1974. *Greek Popular Morality in the Time of Plato and Aristotle.* Oxford: Basil Blackwell.

Garcia, Ernesto V. August 2011. "Bishop Butler on Forgiveness and Resentment." *Philosopher's Imprint* 11.10: 1-19. Available at http://hdl.handle.net/2027/spo.3521354.0011.010

Garrard, Eve and David McNaughton. 2003. "In Defence of Unconditional Forgiveness." *Proceedings of the Aristotelian Society* 103: 39-60.

Griswold, Charles. 2007. *Forgiveness: A Philosophical Exploration.* New York: Cambridge University Press.

Haber, Joram Graf. 1991. *Forgiveness: A Philosophical Study.* Lanham: Rowman & Littlefield.

Hursthouse, Rosalind. 2011. "What Does the Aristotelian *Phronimos* Know?" In *Perfecting Virtue: New Essays on Kantian Ethics and Virtue Ethics*, Lawrence Jost and Julian Wuerth, eds, 38-57. New York: Cambridge University Press.

Hutchinson, D. S. 1995. "Ethics." In *The Cambridge Companion to Aristotle.* Edited by Jonathan Barnes, 195-232. New York: Cambridge University Press.

Johansson, Ingvar. 2009. "A Little Treatise of Forgiveness and Human Nature." *The Monist* 92.4: 537-555.

Kalimtzis, Kostas. 2000. *Aristotle on Political Enmity and Disease: An Inquiry into Stasis.* Albany: State University of New York Press.

Kolnai, Aurel. 1973-1974. "Forgiveness." *Proceedings of the Aristotelian Society* 74: 91-106.

Konstan, David. 2010. *Before Forgiveness: The Origins of a Moral Idea.* New York: Cambridge University Press.

Konstan, David. 2006. *The Emotions of the Ancient Greeks: Studies in Aristotle and Classical Literature.* Toronto: University of Toronto Press.

Kraut, Richard. 2014. "Aristotle's Ethics." *The Stanford Encyclopedia of Philosophy.* Edited by Edward N. Zalta. Accessed March 11th, 2016, http://plato.stanford.edu/entries/aristotle-ethics/.

Leder, Helmut, Benno Belke, Andries Oeberst, and Dorothee Augustin. 2004. "A Model of Aesthetic Appreciation and Aesthetic Judgments." *The British Journal of Psychology* 95: 489-508.

Leder, Helmut and Marcos Nadal. 2014. "Ten Years of a Model of Aesthetic Appreciation and Aesthetic Judgments: The Aesthetic Episode – Developments and Challenges in Empirical Aesthetics." *The British Journal of Psychology* 105: 443-464.

Milliken, John. 2006. "Aristotle's Aesthetic Ethics." *The Southern Journal of Philosophy* 44.2: 319-339.

Moss, Jessica. 2011. ""Virtue Makes the Goal Right": Virtue and *Phronesis* in Aristotle's Ethics." *Phronesis* 56: 204-261.

Murphy, Jeffrie. 1982. "Forgiveness and Resentment." *Midwest Studies in Philosophy* 7.1: 503-516.

Petrochilos, George A. 2002. "Kalokagathia: The Ethical Basis of Hellenic Political Economy and Its Influence from Plato to Ruskin and Sen." *History of Political Economy* 34.3: 599-631.

Proimos, Constantinos V. 2011. "Forgiveness and Forgiving in Rembrandt's Return of the Prodigal Son." *Art, Emotion and Value Proceedings of the 5th Mediterranean Congress of Aesthetics.* Edited by José Alcaraz, Matilde Carrasco, and Salvador Rubio. Mediterranean Congress of Aesthetics: 291-299.

Ricoeur, Paul. 1995. *Figuring the Sacred: Religion, Narrative, and Imagination.* Translated by Davis Pellauer. Edited by Mark I. Wallace. Minneapolis: Fortress Press.Ricoeur, Paul. 1983. "Narrative and Hermeneutics." In *Essays on Aesthetics: Perspectives on the Work of Monroe C. Beardsley.* Edited by John Fisher, 149-160. Philadelphia: Temple University Press.

Ricoeur, Paul. 1992. *Oneself as Another.* Translated by Kathleen Blamey. Chicago: University of Chicago Press.

Vanhoozer, Kevin J. 1991. "Philosophical Antecedents to Ricoeur's *Time and Narrative.*" In *On Paul Ricoeur: Narrative and Interpretation.* Edited by David Wood, 34-54. New York: Routledge.

Weiler, Ingomar. 2002. "Inverted *Kalokagathia.*" *Slavery and Abolition: A Journal of Post-Slave Studies* 23.2: 9-28.

Wood, Robert E. 1999. *Placing Aesthetics: Reflections on the Philosophical Tradition.* Athens, OH: Ohio University Press

Chapter 3

Forgiveness and Warranted Resentment

Frederik Kaufman

Recent philosophical discussions have shown forgiveness to be a frustratingly protean concept and woe to those who seek tidy formulations. Still, a few conditions are necessary for forgiveness to be an intelligible idea at all. One is that there must be an actual offense, not merely an imagined one, to which the victim of the wrongdoing reacts with a range of hard feelings, such as resentment, anger, or disappointment. If there is no genuine offense, then there is nothing to forgive the (alleged) wrongdoer for. Second, because of a genuine offense, the victim's proportionate hard feelings are entirely legitimate or warranted under the circumstances; I am well within my rights to resent you for what you did to me. Third, in order to forgive, the victim must relinquish, overcome, or at least modify her negative attitudes toward the wrongdoer. It makes no sense to say that I have forgiven you if I remain just as angry or resentful as before; perhaps I tried to forgive and failed, but that is a different matter. Moreover, why I abandon my hard feelings seems crucial; forgetting about the wrong you did to me or taking a pill to get over my resentment do not count as my forgiving you. So fourth, in order to forgive, I must overcome my hard feelings for moral reasons (Murphy 2003, 16).[53]

---

[53] Jeffrie Murphy writes, "I propose, then, to understand forgiveness as the overcoming, on moral grounds, of what I will call the vindictive passions—the passions of anger, resentment, and even hatred

This distinguishes forgiveness from other ways in which victims can abandon their moral anger. Fifth, and most perplexing, in order to forgive, the victim must relinquish her hard feelings while at the same time holding the transgressor fully morally responsible for the wrong. The forgiver does not excuse or diminish the moral culpability of the wrongdoer in any way, nor does she condone, minimize, or overlook the wrong. She straightforwardly regards the wrongdoer as morally at fault. She keeps the transgressor's moral culpability firmly in mind, yet still seeks to relinquish or at least modify the hard feelings to which she has every right because of the wrong (Allais 2008, 33).[54]

I shall consider only those transgressions where overcoming one's hard feelings is not expecting too much from people, putting aside cases of grave moral evil where forgiveness is either not normally humanly possible or perhaps even wrong. I also acknowledge that relinquishing one's hard feelings can sometimes be a very difficult undertaking. But if forgiveness is ever a rationally defensible response to wrongdoing, not only can the reasons to forgive be articulated, but a rational agent would expect her retributive emotions to respond appropriately. That is, the rational moral deliberator seeks a proper fit between her retributive emotions and her reasons for holding them, and would abandon those feelings which she decides she ought not to have. Even if reason is the slave of the passions, we can still ask in any particular

---

that are often occasioned when one has been deeply wronged by another."

[54] Lucy Allias expresses this common thought: "Specifically, my concern in this article is to make sense of the idea that these metaphors capture a core part of forgiveness, in a way that is compatible with seeing that forgiveness must be granted without changing judgments concerning the wrongness of the offense and the perpetrator's culpability for it."

case whether our emotions are warranted. Indignation, for example, requires the belief that the target of our antipathy is at fault, and that belief is either true or false; if we learn that it is false, then we see that our indignation is unwarranted and we would have to abandon it, on pain of irrationality, since it would be groundless.

In the philosophical literature on forgiveness, several prominent authors appeal to a similar dynamic with respect to the abatement of resentment following an apology: in their view, a sincere apology from the transgressor undermines the victim's legitimate resentment at having been wronged. The victim then abandons her resentment because she sees that it is unwarranted, and this is what it means to forgive, or so it is argued. "Forgiveness," Charles Griswold writes, "does not get rid of warranted resentment. Rather, it follows from the recognition that the resentment is no longer warranted" (2007, 43). Relinquishing unwarranted resentment may well count as forgiveness, at least in a range of cases. Your friend carelessly erases some of your iPhone photos, and you are seething mad at him; he is mortified by his negligence and sincerely apologizes, and then withdraws into guilty silence, avoiding contact with you. After some measured period of time it would be perfectly appropriate for me to say to you that you should forgive your friend; your continued anger is unwarranted. This sounds like a plausible account of forgiveness following an apology in a case of this sort, but I think that the requirement to relinquish unwarranted resentment fails as a general account of forgiveness, since if one's resentment is not warranted, then of course one should relinquish it. Seeing forgiveness only as the abandonment of unwarranted resentment eliminates the elective nature of forgiveness; it would not be something freely bestowed on the transgressor by the victim, it would instead be required of the victim. Necessarily, one should never keep unwarranted resentment. So even if getting rid of unwarranted resentment can sometimes count as forgiveness, as Griswold suggests, it is hard to see why that would be especially praiseworthy or philosophically interesting. It is not especially praiseworthy because I have no choice in the matter but to abandon my unwarranted resentment; and it is not philosophically interesting because in that case I have no right to continued resentment. Much more significant, in my opinion, is a form of forgiveness where, for moral reasons, I abandon resentment that I could legitimately maintain. Or so I shall argue in this paper.

Let's begin with a straightforward case where forgiveness seems like a natural option: someone is wronged (though not egregiously) and the transgressor later repents, apologizes, seeks to make whatever amends are possible, reforms, and accepts responsibility for the wrong. What is the victim now supposed to do? On what seems to be a standard analysis of forgiveness following an apology in the philosophical literature, the victim is now supposed to relinquish her hard feelings because they are no longer warranted. As sketched above by Griswold, this is what forgiveness amounts to; it is the abandonment of unwarranted resentment (and other vindictive passions).

But exactly how is the apology, remorse, and restitution supposed to make continued resentment unwarranted, thus making forgiveness the only rational choice? There are various explanations in the forgiveness literature. Murphy argues that genuine repentance can negate the insulting "messages" (his term) that wrongful acts convey; such acts imply, he suggests, a different moral status between victim and perpetrator—"I count but you do not" (Murphy and Hampton 1988, 25). Negating insulting messages from wrongful acts means that one's resentment is no longer justified; no more insult, so no warrant to resent the offender. For Pamela Hieronymi, resentment is a kind of protest against a past action that continues to pose a threat, one which loses its point once the transgressor renounces the deed, since there is now no longer a threat to protest against. She writes, "If we understand resentment in this…way, we can start to see how an apology might lead to a change in view or revision of judgment that would rationally undermine it. Once the offender himself renounces the deed, it may no longer stand as a threat to either the public understanding of right and wrong, to his worth, or to one's own. It has been cut off from the source of its continued meaning. The author has retracted his statement, and anger loses its point" (2001, 25). If moral anger loses its point, then it must be relinquished since, as she claims, it has been "rationally undermined." If it has been rationally undermined, then the victim would not be justified to persist in holding it.

For Margaret Holmgren, by taking the necessary steps to address the wrong and to protect ourselves from further abuse, the offended person now has "no reason to resent the offender or to regard his implicit claim about us as a threat" (2012, 75). Again, if after working through the process of addressing the wrong the offended person has no reason to resent, then resentment is unwarranted and so must be relinquished, since it is no longer justifiably held. And Adrienne Martin regards resentment, like P.F. Strawson, as the perception of inadequate interpersonal commitment, which the wrongdoer can overcome by apologizing, thus depriving resentment of its proper object. She writes, "Resentment's primary target is the wrongdoer's inadequate interpersonal commitment, as an ongoing state. If one is persuaded that the wrongdoer now has an adequate commitment…then resentment no longer has its primary target"(2010, 545). But again, if resentment no longer has its primary target, then it cannot be legitimately maintained and so must be relinquished.

These accounts of resentment—insulting message, protest against a threat, threat, inadequate interpersonal commitment—all seek to explain how we lose a legitimate claim to our hard feelings once the wrongdoer apologizes, since an apology (along with repentance and restitution where possible) in one way or another deprives our resentment of its proper object. If our resentment lacks its proper object, we no longer have warrant to it and so our only reasonable option is to abandon it. According to these accounts, that's simply part of what it means to forgive: it is to abandon unwarranted resentment, a negative attitude which we can no longer legitimately hold because the offender has apologized and made good for the wrong.

But again, if our resentment is no longer warranted, then of course we should relinquish it; it is a vindictive passion to which we have no legitimate claim and to persist in holding it is surely an abuse of it. Prior to the apology and any possible amends, maybe we had a legitimate claim to it, but not any longer on this view. The relinquishing of unwarranted resentment account of forgiveness makes forgiveness a dubious virtue (if it remains one at all), since seeking to relinquish something which we hold unjustifiably is hardly the mark of a morally praiseworthy person, nor should we be commended for finally succeeding in relinquishing it, if we are not entitled to hold it.

One might object to the thought that it is not commendable to relinquish something held without right. We do commend the person who turned a wallet full of money in to the lost and found despite his strong desire to keep it. So by analogy we might think the forgiver on the relinquishing of unwarranted resentment account of forgiveness is admirable after all because he managed to relinquish a powerful but unwarranted emotion many of us would be inclined to maintain. But if a sincere apology makes continued resentment unjustified, as explained in the various accounts mentioned above, then forgiveness would involve overcoming an irrational tendency to which we are prone, namely, a propensity to unjustifiably maintain various vindictive passions. So understood, forgiveness becomes primarily an internal struggle for the victim, since he now knows that he has no right to his resentment because it has no appropriate target; he must fight his propensity to maintain it, just as the person who found the wallet knows that he has no legitimate claim to it and must fight his desire to keep the money.

This strikes me as an inadequate account of forgiveness following an apology because it has little to do with forgiving the transgressor who, it seems, has now dropped out of sight; it focuses instead on my internal struggle to rid myself of feelings that I acknowledge it is illegitimate for me to hold. The interpersonal dynamic has shifted profoundly: the apologetic transgressor is in the clear and now the problem is all mine, as it were, since I must try to overcome an emotion that I realize is unjustified. Maybe finally doing so is commendable, but that is an achievement of my character. In some sense I am acting rationally, since I am responding to the knowledge that I have no right to my continued resentment, but to a rational moral deliberator, there is no question that I should abandon unwarranted retributive emotions, and the only question at this point is how best to do so. Indeed, once I realize that my retributive emotions are unjustified because the transgressor's apology deprives them of their proper target, and that I should therefore abandon them forthwith, then taking a pill to get rid of them should count as forgiveness as well. It is thus not clear that I get rid of my resentment for morally credible reasons, on the abandonment of unwarranted resentment account of forgiveness. In fact, in this view I wouldn't abandon my resentment just because the transgressor apologized; there appear to be two steps: first, the transgressor's apology makes me realize that my continued resentment is without justification, and second, I abandon it for that reason.

On the abandoning of unwarranted resentment account of forgiveness, the offender's apology would have the same effect on the victim's relation to her resentment as discovering that the offender was not actually morally responsible for the alleged wrong. Learning that the person who, say, insulted you was deranged or excused in some other way (he was hypnotized or practicing his lines for the school play) means that any resentment you feel is baseless, held without right, and ought to be relinquished immediately. The same would hold if the wrongdoer's apology somehow made our hurt feelings unwarranted, irrespective of how hard it would be for us to relinquish them.

Consider an analogous situation with anger. A man might recognize that he is prone to disproportionate anger at the slightest provocation. He might learn to control the intense waves of anger that he acknowledges are unjustified. This is commendable, but his struggle to do so is his problem, and if he is successful it is an achievement of his character. Similarly, perhaps a person prone to holding grudges could learn to become more forgiving; maybe this too is commendable, but here the focus is on becoming a certain kind of person, not on what it means to forgive. If forgiveness essentially involves abandoning our retributive emotions for morally credible reasons, it is hard to see why giving up something which we acknowledge we hold illegitimately—our unwarranted resentments—should count as especially morally credible. It is true that in giving up our unwarranted resentments we do the right thing, just as the man who returns the wallet does the right thing. But to my mind, much more praiseworthy is freely choosing, for moral reasons, to do more than the minimum to avoid the irrationality of maintaining unjustified resentments.

I think it is important to realize that the legitimacy of our feelings is not automatically undercut by what the apologetic offender does to try to compensate for the wrong he inflicted on us. Relinquishing our hard feelings because they are no longer warranted is different than relinquishing them for morally laudable reasons, which is at the core of forgiveness, or at least at the core of forgiveness that is especially morally praiseworthy. It is the difference between giving up one's hard feelings *because* they have no legitimate basis and giving them up *despite* their having a legitimate basis; the latter seems to me to be a more morally significant form of forgiveness. That is, one elects for moral reasons to abandon one's hard feelings even though one could legitimately maintain them. Surely that would make forgiveness truly praiseworthy; it is not something that one has to do to avoid the irrationality of maintaining unwarranted resentments, but instead chooses to do for the appropriate kind of reasons.

We can thus distinguish between mandatory forgiveness following an apology, where the forgiver recognizes that her resentment is unwarranted and is therefore required to give it up, and what we might call elective forgiveness, where one's resentment remains warranted and so the victim is not rationally required to give it up. Here the forgiver recognizes that her resentment remains warranted irrespective of an apology, but nevertheless chooses to abandon it for morally credible reasons. She could legitimately continue to hold her resentment, but she still does something that she does not have to do: she elects to give it up.

It would seem that elective forgiveness is most appropriate with the more serious offenses, offenses where sincere apologies cannot readily undermine the legitimacy of the victim's resentment. In these cases the question of whether to forgive the wrongdoer calls for the most sensitive and careful consideration by the victim, since the harm of the wrong is greater thus grounding one's resentment more deeply, making retribution a more plausible option. Indeed, with serious wrongs a quick forgiveness can itself be wrong. As Murphy notes, self-respect and respect for the moral order can be at stake (2003, 19). Whereas in more trivial cases, it is easier to see how the transgressor's sincere apology can undermine the victim's warrant to her resentment, so that continued resentment amounts to holding a grudge. If I resent you for damaging my lawnmower you borrowed last week, but you've sincerely apologized, had it professionally repaired and returned it along with a case of my favorite beer, yet I still resent you, then I am holding a grudge. You've done more than enough to make my continued resentment unreasonable. I should give it up.

But the more serious the offense, the harder it is to see how the transgressor can do enough to make up for the wrong and thereby make the victim's resentment unjustified. If a rape victim forgives the rapist, this is not obviously a matter of the rapist having done enough to make the victim's continued resentment unjustified, so that she must relinquish it on pain of irrationality were she to maintain it. In such serious cases it is much harder to imagine the victim coming to hold a grudge precisely because it is harder to see how the transgressor can make the victim's resentment unwarranted. But the difficulty or even the impossibility of doing so need not preclude forgiveness. That is, forgiveness does not require the victim coming to see that her resentment is unwarranted in order to give it up. The forgiving rape victim abandons her resentment *despite* the legitimacy of holding on to it. So while abandoning unwarranted resentment can count as a kind of forgiveness in more trivial cases, it seems that the interesting type of forgiveness involves abandoning warranted resentment for serious kinds of transgressions.[55]

Why might one waive one's legitimate claim to resentment? The rational forgiver should be able to explain why, in any particular case, waiving one's right to continued resentment is the proper choice. Forgiveness is an intentional act, one for which reasons can be given and evaluated. Unless something like this is possible, then we are dealing with emotional forces that play themselves out in various ways independent of rational assessment. The moral emotions relevant to forgiveness, such as resentment and anger, are not mere sensations. They involve judgments; I feel moral anger because of my beliefs about the wrong that you did to me. Moreover, given what you did, I regard my anger as a justified response, not merely a causal consequence of your action. No doubt time alone or some other non-rational process can bring

---

[55] In my view, whether there can be unforgivable transgressions depends on whether an offense is so serious that it would always be wrong to relinquish one's warranted resentment, not on whether it is impossible for the transgressor do enough to make the victim's resentment unjustified.

about a moderation of hard feelings, and perhaps this too can count as a minimal form of forgiveness. Without a full conceptual account of forgiveness we should not rule that possibility out *a priori*. However, our interest here is on what has emerged as the starkest and most interesting form of forgiveness, namely, cases where the victim voluntarily relinquishes her warranted resentment, what I've called elective forgiveness. Mandatory forgiveness, by contrast, is far less interesting, since it is clear what the victim must do about her resentment: she *must* relinquish it, since she holds it without right.

An apology is obviously an immensely important factor for victims trying to decide whether or not to forgive. But rather than an apology undercutting the legitimacy of one's hard feelings and thereby one's claim to maintain them (thus forcing one to abandon them on pain of irrationality, as the abandonment of unwarranted resentment account of forgiveness has it), perhaps apologies can work differently in those cases where they do not function to make one's resentment unwarranted. They might instead give victims an opportunity to reflect on their choices. Recall the accounts of resentment considered earlier: threat, insult, inadequate commitment to interpersonal relations. Perhaps an apology can shield the victim from further assault (so to speak) by quarantining the source of the wrong; it lets her know that she can emerge from her defensive psychological crouch and consider her options, just as you can reconsider how to react emotionally to the criminal who is now sequestered in jail after he assaulted you; he no longer poses a threat, but that does not mean that your resentment for what he did to you is baseless.

Similarly, an apology might give the person wronged an opportunity to reflect on the choices at hand: backward-looking reasons can favor continued hard feelings to which the victim has every right, since this person, the offender, after all, wronged you; forward-looking reasons can counsel abandoning them because (we are assuming) the offender has reformed, made restitution to the extent possible, and expressed his remorse. At this point the victim must choose between maintaining her (warranted) hard feelings and waiving her right to do so. To be clear: we are considering cases where the legitimacy of the victim's resentment is not undermined just because of the apology, rather, the apology now means that she has to decide whether to exercise her right to continue her resentment or not. As I see it, where an apology does not undermine the legitimacy of maintaining one's resentment, forgiveness can be understood as the victim waiving her legitimate claim to continued resentment for morally credible reasons. This makes forgiveness elective, a matter of true choice for the victim, rather than something required on pain of irrationality.

Given that in its most interesting form, forgiveness requires freely choosing to relinquish warranted resentment for morally credible reasons, what might those reasons be? One reason to waive the claim to one's hard feelings is for the sake of a greater moral good at stake in the situation. In this case, the offended person has a clear conception of the wrong she suffered—it is not overlooked or condoned—she realizes that she has every right to maintain her resentment because of the moral wrong she has suffered—her resentment is proportionate and warranted; but she also understands that maintaining it will threaten something of greater moral significance, so she chooses accordingly, seeking the morally preferable outcome in the situation. Repairing a particular relationship, for example, may be more morally significant than maintaining one's legitimate resentment. It is thus no surprise that proper forgiving requires a good measure of mature practical wisdom.

Another reason for waiving one's claim to continued resentment can be for what Glen Pettigrove has called "grace," an intentional unmerited benefit (2012, chapter 7). The victim would bestow upon the offender something which is not his due or that he can justifiably claim merely because he apologized, but what he should gratefully receive, namely, the fact that the victim has voluntarily and magnanimously waived her right to continued resentment. The offender is treated better than he deserves, because what he actually deserves is the victim's continued resentment. His apology does not force the victim to relinquish her resentment on pain of irrationality because it is now groundless; instead, his apology allows the victim to decide voluntarily to relinquish her claim to it as an act of grace, not as something due or owed to the wrongdoer. This preserves the fundamentally elective character of forgiveness, a feature lost in accounts of resentment where the apology undermines one's right to resent by making the resentment groundless. It is this elective feature that makes forgiveness praiseworthy, if and when it is praiseworthy, because the victim voluntarily chooses to do something for reasons that comport with her other values or her self-conception or her understanding of where a greater good lies, not because her moral emotions are now unjustified.

Macalester Bell supplies yet another reason why the aggrieved might voluntarily relinquish her claim to continued resentment. She realizes that what she calls "reparative activities," which include apologies and reparations, cannot by themselves require forgiveness, since that would undercut the elective nature of forgiveness. What is missing, she argues, is inspiration. To inspire is to fill with hope by vividly sketching alternate possibilities. "Reparation," she writes, "can inspire forgiveness by enacting the wrongdoer's commitment in such a way as to invite his victim's forgiveness" (2012, 212). Although she doesn't put it this way, it seems clear that the power of inspiration presupposes that the victim's continued resentment is warranted. An inspirational apology then supplies yet another reason—a hopeful one—for the victim to relinquish it.

So far we have considered forgiveness when the offender apologizes, repents, and makes whatever restitution he can. But when the offender does not apologize, the situation should now be clear: basically, it does not matter. The victim retains the prerogative to forgive irrespective of whether or not the offender apologizes. It is in this respect that forgiveness is unconditional; it does not depend upon an apology (or upon restitution or repentance or remorse). Absent an apology the victim can still choose to foreswear her warranted resentment for any of a variety of morally salient reasons. Thus is it possible for a victim to forgive the dead. Apology or not, the operative question for the victim will always be whether giving up one's warranted resentment is the morally best choice.

Maintaining one's resentment or other hard feelings because of a wrong is the "default" position to which the victim has every right, a right that only the victim can waive. By making a sincere apology and doing whatever he can to make up for the wrong, the offender in fact acknowledges that right; but his apology does not automatically undermine it by rendering the victim's resentment groundless. As we have seen in cases involving more trivial wrongs, while an apology can perhaps undermine the victim's right to continued resentment, with serious wrongs it does not obviously or easily do so. And it is precisely in the more serious cases where the question of whether we should maintain our moral anger or forgive is most significant. Forgiveness in its purest, most philosophically interesting, and most perplexing form lives, as it were, within the range of justified or warranted resentment on the victim's part. That is what she gives up, by choice. Accounts of forgiveness which hold that apologies function by undercutting the victim's claim to her hard feelings thus fail to respect the victim's prerogative because they compel her to relinquish her hard feelings on pain of irrationality. This distorts the relationship between the victim and the offender and, I submit, fails to acknowledge what is most praiseworthy of the forgiver, if she has voluntarily relinquished warranted resentment for morally credible reasons.[56]

References

Allais, Lucy. 2008. "Wiping the Slate Clean: The Heart of Forgiveness." *Philosophy and Public Affairs* 36.1: 33-68.

Bell, Macalester. 2012. "Forgiveness, Inspiration, and the Power of Reparation." *American Philosophical Quarterly* 49.3: 205-221.

Griswold, Charles. 2007. *Forgiveness: A Philosophical Exploration.* Cambridge: Cambridge University Press.

Hampton, Jean and Murphy, Jeffrie. 1988. *Forgiveness and Mercy.* Cambridge: Cambridge University Press.

Hieronymi, Pamela. 2001. "Articulating an Uncompromising Forgiveness." *Philosophy and Phenomenological Research* 62.3: 529-555.

Holmgren, Margaret. 2012. *Forgiveness and Retribution.* Cambridge: Cambridge University Press.

Martin, Adrienne. 2010. "Owning Up and Lowering Down: The Power of Apology." *The Journal of Philosophy* 107.10: 534-553.

Murphy, Jeffrie. 2003. *Getting Even.* Oxford: Oxford University Press.

Pettigrove, Glen. 2012. *Forgiveness and Love.* Oxford: Oxford University Press

---

[56] I gratefully acknowledge written comments on earlier drafts of this paper from Glenn Pettigrove, Lucy Allis, Donna Fleming, and several anonymous reviewers for this volume. I am most grateful to my good colleague Steve Schwartz for his interest, written comments, and critical discussions on this topic.

Chapter 4

Responsibility and Self-Forgiveness in *The Story of Lucy Gault*

Kathleen Poorman Dougherty

William Trevor's novel *The Story of Lucy Gault* tells the tragic story of the Gault family in 1920's Ireland (2002). In the midst of increasing violence, the Gaults plan to leave Ireland, hoping to return someday, but 9-year-old Lucy resists the move. Just before their scheduled move, Lucy runs away in hopes of forcing her family to stay. In a tragic misunderstanding, however, her parents reasonably assume her to be dead and go ahead with their move. When Henry, the loving groundskeeper, finds Lucy in the woods several weeks later, alive but nearly starved, her parents are long-gone. In their grief, the parents cut off contact with their Irish community and settle in a tiny European village to live a peaceful, though melancholy, life together, finding it too painful to return home. After failed attempts to locate and contact her parents, Lucy remains in the family home cared for lovingly by the groundskeeper and his wife. The tragic misunderstanding of Lucy's behavior radically affects all of their lives.

The novel raises numerous significant philosophical issues that warrant exploration. For example, the novel highlights the tenuous relationship between love and human flourishing, showing that loving someone deeply may make us vulnerable to suffering. Likewise, it prompts us to consider questions regarding the role of suffering in good human lives, making clear that living morally and living happily may not go hand in hand. Perhaps most significantly, much of the moral challenge in the novel comes from Lucy's apparent inability to forgive herself for the suffering she has caused both to her parents and to herself, and thus to overcome the sense that she is not entitled to happiness. Though intriguing, not all of these issues can be addressed fully here. This chapter will focus on the ways in which Lucy's inability to forgive herself, and her sense that she needs forgiveness for her action and its consequences, provide insight into the philosophical literature on self-forgiveness, raising numerous challenges to standard philosophical interpretations of self-forgiveness.

First, the literature on self-forgiveness tends to presuppose that, like interpersonal forgiveness, self-forgiveness is necessary only when one has committed a moral wrong. Lucy Gault, however, commits no moral wrong, even though her actions cause considerable harm, both to herself and to her parents. Thus, Lucy's story suggests that standard interpretations of self-forgiveness are incomplete. Second, Lucy's story prompts us to reflect upon the dependence of self-forgiveness on interpersonal forgiveness, for part of what makes self-forgiveness so hard for Lucy is that she cannot be confident that her parents would forgive her, if given the opportunity. This demonstrates that self-forgiveness must sometimes function independently of interpersonal forgiveness. Finally, the novel challenges our sense of the relationship between responsibility and forgiveness, revealing that taking responsibility for our actions and our identities, even when these actions or identities are inescapable, may be tragic and inconsistent with moral well-being. Rather than accept responsibility for her actions, Lucy must relinquish her undue sense of responsibility for harms she could not control, if she hopes to have any possibility of self-forgiveness and thus a restored sense of self.

A non-paradigm case

The standard philosophical understanding of forgiveness is that forgiveness is a moral response to having been harmed or wronged in some way by another (Hughes, 2015). Some descriptions of self-forgiveness attempt to parallel this understanding, thinking that self-forgiveness and interpersonal forgiveness are relevantly similar in requiring wrongdoing. In a typical description of self-forgiveness, the individual in question has committed some bad action, and as a result of this action feels tremendous guilt or shame. To overcome this guilt and shame and be restored to a sense of self-worth or moral self-respect, the individual engages in a process of self-forgiveness. This process of self-forgiveness may also involve attempting to gain forgiveness from the victim, if that is possible, or seeking some kind of reconciliation with the victim. In thinking of paradigm cases of behaviors or actions that challenge us to self-forgiveness, the most plausible candidates are morally reprehensible actions or at least obviously morally bad actions. It is the immorality or the badness of these actions that would seem to make self-forgiveness difficult. These morally bad actions might run the gamut from horrific to tragic to sad. We can imagine, for example, the reformed Nazi sympathizer who now realizes the magnitude of the horror in which he participated, the negligent driver whose inattention causes a tragic accident, the schoolyard bully who later understands what harm she perpetuated, or even the disloyal friend who feels guilt at harming a loved one.

Margaret Holmgren, for example, models her description of self-forgiveness on her understanding of interpersonal forgiveness. She defends a model of self-forgiveness where self-forgiveness is an attitudinal shift toward a wrong; she argues that it is a process of replacing the self-condemnation that arises with the recognition that we have committed a wrong with a "more positive attitude toward ourselves" (2012, 105). For Holmgren, the process can be long and psychologically difficult, consisting of steps that include recognizing and acknowledging the wrong as well as attempting to make amends, but self-forgiveness presupposes that some wrong was committed and that someone was harmed (2012, 106-107).[57] In considering the notion of self-blame, Peter French describes it as "a form of holding oneself responsible, a way of expressing negative self-reactive attitude subsequent to the performance of an action(s)" (2014, 587). Though French is not describing self-forgiveness, self-blame is surely the predecessor to self-forgiveness; if we don't blame ourselves, there is no need for self-forgiveness.

Numerous authors suggest that the need for self-forgiveness may not be predicated on an intentional harm. Zenon Szablowinski points out that "some individuals find it impossible to forgive themselves for wrongs done accidently" (2012, 680). He imagines, for example, the case of a woman who accidentally backs over a young child in her car, killing the child, and cannot escape the sense that she is responsible even though her action was unintentional. Nancy Snow seems to initially suggest that self-forgiveness presupposes a bad action, but then expands the possible circumstances in which self-forgiveness might be appropriate. She tells us that self-forgiveness "restores our capacity to carry on as functioning moral agents even after we have committed moral wrongs or harmed others" (1993, 75). She opens up the possibility that the harm done to others might not have been the result of a moral wrong. She suggests that such wrongs or harms might be intentional, accidental, or the result of weak will or carelessness. Even so, on Snow's view, what characterizes the need for self-forgiveness is that we regret what we have done (1993, 75). Part of what is interesting in Snow's

---

[57] In describing Holmgren's view as paradigmatic, nothing here suggests that it is non-controversial or uninteresting. Holmgren's view is paradigmatic merely in assuming that forgiveness, whether inter-personal forgiveness or self-forgiveness, presupposes a wrong. Her view is quite radical in arguing that forgiveness is always morally warranted.

claim is the distinction between causing a harm and committing a wrong. Lucy Gault's story highlights this distinction and shows the ways in which it plays into our understanding of self-forgiveness.

What makes Lucy's case philosophically interesting and challenges our understanding of self-forgiveness, is that though her action certainly causes tremendous harm, it is by no means a morally bad action. Moreover, it is unclear whether it even makes sense to think of her as responsible for it in any way. Thus, Lucy's case highlights the fact that self-forgiveness may be needed not only when a wrong has been committed, but merely when harm has been caused, even if unintentionally. People are certainly harmed by her action—both she and her parents suffer terribly—but it is not clear at all that her action is morally bad. It is perhaps best thought of as an accident, but perhaps more accurately, it is better thought of as bad luck. Lucy's case helps demonstrate that self-forgiveness, unlike interpersonal forgiveness, may not require an actual wrong at all. Lucy does, of course, regret her action, but just the fact that she regrets it is not enough to say that it was morally wrong. Lucy appears to be struggling with self-forgiveness over something that was simply a terrible misfortune.

Lucy's misfortune stems from having run away from home in an attempt to forestall her family's move. Her actions do, admittedly, have disastrous consequences, but they are consequences she never intended and could never have predicted.[58] Her intention was to forestall her family's move by running to a former, beloved housemaid. However, Lucy falls

---

[58] This may not assuage the strictest of utilitarians, but this is exactly the kind of case that has often been thought to challenge our intuitions about utilitarianism, and would likely give all but the strictest of utilitarians pause.

in the woods, hurting her ankle so badly that she is unable to make it through her journey or return to her family, all the while knowing of the family's impending departure. Complicating matters further, articles of her clothing are found in rocky places near the shore leading her parents to conclude that she has drowned in the raging sea, as was fairly common in their community. Her parents, assuming her to be dead, leave their home. In fact, her mother has even assumed that Lucy committed suicide. In their despair, the Gaults leave Ireland with no final destination in mind; her mother's pain is so acute that they leave and never look back, hoping to escape the devastating circumstances of their daughter's apparent death. Thus, Lucy's impetuous behavior results in a lifetime of her own pain, her parents' pain, and the terrible realization that her action precipitated both. All of the consequent events are certainly the result of Lucy's running away from home, but in no sense could a child have ever thought that this would be the result. Though a particularly stern approach might be to think this is rather impetuous or stubborn, to think Lucy (a young child) responsible for all the harms that followed her escape into the woods would be callous at best.

Robin Dillon argues that it is not only wrong actions that might warrant self-forgiveness. She suggests a wide variety of dispositions or approaches that might call for self-forgiveness, including "[w]rong feeling, wishing, wanting, thinking, reacting, and especially wrong *being*" (2001, 59). Admittedly, Lucy could well be guilty of any number of these wrong dispositions: she certainly felt too strongly, she wanted irrationally, and she reacted hastily. Perhaps most strongly, her one impetuous action was rather typical for her, so that we may think she is guilty not only for one impetuous action, but for having been an impetuous child, that is for wrong *being*. Running away from home was by no means the first time that Lucy had acted impetuously. Her clothes had been found by the shore simply because she had been swimming without permission, and her emotional response to the impending move had been rather irrational. Even so, given that Lucy is only nine years old, we would hardly call these responses serious moral shortcomings. They are neither the result of a settled character, so that we would hold her responsible for having an impetuous character, nor are they such serious actions that they qualify as bad in and of themselves. We do get the sense that Lucy was always perceived as a willful child, often determined to have her own way, which is sometimes enough to be thought bad. Surely, though, even willful children should not endure a lifetime of punishment, either external or self-inflicted.

Lucy's challenge suggests that self-forgiveness can be a serious moral dilemma even when the action is not immoral. Dillon suggests even more strongly that self-forgiveness can be a challenge even without wrong action, being, or feeling. She does argue, however, that self-forgiveness requires agency:

> *[W]here there is no agency there no is (sic) responsibility, and the assumption of responsibility is central to self-reproach. It does, however, make sense to hold character flaws, failures, of virtue or excellence, or inappropriate emotions or dispositions against oneself, since these do implicate agency, and to be devastated by the terrible thing wrought through one's agency, even if it isn't strictly speaking wrong. (2001, 61)*[59]

---

[59] Dillon argues forcefully that just because one feels the need for self-forgiveness, an action is not necessarily wrong. In doing so, she gives a wide variety of examples in which the actions are less than ideal, but not obviously wrong. The kinds of examples she gives include everything from accidents to instances where no decision

Here the question becomes whether it makes sense to say that a nine year old child has agency. Lucy certainly seems to think she does, as she clearly holds herself responsible for her own behavior; whether she is correct in her assessment is an entirely separate matter. How we would assign responsibility or agency here is complicated, and myriad arguments might come down on either side, but I suggest that it is unreasonable to attribute agency to Lucy. If her grave error is simply having been impetuous, then this hardly constitutes a wrong, for being impetuous rather goes hand in hand with being nine years old. Moreover, if it is her *being* that is in question, it is difficult to think of a child as having a settled being or character, especially if we think of being or character as something that is habituated over time.

The Aristotelian conception of the development of virtue (or vice) may provide some insight here. On the Aristotelian account, one develops character traits (virtues or vices) through the repetition of like activity (1999).[60] It is not one action—or even a few actions—that result in virtue or vice, but rather the ongoing repetition of corresponding activities. Moreover, the repetition of actions goes hand in hand with developing the proper modes of thought and feeling. In becoming virtuous, one learns not only how to do the same actions as the virtuous person, but one learns to do them as the virtuous person does them, that is, one acquires practical wisdom. And this takes time. Aristotle even goes so far as to suggest that a young person with practical wisdom cannot be found. Acquiring practical wisdom takes time and experience, which is in part why Aristotle would not typically

---

would be ideal, and the choice may be between the lesser of two wrongs.

[60] For a fuller discussion of my understanding of the relationship between practical wisdom and virtue, see Dougherty (2007).

think of the very young as virtuous. They may have the potential for virtue, but do not yet have settled states of character (Aristotle 1999). In an Aristotelian sense, then, Lucy's way of being is best attributed to temperament or even circumstance, rather than something for which she ought to be thought of as having agency. She may be setting the foundation for a future character or way of being, but to say yet that she has full agency or even a fully developed character trait seems too strong.

That said, Lucy seems to attribute agency to herself, and other characters do describe Lucy as responsible for her circumstances. In fact, Lucy becomes an object of pity, and the plight of the family becomes the stuff of legend, embellished with each telling. The sense of responsibility borne by both Lucy and her parents becomes enhanced and exaggerated:

> *The tragedy called down upon herself by a child, and what had since become her life, made a talking point, and seemed to strangers to be the material of legend. Visitors to the beaches of this quiet coast listened and were astonished.... As often with such travellers' tales, exaggeration improved the telling. Borrowed facts, sewn in where there was a dearth, gathered authority with repetition. (Trevor 2002, 70)*

Whether or not Lucy is actually responsible becomes rather a moot point, when everyone around her seems to describe her as so. Maybe, then, it is not actual agency that matters, but rather the perception of agency. Whether or not Lucy is correct in attributing agency to herself, the fact that she does makes it difficult to forgive herself. What makes the situation even worse for Lucy is that the aspect of herself that she regards as shameful is the only perspective from which she is able to see herself. Lucy is so young that she has never been able to see herself in any other way. She has no grounding moral sense of herself to rely upon, so that her action and its resulting consequences totally constitute her sense of self and understanding of her character. Dillon argues that "wrongs that can be regarded as 'out of character' are less-damaging to one's self-conception," and that what is particularly challenging about actions that cause us to reconsider our own character is that they undermine our sense of self (2001, 64). Lucy, however, has no previous sense of self to be undermined; for her, there is no returning to an otherwise strong sense of self-respect or understanding of herself as a morally upstanding person. She cannot even escape by thinking of her own action as contrary to who she is, for it has come to define her life. Thus, even if she is not properly thought of as responsible for wrongdoing, wrong-feeling, or wrong-being, even if she did not properly have agency, Lucy experiences herself as responsible, and cannot forgive herself.[61]

Even though cases like Lucy's need not radically alter our philosophical interpretations of self-forgiveness, they do prompt a rethinking of standard interpretations. Paradigm cases often influence our understanding of a problem, so that rethinking the paradigm may result in rethinking our approach as well. Lucy prompts reflection regarding the

---

[61] Though Lucy is a literary character, and her experiences are rather extreme, they have certain parallels to reality. A recent *StoryCorps* episode recounted the story of Sean Smith, now 36 years old, who, at age ten, accidently killed his younger sister with a handgun. The children had arrived home alone after school and were looking for hidden video games when they found the handgun in their father's drawer. Just as his sister was telling him to put it away, the gun went off, seemingly in an instant. Though Sean called 911 and tried to revive his sister, she died. To hear him tell his story, it has deeply impacted his life and the lives of his parents. Even though we would not call him guilty or possibly even ascribe agency to him, he experiences guilt and a sense of responsibility. See (Smith 2016).

standard example of the person who needs and strives for self-forgiveness—she is certainly a far cry from the Nazi sympathizer, the negligent driver, the bully, or the disloyal friend. Even so, self-forgiveness is necessary for restoring her moral sense of self.

Self-forgiveness and interpersonal forgiveness

In discussing self-forgiveness, many authors compare it with interpersonal forgiveness in one way or another, under the seemingly reasonable assumption that our understanding of interpersonal forgiveness ought to be at least partially explanatory in an analysis of self-forgiveness. This approach seems to hold some merit even though our relationships with ourselves often differ dramatically from our relationships with other people. Here, however, it is the practical connection between self-forgiveness and interpersonal forgiveness that is of interest. Nancy Snow comments, for example, that "Self-forgiveness can provide a second best alternative to interpersonal forgiveness in situations in which full interpersonal forgiveness is not or cannot be achieved" (1993, 75). In her analysis, Snow describes self-forgiveness as a process that involves "coming to grips with some behavior on my part which harmed, offended, or disappointed another" (1993, 77). This "coming to grips" involves acknowledging our own behavior and being able to move forward with optimism about our chances for self-improvement. Self-forgiveness, on Snow's view, is a process of "self-restoration" akin to the process of restoring a damaged relationship (1993, 76). Self-forgiveness, then, is a process of making the self whole, or restoring the self to wholeness. It is not simply absolving ourselves of our wrongdoing or condoning our wrongdoing, but taking a particular approach to it concomitant with an attempt at altering our future behavior.[62] As Snow suggests, we should not simply acknowledge or accept the wrong and move on, rather, self-forgiveness should be tied to a genuine attempt to remedy the character flaws that made the action possible. This is also consistent with the recognition that all humans have character flaws, but attempting to correct them is part and parcel of maintaining moral agency (Snow 1993, 76).

Numerous elements of this characterization are interesting with respect to Lucy Gault. First, Snow describes self-forgiveness as necessary when we have harmed *someone else*. Though the cases in which someone else has been harmed surely stand out in our minds, it is also worth considering those cases in which we harm ourselves.[63] For Lucy Gault, the harm is certainly both interpersonal and intrapersonal, for her own actions have caused radical self-harm. In fact, it is not obvious who suffers most or who is most harmed. Surely Lucy's parents, Heloise and the Captain, are harmed significantly. The pain for them is so great that Heloise cannot bear the idea of returning to Ireland. However, they build a quiet and dignified life together. Their relationship remains one marked by kindness and gentleness though characterized by their shared solitude and moments of darkness:

> *It was a bad day, the Captain said to himself. In her eyes there was the nagging of what lay at the depths of her melancholy, as always*

---

[62] Paul Hughes argues that it is important to distinguish between condoning, pardoning, and self-forgiveness. See Hughes (1994).

[63] Paul Hughes also suggests that harm to ourselves is important, but claims that harms to ourselves more typically occur in cases that are not all that serious. This would radically understate the case for Lucy Gault. See Hughes (1994, 557).

> *there was on a bad day. She tried to return his smile but could not and, too well, he knew she saw their child allowing the waves to have their way, without resistance because that was their child's choice. His intuition was sharp on bad days; he always knew.... He loved her, more than he could ever have loved anyone, but today, as so often before, she made on her own the effort he could not help her with. (Trevor 2002, 106-7)*

Arguably, of course, it is not only Lucy's actions that cause their suffering. They could have returned, they could have checked in on their former home, but to the best of their knowledge they had no reason to do so. Escaping physically seemed the only way to survive their loss.

Lucy's suffering was arguably even far more profound and coupled with incredible guilt. Her actions resulted in the loss of her entire family and all the innocence of childhood that should have been available to her. She did not have the means of psychological escape open to her parents. She lived out the rest of her life in her small, Irish town with no escape from the prying, judging, and pitying eyes of neighbors. She lived surrounded by the source of her pain—the house she tried to escape, the woods she became lost in, and the eventual understanding of her own terrible tragedy. She certainly harmed her parents, but she probably harmed herself more.

So, self-forgiveness might be appropriate as a response to the pain she caused her parents, but perhaps most for the pain she caused herself and for the tragedy she brought upon her own life. Part of her own tragedy is the seeming inability to allow herself any semblance of happiness. When Ralph, a handsome suitor professes his love to her, and wishes to marry her, she cannot bring herself to make a life with him, for the guilt is too great, telling him, "I am not someone to love" (Trevor 2002, 118). As she confesses more of her life story, she admits that she blames herself for having caused them pain, and that she longs for their forgiveness. No rational argument can persuade her that they would have forgiven her long ago and would want her happiness. Thus, her life remains a constant waiting in her childhood home.

Surely, then, self-forgiveness is also warranted for the harms we bring upon ourselves. In fact, it seems that these are some of the most interesting cases. We harbor guilt over roads not taken, over possibilities not pursued, over effort not made. We frequently blame ourselves (sometimes deservedly) over the paths of our lives. Often we alone have suffered from these failings. Self-forgiveness is sometimes warranted simply so we can move forward more productively, or as Snow would put it, more optimistically. Self-forgiveness would allow Lucy to truly live.

Second, Snow suggests that self-forgiveness might be a "second-best" alternative to interpersonal forgiveness when interpersonal forgiveness is withheld or unavailable. She suggests two ways in which interpersonal forgiveness might be unavailable: the offended might refuse forgiveness, even if forgiveness seems appropriate and reasonable, or the offense might be so great that it is unforgiveable (1993, 79). In these kinds of cases, it makes sense to think of self-forgiveness as an alternative to interpersonal forgiveness, but it is not clear why self-forgiveness should be considered "second-best." Admittedly, we may be skeptical of the person who is too quick to forgive herself when the one she has harmed has yet to forgive her. Self-forgiveness does not seem genuine if it comes too easily; if it does it would indicate that we have not taken the harm done seriously or adequately invested ourselves in the kind of positive change that Snow argues self-forgiveness requires. As Snow points out, following Hare, the self-forgiveness possible in a case like this is likely to remain tinged with guilt, absent interpersonal forgiveness (1993, 79). In cases of wrongdoing that are unforgiveable, Snow argues that self-forgiveness is challenging to say the least, but necessary to continue functioning as a moral agent (1993, 80).

Lucy Gault's case presents another alternative: it's not that her parents are refusing forgiveness or that her action is unforgiveable. For her, interpersonal forgiveness is simply inaccessible. She continues to suffer guilt partly because she cannot know how her parents would respond were they to find her alive and well. Would they be angry? Would they be relieved? Would they pity her and themselves? Without the security of their constant love and attention, she cannot rest assured that finding her alive and well would not now be worse. In fact, when her father finally returns after the death of her mother, it is awkward at best. It pains him, of course, to find that she has been living almost as if time stood still, but his return at this late date cannot repair the damage. The lack of knowing throughout her life seems to make self-forgiveness impossible. In her case, self-forgiveness would have been not just "second-best," it would have been the highest priority. Without forgiving herself, Lucy's life has been effectively on hold; she seems unable to truly live or fully engage as a moral agent without self-forgiveness. The inability to receive interpersonal forgiveness prevents her from having any mechanism with which to forgive herself. Self-forgiveness may happen independently of interpersonal forgiveness, but Lucy Gault's case shows that self-forgiveness is much more difficult, both morally and psychologically, when interpersonal forgiveness cannot be achieved.

The reasons for this may be numerous, but one possibility is that our self-conceptions are often intimately tied to the ways we imagine others perceive us. Genuine self-understanding is often thought to provide some consistency between the way we perceive ourselves and the ways in which others perceive us—a significant disconnect typically is reason to believe that something is amiss with respect to our self-knowledge. Lucy's recognition of the possibility that she deserved forgiveness would have been readily enhanced by the reassurance that her parents also forgave her. In fact had it been possible to assure her of their forgiveness, it might have enabled her to see herself as someone deserving of forgiveness, and thus, provided the first step toward self-forgiveness. Surely interpersonal forgiveness and self-forgiveness need not necessarily go hand in hand, but the willingness of another whom we have hurt to forgive has the ability to make self-forgiveness seem more possible—it allows us a first step.

One might think that had Lucy a stronger sense of self or taken a more rational approach that she might have been able to overcome the lack of interpersonal forgiveness. Possibly someone with a more developed or stronger character could have worked through the challenge and moved forward with self-forgiveness and thus a more engaged life. Samantha Vice's arguments would suggest, however, that such an assessment is psychologically unrealistic. Vice argues that there is an asymmetry which is simply a general feature of persons: coming to understand another more fully typically leads to mercy, coming to understand oneself, however, does not (2006, 94). In order to gain this kind of mercy for ourselves, we would need to be able to view our own lives from an objective point of view, and this is simply impossible. In coming to understand another more fully, we begin to understand not only the other's character and motivations, but also the broader life circumstances that led to action. We are able to see the other in the context of extenuating circumstances and against a framework of a fuller understanding of the human condition; however, "the stance of dispassionate impartiality that does the work for mercy regarding others is immediately unavailable for a person judging her own crimes" (Vice 2006, 104). We are unable to be an impartial judge with respect to our own lives. The challenge is to continue living as the self that our reflection must at the same time judge, which creates a psychological challenge: "One stands before one's own awareness in all one's smallness and moral grubbiness, and it is not another, but one's very self standing, inescapably, there. Because who one essentially is takes up the horizon of awareness, there is no space to move around and judge oneself tenderly or dispassionately" (Vice 2006, 101).

Vice's arguments regard the notion of mercy toward the self with respect to particularly heinous actions, but there are important parallels to Lucy's challenge of self-forgiveness. Though Lucy's action has not been particularly heinous, she experiences it as so morally transformative, that it is unclear whether she is able to make that distinction. Perhaps more importantly, Vice's understanding of the psychological challenges we face in attempting to interpret our own selves from an objective point of view help explain why Lucy finds it so difficult to forgive herself for her actions. It's not just that Lucy needs to come to see herself differently or regard her actions from a different perspective; rather, she needs to be able to interpret her own actions in the context of what is reasonable with respect to a broader understanding of the human condition. She needs to be able to see her own action as a child in the context of the ways in which children behave, of the ways in which consequences are unforeseeable, and the ways in which people must move forward in the face of pain. Vice argues that this kind of approach is impossible in cases of particularly heinous action; perhaps in Lucy's case, without particularly heinous action, it is merely difficult. Imagining her own actions in the context of the human condition would certainly stretch her psychological abilities. Thus, even if she would readily be able to forgive someone else or take mercy on someone else for similar actions, forgiving herself is seemingly out of reach.

Taking responsibility

Finally, *The Story of Lucy Gault* challenges our sense of the relationship between responsibility and forgiveness. Much of the literature on forgiveness suggests that there is an important connection between taking responsibility for our actions and self-forgiveness, assuming that self-forgiveness involves in some important way accepting moral responsibility for what we have done or who we have been.[64] Jeffrey Blustein focuses his discussion on the significance of taking responsibility for our past. As he describes it, "someone who takes responsibility for his or her past appropriates it on the basis of some thematic connection between past and present and constructs a meaning for that past in and through the very act of appropriating it" (2000, 13). In Blustein's view, taking responsibility for our past plays an important moral role, and he suggests that the failure to do so may express a lack of humility or potentially result in a failure of self-forgiveness.

Blustein argues that a failure of self-forgiveness can be a moral defect in a person and that this defect may parallel the failure to take responsibility for one's past, even though the precise relationship between the two may not be altogether clear. He considers numerous possibilities. Forgiving oneself requires taking responsibility for one's past, so that a failure to take responsibility may result in a failure of self-forgiveness. Alternatively, one might be unwilling to take responsibility for the past because one cannot forgive oneself. Thus, it may be unclear where the cause properly lies. The challenge of taking responsibility and for forgiving oneself can be fraught with a variety of psychological barriers, so that it is not obvious which must come first.

Considered in light of the story of Lucy Gault, Blustein's analysis is insightful and interesting but seems incomplete. I think this sense of incompleteness lies with the idea of taking responsibility for one's past. A central element of taking re-

---

[64] Jeffrey Blustein and Margaret Holmgren both discuss the relationship between taking responsibility and forgiveness. See Blustein (2000) and Holmgren (1998).

sponsibility for one's past is the notion of appropriation (2000, 10-12). Appropriation, for Blustein, goes hand in hand with creating meaning out of our pasts. In a sense we create a cohesive narrative about our lives in which we make thematic connections between the events and experiences in our lives so that they build a cohesive whole. In the process, we appropriate actions or events and create meaning out of them. We accept some for the significant role they play in the life we now live and in the cohesive narrative we tell of our lives. Appropriation is a way of claiming the past, making it our own. In making it our own, in making it a part of the history of who we are, that is, in appropriating it, we also take responsibility for it. This sense of taking responsibility is an active way of claiming who we are, of staking our claim in our past actions, characters, habits, and experiences. It's a way of facing things and owning them. Given this sense of appropriation and taking responsibility, it is no doubt that Blustein sees a thorough-going connection between taking responsibility for one's past and self-forgiveness Taking responsibility presupposes self-forgiveness, for taking responsibility for our pasts requires reconciling ourselves to them.

I suggest, however, that Lucy Gault has managed to take responsibility for her past in such a way that self-forgiveness is impossible. Perhaps we should say that she has taken too much responsibility for her past, if that is possible. Lucy has created a narrative for her life, imbued it with meaning, and appropriated her past in such a way that it is part and parcel of who she is, it is an identity she cannot shake. However, the past she has appropriated gives a central place to the most significant event in her life: running away to prevent her family from moving, only for her action to result in a painful severing of her relationship with her parents. Moreover, the events that led to this misunderstanding would all have been avoidable had she been a more obedient and less petulant child. Thus not only does she have events and actions to appropriate, but she also has character traits to attach to those actions that allow the events to have even greater significance. This allows the events to be not only actions she committed, but also to be actions tied up with who she is or was. Consequently it appears reasonable to her to appropriate that understanding even more fully into her personal narrative and assume responsibility for it.

Notably, Blustein suggests that "there are limits to what one can properly appropriate. One cannot properly appropriate and so take responsibility for the influential beginning stages of one's life, since as a young child one does not exert much control over the development of one's character or personality" (2000, 11). In saying this, Blustein seems correct, but these influential, beginning stages can be profoundly meaningful for the path of our lives and the thematic connections that unfold. So, even if taking responsibility is not entirely justified in these cases, it may be unavoidable.

On this interpretation, the challenge for Lucy Gault is not taking responsibility for her past, but rather allowing herself to relinquish responsibility. She needs a narrative or a thematic way of connecting the events in her life that does not give such a central place to her role in the events of that fateful day. She, however, seems to find that nearly impossible. She sees all the terrible consequences of her action as direct results of her own behavior and way of being. She is even incapable of seeing herself in the light of a more objective understanding of human reality, as Vice suggests. Thus, holding herself responsible is the moral challenge that prevents self-forgiveness. And the central role that this too strong a sense of responsibility plays in her future life cannot be rewritten by any form of appropriation or narrative creativity without also seeming disingenuous. It simply has formed the central narrative element in her life no matter how she may attempt to re-describe it. It has become the entire story of who she is; rewriting the narrative would require rewriting her entire sense of self.

For Lucy Gault, rather than accept responsibility for her past, Lucy must relinquish her undue sense of responsibility in order to grant herself forgiveness. And this task seems nearly impossible, even though from our objective perspective as readers we think her worthy and deserving of forgiveness. Taking responsibility generally seems admirable, but sometimes taking responsibility, even when inescapable, can also be tragic and inconsistent with human flourishing.

References

Aristotle. 1999. *Nicomachean Ethics*. Translated by Terence Irwin. Indianapolis: Hackett Publishing.

Blustein, Jeffrey. 2000. "On Taking Responsibility for One's Past." *Journal of Applied Philosophy* 17.1: 1-19.

Dillon, Robin. 2001. "Self-Forgiveness and Self-Respect." *Ethics* 112: 53-83.

Dougherty, Kathleen Poorman. 2007. "Habituation and Character Change." *Philosophy and Literature* 31: 294-310.

French, Peter. 2014. "Self-Blaming, Repentance, and Atonement." *The Journal of Value Inquiry* 48: 587-602.

Holmgren, Margaret. 1998. "Self-Forgiveness and Responsible Moral Agency." *Journal of Value Inquiry*, 32: 75-91.

Holmgren, Margaret. 2012. *Forgiveness and Retribution: Responding to Wrongdoing*. Cambridge: Cambridge University Press.

Hughes, Paul M. 2015. "Forgiveness," *The Stanford Encyclopedia of Philosophy*. Edited by Edward N. Zalta. Accessed June 26, 2016. http://plato.stanford.edu/archives/spr2015/entries/forgiveness/

_____. 1994. "A Response to Snow." *The Journal of Value Inquiry* 28: 559-560.

Smith, Sean. 2016. "I Couldn't Help But Blame Myself." *StoryCorps*. Aired on NPR February 5, 2016. Accessed June 26, 2016. https://storycorps.org/listen/sean-smith-and-lee-smith-160205/

Snow, Nancy. 1993. "Self-forgiveness." *The Journal of Value Inquiry* 27: 75-80.

Szablowinski, Zenon. 2012. "Self-forgiveness and Forgiveness." *The Heythrop Journal* LIII: 678-689.

Trevor, William. 2002. *The Story of Lucy Gault*. New York: Penguin Books.

Vice, Samantha. 2006. "Living With the Self: Self-Judgement and Self-Understanding." *Judging and Understanding: Essays on Free Will, Narrative, Meaning and the Ethical Limits of Condemnation*. Edited by Pedro Alexis Tabensky. Hampshire: Ashgate Publishing.

Chapter 5

Forgiveness and Time: Attitudes, Dispositions, and Philosophical Charity

Ryan Michael Murphy

Admirable cases of forgiveness catch attention and command respect because the good will underlying them so greatly transcends the wrongdoing that permits their enactment. In October 2006, a gunman stormed into an Old Order Amish schoolhouse Lancaster County, Pennsylvania where he took ten young school girls hostage, shot eight, and then killed five of the girls before committing suicide (BBC News 2006). Nothing could have provoked this merciless attack, but within just a few days, the community of survivors publicly forgave the shooter. Their forgiveness was less verbal and marked more by acts of compassion and generosity on the part of survivors and victims' family members; they donated money to the killer's wife and children; and several even attended his funeral. Their inclination toward immediate and wholehearted forgiveness surprised many who would have thought revenge or animosity a more fitting sentiment on the occasion. But these survivors serve as humble exemplars for others. Their moral fortitude is an expression of forgiveness in its most robust sense, and it seems unlikely that such an act would arise spontaneously. Instead, I find it more plausible that this was the result of much moral development and the formation of attitudes and dispositions inclined toward forgiveness that had been nurtured by individuals and adopted by the community for quite some time prior to the attack.

How is forgiveness possible when one is a victim of extreme wrongdoing? Are there any preconditions that make one more or less likely to forgive? Is there any sensible way of understanding forgiveness prior to the commission of any wrongdoing?

In this chapter I seek to articulate a kind of dispositional forgiveness that could account for cases like the one described above. My primary aim is to enhance conceptual clarity surrounding forgiveness as it exists through time. Here I accept as exemplary cases of forgiveness those in which victims of moral wrongdoing approach their perpetrators with patience, compassion, and understanding, even though they still see perpetrators as responsible for their actions. This may or may not involve a forgoing of anger or resentment, as some have suggested, as persons who practice exemplary forgiveness might never feel angry or resentful in the first place, even though it might clearly be warranted. An act of exemplary forgiveness might take the place of punishment, but this need not necessarily be the case since not all moral wrongdoings are accompanied by requisite punishment (consider habitual tardiness for dates with friends or infidelity in a romantic relationship). Exemplary cases are often expressed and understood as extraordinarily humble and merciful responses to egregious and seemingly unforgivable acts of wrongdoing. These cases are plentiful and to limit the scope of conceptual analysis to the moment of wrongdoing and the forgiveness that follows are in some ways temporally myopic and structurally incomplete. Conceptually speaking, forgiveness is just as morally and causally relevant in the time prior to an act of wrongdoing as it is in the moments following. Attitudinal or dispositional forgiveness, or what can be called *forgivingness*, accounts for the ways in which forgiveness can exist prior to any act of wrongdoing.

I first introduce what I take to be the standard archetypal or paradigm case of forgiveness and identify the ways in which it differs from several other instantiations of forgiveness.

Once the significant features of the paradigm case have been articulated, I introduce an account of future-oriented forgiveness and argue that it is conceptually congruent with the paradigm case. I also consider the causal relationship between the two cases and suggest that their interdependent nature is a tenable explanation for exemplary forgiveness cases, such as the Amish. The final turn in this chapter seeks to motivate future-oriented forgiveness as a force in philosophical methodology, namely as the moral architecture that supports the principle of charity. This temporal analysis and application of forgiveness gives philosophers a new way to consider the moral dimensions of philosophical methodology while simultaneously pointing toward the pragmatic outcomes it yields.

Paradigmatic forgiveness

When you forgive, you in no way change the past—but you sure do change the future.

—Bernard Metzer

Although forgiveness is a complex moral phenomenon, there are several features that many agree are present in the paradigm case. First, forgiveness is applicable only in cases that involve moral wrongdoings. Second, forgiveness involves a recognition and acknowledgement that wrongdoing has occurred; it is neither an explanation nor an excuse (Roberts-Cady 2003, 293). Third, forgiveness is morally significant not only for the wrongdoer, but also the victim of wrongdoing. Finally, forgiveness can involve a combination of both actions and sentiments (Zaibert 2009, 365-93).

In addition to the ethical features listed above, the paradigm case of forgiveness follows a specific temporal order: some wrongdoer commits a wrongdoing, then the victim of wrongdoing chooses to forgive the wrongdoer, and finally, some form of reconciliation or overcoming is achieved. The temporal structure of the paradigm case situates the forgiveness event after wrongdoing.[65] I argue that forgiveness, or the same salient features that constitute the paradigm case of forgiveness, can be cultivated and be present prior to the commission of any wrongdoing. In the standard temporal ordering of the paradigm case, the power of forgiveness is only possible after one has suffered wrongdoing. But just as traditional views of post hoc forgiveness extend the relevance of forgiveness forward in time beyond the moment of wrongdoing, attitudinal/disposition forgivingness extends the moral relevance of forgiveness backward in time before the same moment.

Beyond the paradigm case: forgiveness and pseudo-forgiveness

Though the paradigm case of forgiveness is nicely ordered and lends itself well to analysis, the notion and terminology of forgiveness is readily applied in numerous other contexts. I introduce and consider these alternative contexts in order to more clearly demarcate the paradigmatic species of forgivingness I have in mind, from the broader discourse on forgiveness and references to dubious cases of pseudo-forgiveness.

While the paradigm case pertains to moral wrongdoing, forgiveness is widely incorporated into the related field of *criminal law*.[66] This also includes discussion of forgiveness

---

[65] Perhaps the greatest example of pre-emptive forgiveness, or situating forgiveness prior to the wrongdoing, is the theological centerpiece of Christianity, namely Jesus's self-sacrifice upon the cross for the sins and transgressions of all humanity (including future generations). Despite this familiar example, examples of future-oriented forgiveness are scarce in philosophical literature, and my committed focus to developing the latter comes at the expense of more fully explicating the former.

[66] Related notions and relatives of forgiveness in criminal law include pardon, clemency, amnesty and exoneration. While some of

in relation to punishment, which I do not take up here on risk of shifting from discussing the definition of forgiveness to debating its justification. Of course, there is often much overlap between standards of morality and the criminal code, but there are just as many cases of criminal laws that do not seem to comport so well with any moral system. Consider a political prisoner who is convicted by a dictatorial regime of having violated a criminal law against "treason" by speaking against the government and advocating democratic reforms. While this person is technically guilty of violating a criminal law, it is far less clear that the reformer has committed a moral wrongdoing. Suppose that after enduring a short prison sentence, the regime decides to "forgive" or pardon the reformer for violating the law in order to avoid scrutiny from other nations. Although the term "forgiveness" could be invoked by the regime, this notion of forgiving is categorically distinct from the paradigm case because it misses the mark in tracking moral value and is instead an instance of pseudo-forgiveness.

In the paradigm case of forgiveness, the wrongdoer must commit some actual moral wrongdoing, but the case of the dictatorial regime merely suggests the possibility that not all criminal laws criminalize moral wrongdoing. In fact, they may sometimes reward moral wrongdoing and punish morally praiseworthy efforts. This is not to suggest that all criminal law is divorced from moral values, but rather to indicate the most extreme and obvious cases of such a divide, in order to argue that the use of the term 'forgiveness' in criminal

---

these cases might qualify as true paradigm forgiveness cases, this falls beyond the focus of this chapter. My reference to criminal law here serves primarily to indicate that this domain exists with respect to forgiveness, but is not always identical with the paradigm case.

law does not always carry the same meaning as it would in a strictly moral context.

Relatedly, forgiveness terminology surfaces in the context of *social norms and etiquette*. Although some social norms seem to hold morally significant dimensions, it is clear that many simply do not. Imagine a young debutante who arrives at a highbrow dinner function and has never learned Euro-American dining etiquette. Perhaps she uses the dinner fork instead of the salad fork to eat her salad, she slurps her soup up loudly, and starts eating her entrée the moment it is served, while the other guests wait patiently for the host to propose a toast. While the more finessed dinner guests might "forgive" the debutant for her actions, the notion seems inapplicable here. At best, she might be excused for her lack of understanding these social norms, but the moral features that constitute forgiveness are notably absent in this case. Rules of etiquette do not track moral judgments in any consistent way. Although standards of etiquette might coincide with ethical standards (perhaps regarding vulgar speech), the lack of consistent tracking between them renders etiquette a relativistic and sometimes arbitrary standard of measure. Forgiveness is neither an excuse, nor exception, nor allowance; nonetheless, common understandings of forgiveness in the realm of social norms tend to take these forms.

A third category of cases in which the terminology of forgiveness is deployed occurs in cases of *financial transaction*, particularly when balances of outstanding debt are written off or discharged. The forgiveness of financial debts could arise in several different situations, but Nancy Holmstrom considers 'forgiveness' as a moral term to describe fiduciary transactions and finds it to be an incorrect and misleading use of the term (2015, 41-3). Most importantly, Holmstrom points out that forgiveness implies that the person being forgiven has committed some kind of wrong, but most debts are incurred through no wrongdoing whatsoever. As such, she calls for replacing the use of the term 'debt forgiveness' with a more accurate term, such as 'debt cancelation' or 'debt liberation' (Holmstrom 2015, 41).

Holmstrom's argument underscores the defining moral aspect of forgiveness by decoupling it from economic transactions. In a yet further contorted usage of the terminology of forgiveness, she notes that debt forgiveness is invoked even in cases of debt bondage or other situations in which it is the lender, not the debtor, who appears to be in the moral wrong. Pointing toward examples such as debt from medical bills and student loan debts, Holmstrom argues that reference to debt forgiveness should be avoided and instead we should question if these debts, "shouldn't...be seen as invalid in the first place" (2015, 42). In cases of immoral or exploitative debts, the terminology of forgiveness is highly problematic because it seeks to represent, and potentially legitimize, inverted moral structures in which lenders are in the moral wrong, but borrows are the ones who seek forgiveness.

The misapplication the term 'forgiveness' in this case arises from the divergence of economic values from moral values and could be characterized as pseudo-forgiveness. But not all agree that the moral discussion of forgiveness should be decoupled from its financial counterparts. Despite Holmstrom's contention that the terminology of forgiveness in economic considerations is inappropriate, Brandon Warmke argues that the language and structure of moral forgiveness is shaped by and best understood within an economic framework. Rather than importing the terminology of forgiveness into economics, Warmke extrapolates from economic structures an economic model of forgiveness (2015, 1-20).

Warmke's economic model of forgiveness is motivated by the framework of fiscal debt-cancellation and offers an account of how forgiveness cancels moral debts. Important to this model is the difference between debt and guilt:

> *Moral debts between persons may be eliminated by moral-debt forgiveness, just like in the economic case. But eliminating a moral*

> *debt does not eliminate one's guilt. That one is guilty for committing a wrong is, as it were, simply a matter of fact about one's moral ledger. (Warmke 2015, 14)*

While Holmstrom claims that the moral vice of infusing financial language with the language of forgiveness is that it fails to connect with moral value, it seems conceptually pragmatic to use the language of economics to describe moral forgiveness insofar as it helps to account for how forgiveness is understood as simultaneously holding a wrongdoer responsible while also moving beyond the wrongdoing. My intent here is not judge the success of Warmke's model, but rather to point out a few ways in which it helps to clarify the project of conceptual accounting at hand.

Part of Warmke's economic model of forgiveness depends on the distinction between what, "on one hand can be called the *practice* of forgiveness, and on the other hand, the *product* of that practice, the debt-forgiving event, which can be called *forgiving*" (2015, 4). Cast in this light, there is a tight causal connection between practices and the products to which they lead—this is a phenomenon I will explore in greater depth later. Beyond this causal connection between practices and products, occurrences of forgiveness have "a home in a larger constellation of behaviors and attitudes that constitute the practice of *forgiveness*" (Warmke Ibid.). If any account of forgiving-events must draw upon a broader constellation of attitudes and behaviors broadly called forgiveness, shouldn't there be an account of this broader constellation? After all, if the *explanandum* seems clear by gesturing to a broadly defined *explanans*, then the explanation is perhaps less precise than it purports to be. But this is not necessarily a theoretical shortcoming, rather it is an invitation for further conceptual clarity.

Similar to the ways in which I have just described various distinct meanings and uses of forgiveness, Charles Griswold defines the following five categories of forgiveness: political

Forgiveness and Time   117

apology, economic forgiveness, political pardon, judicial pardon, and metaphysical forgiveness. While Griswold's seminal work centers on forgiveness in the sense of political apology, my focus in this chapter falls under the heading of "metaphysical forgiveness," although my aim is primarily in conceptual clarification. Griswold suggests that these and other modulations of forgiveness "may usefully be thought of as bearing a Wittgensteinian 'family resemblance' to one another" (2007, 136-137). This is a helpful way of categorizing the various notions of forgiveness, but the family resemblance metaphor can be understood in another, perhaps more elucidating, way.

Although Griswold and Wittgenstein understand "family resemblance" to be the kind of "complicated yet perceptible nexus of between family members in a family," I find it helpful to consider how the term "family" could be understood as a level of biological taxonomy (Griswold 2007, xvii). The shift of meaning here serves not as an equivocated term for argumentative sake, but rather to better conceptualize the nature of categorization that best applies to the type of future-oriented forgivingness I seek to describe. As a biological category, families contain subgroups including genus and species. This hierarchical structuring of family resemblance suggests that although all members of the family hold some basic structures in common, they have less in common with any member chosen at random than members of the same genus or species.[67] The claim I seek to defend is that future-

---

[67] Consider the biological family, *canidae*, which includes animals as diverse as foxes, wolves, jackals, and dogs. The sub-group, genus *canis*, includes wolves, coyotes, and domestic dogs (but does not include foxes). Finally, the species *canis lupus* refers specifically to the gray wolf, and none other. My point here is that the philosophical suggestion that concepts bear "family resemblance" could mean either a close family resemblance (as in siblings and first cousins) or it could imply a much broader taxonomic classification that in-

oriented forgivingness bears not only a family resemblance with the paradigm case, but is part of the same genus; and if understood in a temporally sensitive light, the same species as well.

Forgiveness in Time: Future-oriented forgivingness as attitudes and dispositions

"Forgiveness is not an occasional act, it is a constant attitude."

—Martin Luther King, Jr.

Given the array of scenarios in which the terminology of forgiveness is used, I will argue that future-oriented forgivingness is categorically more similar to the paradigm case than any of the other cases or modulations described above. My argument here is two-pronged: first I will argue that the paradigm case and future-oriented forgivingness are categorically congruent; and second, I will argue that the causal interplay between these two cases is one of interdependence. In short, these cases ought to be understood as being equal in terms of being part of the same family or genus of moral phenomena, but also as being inseparable in causal terms. While the claim of causal interdependence is one that could, in theory, be subject to empirical study, I reference it here because it provides concepts and vocabulary with which to more accurately describe future-oriented forgivingness.

---

cludes a wide range of distinct specimens that may be loosely associated. Future-oriented forgiveness and the paradigm case are not only members of the same family; they are in fact members of the same species.

An initial formulation of what I have in mind when I speak of future-oriented forgiveness includes attitudes and dispositions, or the tendency one has toward forgiving, especially before any wrongdoing has occurred. Related or similar moral phenomena could include mercy and compassion.[68] Alternatively, Robert C. Roberts argues that, "forgivingness is the disposition to abort one's anger (or altogether miss getting angry) at persons one takes to have wronged one culpably, by seeing them in the benevolent terms provided by reasons of forgiving" (1995, 290). These accounts of forgiveness-as-virtue draw heavily on sentiment and moral psychology. The conception of future-oriented forgiveness, or what I shall call *forgivingness* (in borrowing the term from Roberts), is the quality of persons who are *more likely* to forgive any wrongdoing because of deliberate intention and the cultivation of social attitudes framed around forgiveness, benevolence, and charity.

Forgivingness is attitudinal in the sense that it exists both cognitively and emotionally. It is an attitude of which the holder is aware and which the holder chooses to build, develop, and maintain. Often, attitudes are understood as being malleable and selectable by choice, hence attitudinal forgivingness is chosen by those who hold it and is selectively developed so as to apply in a wide range of cases.

As an attitude, forgivingness is held with a large degree of generality or universal applicability. On one hand, forgivingness is forgiveness in its potential form, but on the other

---

[68] Jeffrie G. Murphy and Jean Hampton explore the relationship between forgiveness and other sentiments such as mercy and compassion in *Forgiveness and Mercy* (Cambridge: Cambridge University Press, 1988). I mention this here because rather than treating these as orthogonal moral phenomena, I instead wish to focus my conceptual distinctions on forgiveness *simpliciter*, albeit from a more temporally expansive perspective.

hand it is simultaneously a realized attitude which is known and felt by those who hold it. The potent duality of expressed and potential forgiveness persisting attitudinally through time allows for the ascription of, "the virtue of forgivingness to a person, for it should be clear enough across an extent of time, whether a person is seriously just and has self-respect" (Roberts 1995, 296). The essence of an attitude is that although it can be expressed in a momentary instance, attitudes are generally held and developed over a period of time. Likewise, when attitudes are ascribed to individuals and groups (i.e. "she has a good attitude toward working with others," or "they have a bad attitude toward eating new foods"), they tend to describe ongoing or developed belief states. Attitudinal forgivingness might also encompass what Warmke refers to as the "practice of moral forgiveness," or "the set of attitudes and behaviors that are informed by a certain shared set of general concepts and norms" (2015, 4). Although attitudinal forgivingness can be expressed through behavior and is informed by concepts and norms, it can be realized without being enacted. Once enacted, it could perhaps be better described as a disposition.

Dispositions differ from attitudes in that they are more predictive of actual outcomes in any given circumstance. Whereas an attitude is primarily felt and known by the holder, dispositions are primarily realized as reliably predictive indicators that may or may not be known to the holder. Nonetheless, they can be expressed and analyzed in causal terms for any set of events. Dispositional forgivingness, then, is the measure of the likelihood that one will forgive a wrongdoer in a hypothetical case of future wrongdoing. Whereas attitudinal forgivingness is general and universal in scope, dispositional forgivingness is predictive of particular instantiations of forgiveness in cases of future wrongdoing.

Considered jointly, attitudinal and dispositional forgivingness comprise the phenomenon of future-oriented forgivingness. The need for such an account is significant for explanatory terms in the paradigm case of forgiveness. Why is it that some individuals are more likely to forgive a wrongdoing while others are more likely to bear a resentful grudge? An account of forgivingness also provides the groundwork for describing and potentially prescribing the predictive moral *qualia* that will lead individuals to be more forgiving and less resentful with respect to future events. Together, this justification minimally offers a more comprehensive account of the phenomenon of forgiveness, and more broadly seeks to articulate an otherwise ambiguous aspect of moral development. On one hand, this project aims at conceptual clarification of the virtue of forgivingness; on the other hand, I argue this particular description carries with it prescriptive value, particularly in the realm of discourse and methodology in philosophy.

Categorical congruence: forgivingness and the paradigm case

Having thus far focused on the concept of forgiveness of the paradigm case and introduced the notion of forgivingness as attitudinal and dispositional, I argue that these cases should be understood as categorically congruent. While the notion of equivalence would be a stronger linking of concepts, it is not the most appropriate way of describing the relationship between terms because equivalence here would imply tautology. Although the concepts are incredibly similar and linked in interesting ways, the differences permitted by the concept of congruence give this theory its explanatory significance.

Akin to mathematical uses of the term, congruence between states of affairs permits difference and variability in some properties, while at the same time insisting other invariable properties must be identical in all cases.[69] Comparing the paradigm case of forgiveness with future-oriented forgivingness, there are many obvious *variable* properties: the location or point in time at which they occur; the orientation they take toward the person being forgiven; and the breadth of responses that would qualify as forgiveness or forgivingness for any particular wrongdoing. At the same time, there are several invariable properties in both cases: they both respond to moral qualities; they both seek to recognize wrongdoing; and they both serve to empower the victims (or potential victims) of wrongdoing.

Understood holistically, the variable properties between the paradigm case and future-oriented forgivingness allow for the multiplicity of possibilities in particular cases of forgiveness. At the same time, the invariable properties shared between the two cases define these cases as congruent. Paradigmatic forgiveness accounts for a bedrock of shared theoretical commitments, while forgivingness in time permits the theoretical plasticity allowed by congruence. In the same way that congruence is both an equivalence of invariable properties and permits a space for divergence among variable properties, so too does the taxonomical definition of species permit variability among specimens while simultaneously holding that they all belong to the same fundamental category.

---

[69] The Oxford English Dictionary defines congruence as, "the fact or condition of according or agreeing; accordance, correspondence, harmony," or being in accordance with reason. I take this definition to be minimal in describing the congruent relationship between the paradigm case and forgivingness. Additionally, I seek to describe not only the harmonious points of agreement between cases but also to describe the points of divergence which, although different, do not disrupt this harmony.

Of course, one might object that the properties I have identified as either variable or invariable could have been selected otherwise and, hence, are arbitrary. But this not the case because the list of invariable properties is precisely the same list of properties that define the paradigm case and which are notably absent (either in whole or part) in each of the other non-paradigm cases described. As such, the congruence between future-oriented forgivingness and the paradigm case of forgiveness is significant because the invariable properties they share are the same properties that are generally recognized that define the paradigm case. In other words, future-oriented forgivingness is an instantiation of the paradigm case.

Forgivingness and time: causal interdependence and explaining exemplary forgiveness

Situating forgivingness within the broader constellation of forgiveness accounts only for the categorical axis of my conceptual description. In addition to the categorical relationship, I also seek to elucidate the temporal dimensions of forgivingness. Understood as a type of forgiveness, forgivingness operates in and through time much as other moral phenomena, and the complexity of the apparent passage of time yields at least two distinct perspectives from which to observe and assess. In a dissection of prudential wellbeing in time, J. David Velleman notes that, "a person has two distinct sets of interests, laying along two distinct dimensions—his synchronic interests, in being well off at particular moments, and his diachronic interests, in having good periods of time and, in particular, a good life" (1993, 343-4). The same distinction helps enormously to clarify the manner in which forgivingness operates in any particular moment for a person, and how it relates to longer periods of time, namely one's lifespan.

Others have also pointed out the ways in which forgiveness operates both synchronically and diachronically. In arguing that forgiveness is an alternative to punishment, Leo Zaibert suggests that, "punishment and forgiveness are mutually exclusive (synchronically)" (2009, 369). In other words, at any given moment one cannot simultaneously punish and forgive another for the same act of wrongdoing. In an entirely different context, Charles Griswold considers the "the diachronic and perspectival dimensions of forgiveness," with respect to the narrative passage of time (2007, 98). Here, Griswold touches on the phenomena of the passage of time as it bears upon the experience of forgiveness, particularly noting the ways in which "the narration of is not the same thing as being the subject of that experience at that time" (2007, 202). Although entirely different in scope, both Zaibert and Griswold consider forgiveness in its synchronistic and diachronic dimensions, but only insofar as it relates to other phenomena or agents. The following is my synchronic and diachronic analysis of forgiveness with respect to itself and forgivingness, that is to say, forgiveness in time.

Forgivingness is synchronic in that it exists within discreet moments in time. Efforts in developing attitudes of forgivingness occur in particular moments and such attitudes are valuable in those moments. The subjunctive nature of attitudes affirms the potency of forgivingness in any given movement, even if it is only as *potential*. To hold a broad range of attitudes of forgivingness in any particular moment is to be prepared to respond with forgiveness in any possible situation *if one were to arise*. Potential forgiveness is just as morally significant as realized acts of forgiveness, because the only difference here is time and circumstance. Noting this subjunctive feature of forgivingness operating synchronically eliminates the objection that forgivingness is solely instrumental in effectuating forgiveness.

Furthermore, forgivingness operates diachronically in that it works across and through time. In this sense, the passage of time means that forgivingness as an attitude or disposition is cultivated through sequential moments of time (as in t_1, and persists at t_2, t_3, sequentially through t_n). In passing through this sequence of moments, forgivingness also operates across time (as in from t_1 to t_n). In the standard picture of forgiveness, the diachronic explanation describes how an agent's effort in developing attitudes now develops as effects at a later point in time while also being able to describe the larger phenomenal time slice as a single unified whole (forgiving attitudes and acts of forgiving as part of the same single story). The diachronic conception of time accounts for the passage of time in two ways—it accommodates a moment-to-moment narrative of the events, while also permitting the entirety of events to be described as a single narrative. This feature of forgivingness in time produces an interdependent relationship between future-oriented forgivingness and acts of paradigmatic forgiveness.

This relationship of interdependence means that forgivingness causes forgiveness, and also that forgiveness causes forgivingness. Small acts of forgiveness contribute toward the development and maintenance of attitudes of forgivingness. Consider how we might practice forgiving small wrongdoings (e.g. the breaking of a promise by being late for an appointment), and how repetitions of forgiveness on a smaller scale contribute to or perhaps even constitute attitudes and dispositions of forgivingness. In this way, smaller ongoing practices become inextricably linked to broader attitudes and ideals.

Operating in the other direction, developed attitudes of forgivingness are more likely to produce dispositions to forgive when confronted with a serious case of wrongdoing. Roberts suggests that the virtue of forgivingness is "possible because of a certain looseness of fit between the judgments that constitute the cognitive content of an emotion and the emotion itself" (1995, 289). Consider for a moment cases like the Amish schoolhouse shooting mentioned at the beginning of this chapter. Acts of violence, especially when directed toward innocent children, are among the most severe type of wrongdoing, and in the judgment of many, such acts are worthy of contempt, condemnation, and the withholding of forgiveness. Why is it that the affected Amish community was able to forgive the perpetrator so quickly? I suggest that this is less the product of a deliberated instantaneous decision and more likely grew from an ongoing attitude and disposition aimed at forgiveness, humility, and gentleness all stemming from their shared cultural and religious practices. Here I suggest that the "looseness of fit" between emotions and thoughts about emotions as described by Roberts is perhaps a more tightly woven connection, held together by relations of cause and effect.

The claim of interdependence between practices of forgivingness and products of forgiveness, although generated through philosophical discourse, is one that I believe is fundamentally a question for empirical observation. A working hypothesis for a scientific inquiry into this claim would hold that that actualized forgiveness-events (or *products of forgiveness*, to use Warmke's language) are more likely to obtain when the agents involved have practiced attitudes of forgivingness. The design of such an experiment would require much planning and require substantial ethical review for the human subjects involved, as they would need to be subjected to some kind of forgivable wrongdoing. Whether such an experiment is possible and whether it might produce results that run parallel to the conceptual account of forgivingness in time for which I argue, I do not know. Nonetheless, I see this as a point of possible collaborative research between empirical science and philosophy.

Considering objections and concerns

There are, of course, several lines of criticism, objection, and questioning that are likely to be directed toward this account of forgivingness. Before carrying this conceptual account into a more applied context, prudence and charity require that I address a few such questions.

A possible concern with the active and perpetual cultivation of forgiving attitudes is that such a practice assumes that future wrongdoing will occur. In other words, this might promote a pessimistic view towards others or life in general that wrongdoing and offense are likely to happen, that we are likely to at some time or another be victim of some wrongdoing, and that this is best addressed by cultivating forgivingness in the present. While it is true that the attitude of forgivingness could be painted as a form of pessimism, it could equally be understood as a way of cultivating optimism that any potential act of wrongdoing could be met with forgiveness. In the same way that an insurance policy could be interpreted as being pessimistic, it simultaneously provides peace of mind that if anything unfortunate were to happen, preparations would already be securely in place.

Another objection argues that forgivingness creates an ethos which cannot prevent wrongdoing; it assumes it will happen, and almost preemptively forgives it. Responses to this could include: 1) the key component of forgiveness that recognizes wrongdoing as wrongdoing; and 2) the claim that if universalized, forgivingness would radially reduce, or under ideal circumstances, eliminate wrongdoing. Forgivingness should not be confused with pre-emptive forgiveness. Whereas attitudinal forgivingness is generalized and applies in a broad range of situations, pre-emptive forgiveness is aimed at a specific act of wrongdoing that is perceived as being highly likely to occur.[70]

Suppose further that even though one has spent time cultivating forgivingness, no forgivable wrongdoing ever occurs. A critic might argue that the effort of developing forgi-

---

[70] Many examples of apparent pre-emptive forgiveness can be understood as attitudinal forgivingness. Consider the Quaker Declaration of Life (http://www.quaker.org/declaration-of-life.html), which asserts that if one were to become the victim of a homicide, the declarant wishes that the murderer not be subject to the death penalty. While this seems to be a case of pre-emptive forgiveness of one's potential murderer, it is more accurately understood as a generalized rejection of capital punishment in all cases.

vingness is, in this case, wasted. Cultivating forgiving attitudes and dispositions requires energy and dedication that could have been spent on other morally worth pursuits. To this, I would respond in a few parts. First, the subjunctive power for forgivingness is that it could be realized if a circumstance arose in which it were needed. The fact that no such case arises does not diminish the power that it in fact has. Relatedly, some hold the view that moral development of some particular virtue does not occur in isolation, but rather is part of a holistic process of personal moral development. Developing attitudinal forgivingness can operate instrumentally to promote personal character development, even if no wrongdoing ever occurs. As forgivingness develops, so too might patience, humility, generosity, and a plethora of other virtues.

A final technical question would ask, how is forgivingness developed or measured? After all, if forgivingness really is a power or potentiality, then there must be some way of quantifying it. It certainly seems that the forgivingness required to forgive a pickpocket is significantly different from the forgivingness required to forgive an assailant or the murderer of a loved one. Of course, developing a full-bodied account of forgivingness would involve developing some such metric, but in its absence, I can only suggest that differences in the magnitude of forgivingness could be best measured through the ways in which people actually forgive. If this is the case, then forgivingness could only be measured retroactively. A further related question might ask if and how a metric of forgivingness could be expressed in standard terms between people. Clearly, these questions are significant and voluminous enough to justify another investigation; however, given the limitations of this chapter, I must leave these questions stated but unanswered.

From concept to practice: philosophical method and forgivingness

Forgive me my nonsense, as I also forgive the nonsense of those that think they make sense.

—Robert Frost

Up until this point, my work has focused entirely on the theoretical and abstract dimensions of forgiveness. Opening with an explication of the paradigm case, non-paradigm cases, and pseudo-forgiveness, I have situated future-oriented forgivingness within the broader constellation of related concepts and argued for its congruence with the paradigm case. Further, I have argued that the causal interdependence between the two explains exemplary acts of forgiveness, and I have considered several anticipated objections to the concept of forgivingness that I propose. At this juncture, I shift from primarily theoretical focus toward an applied context.

The Irish philosopher and novelist, Iris Murdoch, reminds readers that, "moral philosophy should be inhabited" (1970, 47). I take this not as a mere suggestion, but rather as normative statement that moral philosophy (as theory) is inseparable from practice and action. Thoughts from the proverbial armchair may resonate with truth and clarity, but because they take as their subjects the actions and attitudes humans carry throughout life, they can only be successful when they inform, direct, and justify the choices we make. Forgivingness is already embodied in philosophical methodology, in particular, through a broad understanding of the principle of charity.

The final shift in this chapter is not a tangential foray from my chief argument; rather, it is a two-fold support for it. First, by understanding attitudinal forgivingness in this context, I hope to articulate as clearly as possible the concept I have in mind. Second, I have selected this application as one that is relevant to philosophers because moral philosophy and inquiry into ethics cannot be divorced from the practice and practical concerns of action.

The principle of charity in philosophy dates back at least to W.V. Quine, and is often accredited, in large part, to Donald Davidson. For Davidson, the principle of charity is one that is necessary as a matter of interpretation and understanding other thinkers. Others have expanded the meaning of this principle to imply that we ought to attempt to understand the ideas of others with maximal truth and in the strongest argumentative form possible. On this account, the principle becomes less a necessary condition for interpretation and more of a heuristic device by which thinkers are better able to consider new and unconventional ideas. My aim in this chapter is neither to adopt nor advocate any particular formulation of the principle of charity, but rather to frame it in broad strokes as I characterize the essential features of the principle(s) as being an enacted form of forgivingness.

Davidson's sense of the charity principle bears four significant and distinct features: 1) the principle welcomes divergence and disagreement; 2) it makes any disagreement substantive and significant; 3) it is an expressed attitude toward both thoughts and thinkers; and 4) it is a necessary component of interpretation and discourse. Although these components of Davidson's principle arise as linguistic and epistemic necessities for his broader theories of truth, interpretation, and mental phenomena, they bear normative implications similar to those I have described as forgivingness.

To be charitable does not force thinkers into an ideal of agreement; rather, "charity invites departures" (Davidson 2006, 177). This is possible because Davidson's principle doesn't concern so much what we believe, but rather how we go about interpreting and understanding the beliefs of others. In the same way that an agent's disposition of forgivingness concerns a wide range of possible responses to the actions of others, Davidson's principle of charity concerns the wide range of possible ways of understanding the beliefs and assertions of others. Forgiveness similarly produces a multitude of reasonable responses to any given set of events. In fact, "it is not possible to delineate with precision the practical wisdom possessed by the ideally forgiving person," but thoughtful discussion about the virtue of forgivingness "begins to indicate roughly the boundaries" (Roberts 1995, 302). Neither forgivingness nor charity dictates a singular response to any given case; instead, they draw reasoned limits around a range of acceptable responses.

Although Davidson's principle of charity permits divergent beliefs, it does constrict the number of reasonable interpretations given to any belief or thinker in that the interpretation must seek to maximize consistency in the beliefs being interpreted. In other words, the principle of charity holds that we should try to understand others as being consistent because, "crediting people with a large degree of consistency cannot be counted mere charity: it is unavoidable if we are in a position to accuse them meaningfully of error and some degree of irrationality" (Davidson 2011, 221). In this way, charity allows for meaningful disagreement because it eliminates the possibility of misunderstanding in disguise as disagreement. Similarly, paradigmatic forgiveness and forgivingness respond to wrongdoing powerfully because they are distinct from other responses such as excuse, exception, or allowance.

Just as theorists of forgiveness argue that forgiveness targets wrongdoers and not their actions, Davidson's principle takes into consideration not only thoughts, but also the thinkers who hold those thoughts. An important element in the charity principle is the presumption that the ideas a thinker holds are consistent, and consequently that the thinker is, herself, rational and consistent. In describing a hypothetical encounter with an alien, Davidson argues that, "just as we must maximize agreement, or risk not making sense of what the alien is talking about, so we must maximize the self-consistency we attribute to him, on pain of not understanding him" (2006, 163). Forgiving a wrongdoer expresses a similar kind of respect for the wrongdoer in that they are respected as a reasonable person who can be held responsible and is worthy of praise, blame, and forgiveness (as opposed to unreasonable beings who can only be excused). As a methodological approach in philosophy to understanding and considering the ideas of others, a lack of charity is not just a misunderstanding of ideas; it's also a lack of respect and the patience to understand other thinkers.

The fourth component of Davidson's principle of charity is perhaps the most significant because it holds that being charitable in interpretation is not a choice, but is instead an imperative. Davidson is clear in stating, "charity is forced on us; whether we like it or not, if we want to understand others, we must count them right in most matters" (2006, 207). Elsewhere in the same essay, the claim of necessity is similarly stated, "since charity is not an option, but a condition of having a workable theory, it is meaningless to suggest that we might fall into massive error by endorsing it" (Ibid., 207). The necessity of charity in interpretation stems from the linguistic and epistemic need to hold other authors and their thoughts as being mostly reasonable, if there is to be any meaningful disagreement at all. If such charity were optional, then interpretation would in no way be necessarily bound to reason. This final condition of necessity has a normative operation for the principle of charity in Davidson's broader philosophy—that is to say, it is a principle that must be followed. The question at hand is whether the call to forgivingness has the same necessary moral pull.

This is one space in which forgivingness might differ from the principle of charity, because while the principle of charity is a necessary condition for understanding and interpretation, it seems that the call to cultivate forgivingness might not be so strong. After all, one could be a forgiving person on some particular occasion of wrongdoing without having ever worked to be a forgiving person. Additionally, some might see forgivingness as a character trait[71] which is praiseworthy to possess and develop, but for which one might not be blamed for not cultivating. This question aligns itself with the ongoing debate over the moral status of forgiveness as being a praiseworthy act of charity and generosity versus an obligatory act that is expected. Although an adequate address of this question would require more space than is afforded here, I am drawn to the element of necessity present in Davidson's articulation of the principle of charity. The implications of arguing for the necessity of cultivating forgivingness would be far reaching, but I cannot cast that argument here.

The principle of charity in philosophy can be understood more broadly than in Davidson's particular version aimed at interpretation and understanding. Some suggest the principle of charity is not merely a necessary condition for understanding and substantive disagreement, but that it also calls for understanding the arguments of others with valid and sound interpretations (Lander Philosophy 2000). Again, going beyond what Davidson holds, some argue that philosophical charity involves a suspension of one's own belief in order to consider new or foreign ideas. This formulation of the principle of charity moves away from the strictly necessary sense of being a precondition for interpretation as stated by Davidson, and adopts a more generous ethos of reading and interpreting the ideas of others in a way that is most palpable for the reader.

---

[71] For such an account, see Margaret Holmgren, *Forgiveness and Retribution: Responding to Wrongdoing* (Cambridge: Cambridge University Press, 2012).

Although I sympathize with this sentiment and the pragmatic consequences of this approach to understanding philosophy, I have concerns that this model of implementing the principle of charity goes too far. If the way of measuring a new idea and affording it due charity is to interpret it in a way that is the strongest or most acceptable for oneself, this risks becoming a departure from forgivingness towards the subtle assertion that new ideas must accord with one's preexisting standards in order to be adopted. The most critical risk here is that although we may interpret ideas such that they accord with our own views, we risk misinterpreting them when we do so. When affording strength to an argument becomes the paramount concern of the charity principle, charity may diverge from methodological forgivingness, and fall hostage to ego-oriented interpretation.

Forgivingness and the principle of charity both suggest a future-oriented approach to adopting attitudes in the present that influence interpretations and responses to future contexts. Forgivingness enacted in the context of philosophy can be understood as the principle of charity in its most basic form. To be charitable in interpretation is a precondition for understanding and meaningful disagreement. When philosophers and philosophies speak past one another, what they are missing is this methodological commitment to seeking understanding and the willingness to forgive some differences, if it allows for more significant and philosophically rich debate. Among the various philosophical methodologies, the principle of charity should be understood as the common denominator because without it, insular methodologies devolve from dialogue to monologue.

In addition to structural similarities and conceptual overlap between forgivingness and the principle of charity, both can also be justified in terms of the consequences they bring about. When forgivingness manifests in moments of wrongdoing as forgiveness, it leads to overcoming feelings of resentment; it can promote reconciliation between victims and wrongdoers; and among other consequences, it can halt the negative consequences of the wrongdoing itself. Even without any actual wrongdoing, the development of forgivingness can promote the development of other amenable character traits. The principle of charity, understood as philosophical methodology yields a similar list of desirable consequences.

First and foremost, the principle of charity encourages a better understanding of one another. Any philosopher who values disagreement should value it because it is a substantive disagreement and not merely a misunderstanding or a refusal to take it seriously. Philosophical disagreement arising from within a shared commitment to the principle of charity is substantive and productive in that it defines questions to motivate future research. Alternatively, disagreement and divergence that is not charitable often presents itself as misunderstanding or, worse yet, deliberate straw man argumentation. The commitment to charitable methodology preserves the potency of disagreement as a progressive force in philosophy.

A commitment to the principle of charity also allows for the emergence of new or unorthodox ideas because this methodology demands that even the most seemingly absurd claims be taken just as seriously as those that strike us as intuitively obvious. Ideas should not be rejected simply because they are unpopular or they challenge the status quo. After all, many of the most commonly held beliefs of today were at one time controversial and unconventional. Rather than discounting and summarily dismissing a challenging theory, the principle of charity demands that we take challenges seriously so that any true disagreement can surface as a meaningful source of inspiration.

Related to the willingness to consider new ideas is the benefit that the charity principle prevents the ongoing adherence to problematic views or debates merely because they are canonical or widely accepted. This implies that those who practice charity in philosophy accept a kind of vulnerability, namely the vulnerability to recognize and accept reasons to abandon faulty beliefs. Without the willingness to give up faulty beliefs, philosophy risks becoming dogmatic, and the principle of charity guards against this by ensuring that we take the ideas of others just as seriously as our own.

Considered jointly, the last two consequences that: 1) ideas not be rejected because they are unpopular; and 2) that the mainstream ideas we hold can be called into question, implies a philosophical methodology that is less domineering and more genuinely inquisitive. Even if this methodological approach does not lead to groundbreaking ideas right away, it is an attitude or disposition that is well primed to respond when the opportunity arises. At the very least, the principle of charity promises that we cannot ignore the potential merit of new ideas because of the blindness created by ideas already held.

These practical advantages depend on one's willingness to adopt the principle of charity as a methodological approach. This is a form of forgivingness in that it is a type of preparing oneself to thoughtfully encounter and respond to ideas that may contradict beliefs one already holds. In the same way that the virtue of forgiveness is unlikely to be realized by someone who has never practiced forgivingness, the advantages of charity are not as available to philosophers who do not practice charity.

Before concluding this application of forgivingness as instantiated in the principle of charity, it is worth recognizing that many advances in philosophy have been fueled by a dialectical approach of question/response and criticism/refutation in the Socratic tradition or the Hegelian progressions of thesis, antithesis, and synthesis. Critics might suggest that my advocacy of charity in methodology would forgo this somewhat adversarial tradition and the wealth of philosophical advances it has produced. On the contrary, I agree that these modes of discourse are worthy and yield fruitful insight. But these insights and breakthroughs are best produced when dialectical dialogue is rooted in charity because disagreement arising in such contexts is guaranteed to be meaningful. Charity and opposition are not mutually exclusive; rather they operate synergistically as long as one does not eclipse the other.

Conclusion

Forgiveness is the key to action and freedom

—Hannah Arendt

Charity requires that I welcome criticism of the interpretations and arguments I have offered in this chapter, and because I believe in the productive force of disagreement I am happy to do so. The primary goal of this work was to articulate a theory of congruence about certain cases and qualities of philosophy, so as to help better define the full breadth of the temporal contours of forgiveness. To the extent that I have been successful, I hope to both broaden the discourse about forgiveness, especially with respect to the complexity of temporal dimensions, and to give philosophers reason to approach the ideas of others with due care. Additionally, I hope to have posed a substantial lead for empirical researchers who might be motivated to test the hypothesis that there is an interdependent causal link between attitudinal forgivingness and acts of forgiveness. Finally, I hope to have presented this new conceptual analysis in a way that is relevant to philosophers and other readers by suggesting a (re)formation in charitable attitudes in philosophical methodology.[72]

---

[72] I am grateful to Dugald Owen for commenting on earlier versions of this chapter and providing constructive criticism and questions that sharpened my view. If I have learned philosophical charity anywhere, it has been through observing his practice.

Forgiveness has the power to allow overcoming of wrongdoing that has happened, and while forgivingness may not be able to augment future happenings, it certainly has the power to change the way we respond to them. In the wake of the school shooting, the Amish community manifested forgiveness when many thought it was unwarranted. Amidst such a violent catastrophe, it was forgiveness that gave this community the resilience to stop the suffering with the act of wrongdoing and to build the New Hope School at a new location. Forgiveness and time cannot erase wrongdoing, but to practice forgivingness in time is affirmation that the efforts of today contribute to the freedom of tomorrow, no matter what obstacles we might face.

References

BBC News. October 3, 2006. "Fatal Shooting at US Amish School." Accessed February 27, 2016, http://news.bbc.co.uk/2/hi/americas/5400570.stm

Davidson, Donald. 2011. "Mental Events." *Essays on Actions and Events*, Second Edition. Oxford: Oxford University Press.

_____. 2006a. "Truth and Meaning." *The Essential Davidson*. Oxford: Oxford University Press.

_____. 2006b. "On Saying That," In *The Essential Davidson*.

_____. 2006c. "On the Very Idea of a Conceptual Scheme." *The Essential Davidson*.

Griswold, Charles L. 2007. *Forgiveness: A Philosophical Exploration*. New York: Cambridge University Press.

Holmstrom, Nancy. 2015. "Debt Forgiveness: Who Owes Whom for What." *Tikkun* 30.4: 41-43.

n.a. (Lander Philosophy). 2000. "Philosophy 312: Oriental Philosophy: The Principle of Charity." Accessed February 27, 2016. http://philosophy.lander.edu/oriental/charity.html

Murdoch, Iris. 1970. "On 'God' and 'Good'." *The Sovereignty of the Good*. New York: Schocken Books.

Murphy, Jeffrie G., and Jean Hampton. 1988. *Forgiveness and Mercy*. Cambridge: Cambridge University Press.

Roberts, Robert C. 1995. "Forgivingness." *American Philosophical Quarterly* 34.2: 290-306.

Roberts-Cady, Sarah. 2003. "Justice and Forgiveness." *Philosophy Today* 47.3: 293-304.

Velleman, J. David. 1993. "Well-being and Time." *The Metaphysics of Death*. Edited by John Martin Fischer. Stanford, CA: Stanford University Press.

Warmke, Brandon. 2015. "The Economic Model of Forgiveness," *Pacific Philosophical Quarterly* 95.4: 1-20.

Zaibert, Leo. 2009. "The Paradox of Forgiveness," *Journal of Moral Philosophy* 6.3: 365-393.

Chapter 6

Betrayal, Forgiveness, and Trusting Again

John McClellan

I. Introduction

"Once a cheater, always a cheater:" a sweeping generalization of the romantically unfaithful that cannot, of course, be strictly true. Still, the fact that a person has already committed a serious betrayal does not exactly bode well for his/her future trustworthiness. But then what about second chances? What about forgiveness? What about those whose love and desire for continued intimacy with their betrayers compels them to stick it out and trust again? Are they just gluttons for punishment? Or, to introduce the central question of this chapter, is their renewed trust in their loved ones not, at the very least, *epistemically unjustified*?

I hope to show that there is a plausible way to view "trusting again" as epistemically justifiable even when it is not proportioned to the evidence of the betrayer's future trustworthiness. I warn my reader at the outset that my approach will strike many as lying too far outside the bounds of legitimate epistemological analysis. The conclusion for such readers may well be that there is an irreconcilable tension between epistemic norms and a very admirable form of forgiveness.

II. Forgiveness and trusting again

Betrayal and mistrust naturally go hand in hand, but the depth, breadth, and longevity of mistrust exhibited in the aftermath of betrayal varies widely. For some persons, a particularly hurtful wrong incurred in a close relationship (e.g., from a parent) leaves them generally suspicious of others in ways that make it difficult to cooperate in various social contexts and virtually impossible to forge meaningful intimate relationships. Other persons, though, seem to come through what they ought to perceive as a most serious betrayal perfectly eager to trust again. While it is for the cognitive scientist to determine what explains these discrepancies in our individual responses to betrayal, it is for the philosopher to determine—or at least to inquire into—what sort of trusting after betrayal is appropriate in light of moral and/or epistemological norms.

My interest in this chapter is primarily epistemological, and my focus will be on a certain subclass of the potential *overtrusters*, namely those who find themselves trusting again the very persons who have betrayed them in the past. Moreover, I will focus on trusting again as it occurs within the context of particularly close relationships such as committed romantic partnerships and intimate friendships. It is in this context that the impetus to trust again often stems from one's continued deep affections for one's own betrayer. Consequently, it is here that the ideals of unconditional love, forgiveness, compassion, and (in an irony of sorts) passionate commitment to another person threaten to clash head-on with epistemic norms. An epistemically appropriate trust would seem to be based on strong evidence of the trusted's trustworthiness, but a committed lover or friend who forgives and trusts again will not typically base her assessment of her lover's or friend's trustworthiness on a cool-headed survey of the evidence—evidence that, from an objective point of view, would likely not support a high degree of confidence in that person, in light of his/her past behavior. And yet she must find a way to place her confidence in that person again, so long as she desires to restore intimacy in the relationship.

It is probably not the place of the philosopher to baldly assert claims as to what intimacy requires when such claims might be thought the proper purview of the social sciences. But the claim that intimacy requires trust should at least have enough initial plausibility, I think, to justify exploring its epistemological implications. To be clear, it is only in the particular context of intimate relationships that I presume there is a connection between forgiveness and the need to trust again. It would be a mistake to think that forgiveness *as such* involves a requirement to trust one's betrayer again. Indeed, it is a plausible view that forgiving a betrayer is consistent not only with a permanent loss of confidence in that person but even with outright termination of the relationship. But matters are different, I think, when both parties to the betrayal desire an ongoing or renewed intimate relationship together. Speaking for myself at least, it is unfathomable to me that I would think someone a *close* friend if I did not trust him significantly. If, for example, I am never willing to speak with him about deep personal matters because I am not confident he would refrain from relaying what I say to a third party for a good laugh, I would not think him a close friend no matter how much I enjoy his company. That is not to say I expect those closest to me to be perfect, but I do consistently trust them to do right by me when it matters most.

By the same token, it is important to me that they trust me deeply. While my wife, for example, has every reason to expect I will continue to commit my share of wrongs towards her (e.g., occasional careless comments, moments of neglect, etc.), it is crucial to me that she is confident I would not look her in the eye and lie to her about some serious matter, nor abandon her in her hour of need. And if I were to seriously betray her trust in me, and if she were subsequently gracious enough to forgive me and seek reconciliation, I would not think our bond truly restored until I had secured her trust in me again. I realize that nothing in this bit of psychological autobiography constitutes an *argument* for the claim that intimacy requires trust, but it does illustrate what I expect is a common sentiment behind what, again, I only ask my reader to take as a working assumption.

III. Two kinds of trust

If we are to investigate the epistemic status of trusting a "former" betrayer,[73] we would do well to know, at least roughly, what we mean by *trusting*. As is typical in philosophy, the literature on trust reveals that it, like other ubiquitous phenomena (e.g., knowledge, personal identity, etc.), turns out to be a rather difficult thing to pin down. This is not the place to delve deeply into the conceptual difficulties that arise in attempts to precisely state the necessary and sufficient conditions for proper application of the term 'trust', but it will at least be helpful to distinguish between two related but separable phenomena that go by the same name.

There is first a type of trusting characterized by one's willingness to assume a position of *reliance* on another person, whereby one places some good or task under her purview and relies on her to take care of that good or to perform that task.[74] Second, there is trusting in the *doxastic* sense, whereby one has confidence in another that she will (or would) come through for one in some respect.[75] These two forms of trust—which I will call "reliance-trust" and "doxastic-trust"—often coincide, as when I choose to rely on a neighbor to take care of my dog for a few days while being fully confident that he will do a good job. But they can just as easi-

---

[73] I will often refer to the betrayer as a *former* betrayer to indicate that the truster trusts that the betrayal is not ongoing. I put aside cases where the betrayal is known to be ongoing since I presume that even though forgiveness is possible in such cases, intimacy is not. That said, I recognize that there is another sense (sadly) in which a person who commits a betrayal is always one's betrayer no matter how trustworthy he remains thereafter. Thanks to Court Lewis for pointing this out to me.

[74] The preeminent statement of the view that trust is a certain form of reliance is given in Baier (1986).

[75] This type of trust features in McGeer (2008).

ly come apart. As is often pointed out in the literature, we sometimes have reasons to rely on others even though we lack confidence in them. Consider, for example, "parents deciding to trust their teenagers with the house or family car, believing that their offspring may well abuse their trust, but hoping by such trust to elicit, in the fullness of time, more responsible and responsive trustworthy behavior" (McGeer 2008, 241). But it should also be acknowledged that reliance-trust and doxastic-trust can come apart the other way too, since we might choose to refrain from relying on certain persons even though we have ample doxastic-trust in them. I might, for example, rely on my neighbor to take care of my dog instead of my best friend only because I think it would be more inconvenient on the latter, and I do not wish to burden him. My decision not to rely on him clearly does not indicate any lack of trust *in* him.

Some commentators have suggested that reliance-trust is more central to the concept of "real" trust than doxastic-trust, and hence, they think that trusting is properly subject to moral and pragmatic norms but not really to epistemic norms.[76] But the fact that it makes perfect sense in the previous example to say that I trust my friend completely with respect to taking care of my dog, even though I choose not to rely on him, indicates clearly enough that doxastic-trust is at least as deserving of the name "trust" as reliance-trust. Thus epistemic concerns about trust *per se* cannot be easily shirked.

This is especially true for those seeking to restore intimacy after betrayal, since both reliance-trust *and* doxastic-trust will need to be restored if our working assumption is correct. A husband, for example, who decides to forgive his wife and rebuild intimacy after discovering she secretly mishandled

---

[76] See Holton (1994) and Jones (1996).

their finances to support a leeching relative (for which she has sincerely repented) will need to both accept vulnerability to possible future harms from her and find a way to believe in her again. While we might expect that his willingness to engage in reliance-trust (e.g., entrusting monies to her discretion again) before his suspicions of her wane, true intimacy eventually demands his renewed confidence in her too. And while both forms of trusting again are risky business in that they subject the forgiver to various harms from future betrayal, it is at the onset of doxastic-trust in a former betrayer in particular where the markedly *epistemic* risk that constitutes the focus of this chapter arises. Hence, I will have doxastic-trust in mind when speaking of trust in what follows.

IV. Trusting again as an instance of epistemic partiality

It would be a mistake to think that a forgiver who seeks intimacy with a former betrayer will be required to somehow talk herself into being confident in that person again or else forever remain in a state removed from true intimacy. While I do not doubt that we have at least some capacity to induce/sustain beliefs we think we *ought* to have (at the very least, to suppress doubts we wish not to entertain), I think the best explanation for the impressive capacity of forgivers to renew their trust in their former betrayers in the context of close relationships lies in a much less intentional process. That is, as forgiveness sets in, and the pain of betrayal begins to fade, I think it only human that the strong affections one has for a person would have a way of spurring one's renewed confidence in him/her. On my understanding, then, trusting again is really just a special case of a more general phenomenon that permeates interpersonal relationships, namely our tendency to form relatively favorable beliefs about persons we care deeply for—i.e., beliefs that are favorable relative to the beliefs unbiased observers would likely form about them. As John Heil puts it, "One simply does not *draw* certain conclusions about one's friends or loved ones in the way one draws conclusions about others. This need not be a matter of effort or deliberate calculation. Rather, it is, typically at any rate, perfectly natural and unselfconscious" (1983, 762). So, much different from thinking of the forgivers at issue here as those who are eventually able to *force* themselves to trust a former betrayer again, I suggest we think of them as those who more so *find* themselves trusting again.

The epistemological dilemma is not at all dissolved by this clarification, though, as the fact that a psychological process comes natural to us does not at all mean that it is epistemically justifiable. It is to be expected that onlookers who were privy to the original betrayal in the sort of case I have in mind, and who do not share the forgiver's affections for that person, will tend to remain much more suspicious of him, and, consequently, fear for irrationality on the part of the truster. And she herself may wonder at times if her love is blinding her to the harsher realities of her loved one's virtues and vices, and thereby, overriding her rational faculties.

A number of philosophers have recently discussed the questionable epistemic status of the sort of doxastic bias described by Heil under the label "epistemic partiality." The discussion was initiated by a pair of independently published papers by Simon Keller (2004) and Sarah Stroud (2006), each of whom argue that a healthy friendship *requires* doxastic biasing in ways that are at odds with traditionally recognized epistemic norms. Those norms are commonly thought to require a level-headed proportioning of belief to evidence, whereas friendship, say Keller and Stroud, requires a more passionate willingness to go *beyond the evidence* in the interest of forming comparatively favorable beliefs about one's friends. Keller illustrates this phenomenon with the case of a man who is compelled to form much more favorable judgments about the quality of his friend's poetry than an unbiased observer would be inclined to make. Stroud provides a case of a friend who is disinclined to accept as true a third-party allegation of her friend's immoral behavior, even though neutral parties would be inclined to accept it. Though Keller and Stroud agree that good friends *ought* to be biased in these ways, and that such a biased doxastic practice is inconsistent with the demand to proportion belief to evidence, they disagree on one important point: for Keller, the take-home lesson is that friendship norms genuinely conflict with our epistemic norms; whereas Stroud suggests that we instead consider revising our understanding of epistemic norms so that they do not require us to dispassionately proportion beliefs about our loved ones so strictly to the evidence. I will make an attempt to follow Stroud's suggestion in the final section of this chapter.

V. Two extant attempts to justify epistemic partiality

It is possible to argue, however, that there is no genuine conflict in the first place between the tendency of a good friend to favorably manage potential counter-evidence against her friend and the epistemic goal of proportioning one's belief to the evidence. Katherine Hawley, for example, suggests that our tendency to think favorably of our friends could be explained by our having privileged access to evidence of our friends' abilities and good natures that outsiders could not be expected to have. "Put simply, we already know a lot about our friends, and this can give us good epistemic reason for treating new information about our friends differently from new information about our non-friends" (Hawley 2014, 2036). This move is anticipated, however, by Stroud who points out rightly, I think, that it does not do justice to the motivational or affective dimension of epistemic partiality. An impartial observer, she suggests, could also have strong inductive evidence of your friend's good character but not feel the same *obligation* and *drive* to interpret the new, potentially contrary evidence in such a favorable light (Stroud 2006, 515-7). Thus the partialist will characteristically tend to come out with more favorable beliefs than the evidence, strictly speaking, supports.

Moreover, Hawley's proposal would seem especially unhelpful when applied to the typical case of trusting again. While it would only be sensible for a forgiver in such a situation to bolster her trust with appeals to any privileged evidence she might have concerning her former betrayer (e.g., her first-hand awareness of his remorse, his otherwise private attempts to reform underlying issues that influenced the betrayal, etc.), there is a pretty straightforward sense in which the overall evidence is not likely to support the committed truster's characteristically *high* degree of confidence in her friend or lover. She is trusting, after all, a person who already proved not to be trustworthy in the past. Furthermore, the reality is that most trusters probably find themselves in relevantly similar evidential situations as she. Most of them probably also think they have some privileged evidence outsiders are not privy to for thinking those they trust are "special" and will not join the ranks of the repeat offenders. Upon realizing that others who were privy to the betrayal do not trust their loved ones quite so much, the trusters will think the others "don't know my friend/lover like I do." That is simply the nature of their love and trust, and it is an admirable form of devotion. But, objectively speaking, there would be no need to think their loved ones were *special* in this respect in the first place, if people in similar situations were not so often mistaken.

This brings us to a deeper problem with Hawley's proposal. If privileged access to evidence were thought to render the average case of epistemic partiality justifiable, it would thereby render the average case of forming less favorable beliefs from a more detached point of view unjustifiable. The reason is as follows: most people will have *someone* close to them who is prone to forming more favorable beliefs about them relative to the beliefs less vested observers would naturally form, and the more favorable believers will naturally take themselves to have privileged evidence for those beliefs. And if we are to think such people really do tend to have access to privileged evidence that overall supports their more favorable beliefs, then whenever we find ourselves in the position of the impartial observer who is tempted to form the less favorable judgment, we would be obliged to think it likely that the total *available* evidence (i.e., the larger body of evidence that the epistemically partial folks are privileged to have) would actually support the more favorable belief. And clearly, it would be unjustifiable for a detached person to hold the comparatively less favorable belief while expecting the larger body of evidence "out there" to be against it. The upshot is that Hawley's proposal exonerates epistemic partiality only at the cost of impugning epistemic *im*partiality, and that seems to go too far.

At least one thinker would disagree, however, with the notion that we should be slow to impugn the less favorable beliefs of impartial observers. In his recent treatise on love, Troy Jollimore, tries to justify epistemic partiality precisely on the grounds that the efforts one makes to form favorable judgments of one's loved ones often lead to more accurate judgments than those made from a dispassionate approach. As he puts it:

> *The tendency to assume the best of a person may indeed lead us astray in those occasional cases when a person is in fact acting badly; but the tendency not to assume the best, to abandon too quickly the effort of seeking an explanation that can rationalize someone's behavior and render it intelligible and even admirable, can also act as an impediment to our efforts to form a truer picture of the world.* (2011, 63; emphasis original)

And, even more strongly:

> *If the lover is blind to certain explanations and interpretations—those that tend to see the beloved in unflattering or negative terms or that perhaps avoid seeing her as an agent*

> or subject—*the detached observer is blind to other, more sympathetic explanations and interpretations. In many cases the detached observer's blind spot will, at the end of the day, be more epistemically disabling. (Ibid, 64)*

In other words, the more favorable beliefs are the truer ones "in many cases," and it is consequently the epistemically partial lover or friend and not the unbiased observer who will come out on top in the pursuit of truth.

As much as I am attracted to Jollimore's approach, I do not think it can serve as an adequate epistemological justification for engaging in epistemic partiality in typical cases, without some further argument for thinking that the favorable judgments formed in the throes of its biased approach tend to be true *at least as often* as those formed from a more dispassionate stance. And that seems too optimistic, especially when applied to my target cases where the persons having the more favorable (trusting) beliefs formed about them are those who have already proved to be untrustworthy in the past.

Moreover, there is a principled reason to think epistemically partial beliefs could not, statistically speaking, *tend* to be true. In principle, for most any epistemically partial belief-forming process that leads to a favorable belief of person S, there could be another epistemically partial belief-forming process leading in the opposite direction. Consider, for example, the very sort of case Stroud and Jollimore discuss in which someone has made an allegation of immoral behavior against your friend. Your bias toward your friend might well lead you to expect that the allegation is mistaken in some way, and Jollimore is quite right that you may turn out to be right. But someone who is a good friend of the one making the allegation—and who, therefore, naturally considers that person a reliable source—would expect you to be quite wrong about that. And, of course, only one of you can be right. In principle, then, an epistemically partial doxastic process could be expected to lead to truth only about half of the time. If this is right, then it would seem the best way to secure beliefs that *tend* to be true would be to accept those an ably-informed impartial observer would tend to accept. So much the worse for the epistemic status of partiality, and hence, the epistemic status of trusting again.[77]

VI. Considering the epistemic value of "trusting again"

I propose, then, that we accept as genuine the tension between the committed friend or lover's trust and the demand to proportion one's confidence to the evidence. If trusting again is to be viewed as epistemically viable, I suggest we focus on the bigger picture of epistemic goods made possible by intimacy and, in turn, by trust. This reveals a way to view a state of biased trust as at least epistemically *valuable*—and in turn, I hope, *justifiable*—even though it is not proportioned to evidence of trustworthiness. As I warned at the outset, though, this strategy is not likely to move those who prefer to think of epistemic justification in usual terms, but it seems worth a shot given the admirable nature of trusting again (in typical cases).

My proposed strategy makes use of three crucial claims, each of which I expect to be more controversial than the last.

---

[77] Jollimore acknowledges a difficulty very close to this one (2011, 61). He points out that the friend of the accused in such a case will often seek to vindicate the accused and actively seek to discredit the accuser. But he thinks this worry can be avoided if the friend were to simply focus her faculties on the former partialist task rather than the latter. I do not know how consciously separable these tasks are, but supposing it can be done, this would not mitigate against the particular worry I am raising, since I am imagining two different partialists whose beliefs would still be in direct opposition even if they were each focused only on favoring their respective friend's position.

Claim 1: Important truths are *epistemically* more valuable to obtain than mundane truths.

This claim is common among contemporary epistemologists, as noted by Jason Baehr:

> *[O]ne often finds comments to the effect that what is good or desirable from an epistemic standpoint is true belief, but not true belief simpliciter or true belief about just any old subject-matter. For instance, true beliefs about the number of blades of grass on the neighbour's front lawn, grains of sand in a cubic foot of the Sahara, or listings in the Hong Kong telephone directory, are not, it is standardly claimed, part of the epistemic goal. Rather, what is good or desirable from an epistemic standpoint is true belief about subject-matters or facts which are epistemically significant, worthy or interesting.*
> *(Baehr 2012, 5)*[78]

Thus while beliefs about the telephone directory would be epistemically justified in the evidentialist's sense of being formed on the basis of solid evidence (i.e., looking directly at the records), there is a broader and more important sense in which one who devotes all his time to learning such facts is engaging in an epistemically *un*justifiable doxastic process. He is doing what he ought *not* do, not just from the moral or prudential points of view, but also from the epistemic point of view.

---

[78] For a fuller treatment of this view see Riggs (2008).

The second claim in my proposed strategy is likely more controversial.

Claim 2: It is only in intimate relationships that we can acquire some of life's most important truths.

While one can perhaps learn many things about love and friendship from a distance, I do not think it too much a stretch to say the deeper truths offered by intimate relationships are only to be learned "from the inside." If so, then there can be significant epistemic merit in trusting a person beyond the evidence given our working assumption that intimacy requires trust.

One worry for Claim 2 is that much of what I want to call the important "truths" acquired in intimate relationships are probably not propositional in nature. That is, intimacy affords one with direct *acquaintance* with important realities including, not least of all, direct acquaintance with one's friend or lover his/herself. I expect some would be hesitant to think of such acquaintance as a markedly epistemic state, given the propositional bent of contemporary epistemological analyses. Even so, I would think there are *some* important propositional truths that can only be obtained via an intimate relationships, if only important truths about one's friend or lover that would not be available to less familiar acquaintances. For example, a person might disclose to you some deep hurt or need, only if she considers you a close and trustworthy friend. This is important information you would not be privy to absent your trusting bond.

Along these lines, there is also a more subjective sense in which intimacy enables one to acquire an encyclopedic amount of important propositional truths about one's friend or lover. I say "subjective," because I have in mind information about a person that will only be regarded as important to someone who cares deeply for that person. For example, it matters a great deal to me to know what my wife wanted to be when she grew up and what she likes to do on a typical Saturday, but I do not expect ignorance of these truths to matter much to my reader. The reason is, of course, that when you love someone, all sorts of otherwise mundane trivia about them become meaningful subject-matter *to you*, though philosophers could debate whether such information has much in the way of genuinely epistemic value. In sum, it seems to me that these considerations together generate adequate support for Claim 2, but I recognize that there is room for a good deal of debate.

Supposing that Claims 1 and 2 are true, we are now in position for the final and most controversial claim in my proposal.

Claim 3: Whether a doxastic state—e.g., trust—is epistemically justified depends, at least in part, on its epistemic consequences.

It is widely accepted among philosophers that one's overall moral justification for performing a certain action is at least sometimes dependent on the morally-relevant consequences at stake, but it is not at all common to say that a person is sometimes epistemically justified in holding a certain belief by virtue of the epistemically relevant consequences at stake. Philosophers tend to keep epistemic evaluations of beliefs isolated from considerations of future epistemic gains. They focus on a certain belief and ask whether the believer has good evidence for thinking the belief is true. Or (to take an "externalist" line), they might ask whether the belief was formed by a reliable belief-forming process, where reliability is understood as producing a preponderance of true beliefs of the belief-type at issue—e.g., beliefs that a former betrayer is trustworthy. It is not also asked if a person's holding that belief—whether well evidenced or poorly evidenced, and whether reliably formed or unreliably formed—enables her to acquire a certain class of important truths such as those trust enables her to acquire in an intimate relationship.

This issue was at least broached by Roderick Firth in his 1981 presidential address to the American Philosophical Association (1981). He points out that a belief can fail to have what he calls *intrinsic* epistemic merit, meaning that it fails to be well-supported by the evidence, and yet have a great deal of *instrumental* epistemic merit, meaning that the belief is causally related to the acquisition of other beliefs that are well-supported.

> *Consider, to take just one dramatic example, the belief that human beings are created and sustained by God for the primary purpose of expanding human knowledge. This belief might have no intrinsic epistemic merit at all... Yet it might have a very high degree of instrumental epistemic merit. If the belief were a common one, it might alter human motivation in a way that would produce un-dreamed of advances in human knowledge (Ibid, 8).*

Firth claims that these two forms of epistemic value are "irreducibly distinct" and that they, therefore, afford us two irreconcilably different epistemic appraisals to make in a given case.

I wonder, though, why we should not expect there to be a higher-level epistemic norm (or set of norms) that takes both kinds of epistemic merit into account and makes all-things-considered *epistemic* prescriptions for our belief. This, after all, is how many of us think ethics works. We have strong deontological inklings regarding respect for persons, but we nonetheless recognize that morally relevant consequences sometimes factor into the all-things-considered moral requirement in a given case. We will say, to take an extreme example, that despite the fact that killing an innocent person has a great deal of intrinsic moral *dis*value, even that can be what we all-things-considered morally ought to do under certain momentous circumstances in which killing that person would have extreme instrumental moral value. It seems reasonable to wonder, then, why there would not be a parallel all-things-considered epistemic norm that would take into account both the intrinsic epistemic disvalue of trust in a given case (i.e., the degree to which a given trusting belief goes beyond the evidence) and the instrumental epistemic value at stake (i.e., the epistemic goods one stands to gain by that trust).

It is worth stressing that the epistemic disvalue of a typical case of trusting again will not be nearly as high as the intrinsic moral disvalue of killing an innocent person. Whereas killing an innocent person is gravely at odds with standard moral norms and can thus only be justifiable when the morally relevant consequences favor it in a most significant way, the degree to which confidently trusting a former betrayer will be at odds with one's evidence will typically be much lower. Thus if epistemic stakes *were* recognized to play a role in the epistemic justification of a given belief, the valuable epistemic consequences of trust stand a good chance of being high enough to overcome the typical case of disproportionate evidence of trustworthiness.

VII. Conclusion

The above strategy is admittedly questionable and incomplete. Not only does it require taking a non-standard approach to epistemological analysis, there are likely other challenges to face in applying it to actual cases of trusting again. For example, even if we allow that trusting belief itself can be epistemically justified (at least in part) by virtue of the epistemic consequences of intimacy, it does not follow that trusting belief *in one's former betrayer* will be justified. One might argue that the forgiver could just as well pursue intimacy with someone else who has a better track record and learn her important truths that way. That would not sit well with a forgiver, of course, since she wants intimacy with a particular person (and *that* person's truths) and not just intimacy as such. So this objection puts the onus on a defender of my strategy to argue that what I called the "subjective value" of certain truths really does factor into determinations of overall epistemic value. I am optimistic that this can be done, but again, this is just one of the complications my strategy would face.

Suppose it turns out that this strategy is unsuccessful. Suppose, moreover, it turns out there is *no* viable strategy for rendering trusting again epistemically justifiable in the sorts of cases I am concerned with. That would leave a forgiver who desires continued intimacy with her former betrayer with a serious choice. She must choose whether to privilege her pursuit of intimacy with a person she cares for deeply over her own epistemic rationality. I, for one, aspire to love those closest to me unconditionally. To me, that means I aspire to be a person who would give a second chance after even a serious betrayal, and allow myself to trust again without concern for proportioning my belief strictly to the evidence. If that means I aspire to be the sort of person who would flout his epistemic duties for the sake of those he cares about most, then I suppose I will own that aspiration. It would doubtless be difficult to trust again, and it would certainly be risky, but it is also exactly what I hope those whose love and trust I cherish most would do for me. Now, if only there were a Golden Rule in epistemology.

References

Baehr, Jason. 2012. "Credit Theories and the Value of Knowledge." *The Philosophical Quarterly* 62: 1-22.

Baier, Annette. 1986. "Trust and Anti-Trust." *Ethics* 96.2: 231-60.

Firth, Roderick. 1981. "Epistemic Merit, Intrinsic and Instrumental." *Proceedings and Addresses of the American Philosophical Association* 55.1: 5-23.

Hawley, Katherine. 2014. "Partiality and Prejudice in Trusting." *Synthese* 191: 2029-45.

Heil, John. 1983. "Believing What One Ought." *Journal of Philosophy* 80.11: 752-65.

Holton, Richard. 1994. "Deciding to Trust, Coming to Believe." *Australasian Journal of Philosophy* 72: 63-76.

Jones, Karen. 1996. "Trust as an Affective Attitude." *Ethics* 107.1: 4-25

Jollimore, Troy. 2011. *Love's Vision*. Princeton, NJ: Princeton University Press.

Keller, Simon. 2004. "Friendship and Belief." *Philosophical Papers* 33.3: 329-51.

McGeer, Victoria. 2008. "Trust, Hope, and Empowerment." *Australasian Journal of Philosophy* 86.2: 237-54.

Riggs, Wayne. 2008. "The Value Turn in Epistemology." *New Waves in Epistemology*. Edited by Vincent F. Hendricks and Duncan Pritchard. New York: Palgrave Macmillan.

Stroud, Sarah. 2006. "Epistemic Partiality in Friendship." *Ethics* 116.3: 498-524.

Chapter 7

The Asymmetry of Forgiveness

Mariano Crespo

A careful analysis of our moral life shows that we have different kinds of moral experiences. Some of them arise at the borders of our moral conscience while others play a more central role. For example, the experience of thanking belongs to the first type of act. It is important, but its importance does not seem as decisive as other moral acts, which are, so to speak, at the center of our moral life.[79] Forgiveness, in contrast, belongs to these more central moral experiences. Forgiving a wrongdoer reveals a special depth in the person's moral life: it becomes impossible to forgive him or her and at the same time experience a desire for revenge against the one who has done wrong. If we did harbor such a desire, we would have a good reason to doubt the authenticity of our forgiveness. Without dealing here with the difficult issue of whether there are moral experiences which are more central or deeper than forgiveness, one thing is clear: a genuine act of forgiveness "colors" our whole moral life. It is not a secondary or "peripheral" experience in a person's moral life; rather, it is linked with her most central nucleus.[80]

In this paper I would like to defend, on the one hand: a) that in every genuine act of forgiveness there are two central

---

[79] This idea of a central subject (*Ich-Zentrum*) with a series of concentric layers is to be found, for instance, in Alexander Pfänder, an author belonging to the phenomenological school. Cf. (Pfänder 1913); (Pfänder 1916); (Ferrer 2002); (Crespo 2009).

[80] On this kind of experience, cf. (Zirión 2012).

elements; and b) that these two elements are in what I will call an "asymmetric" relationship. I will conclude by pointing out that the analysis of both of these elements has important consequences for the theory of action and, I believe, for the metaphysics of the human person.[81] The first of the two elements I mentioned has to do with the fact that the one who forgives renounces a certain moral claim with regard to the wrongdoer and "closes," so to speak, the "guilt account" he had maintained concerning the one who is forgiven. We can call this first element "the purification of memory."[82] While forgiving the wrongdoer, the forgiver breaks the logic of "an eye for an eye" and lets the one who is forgiven know that he will not take the wrongful act into account.

Here raises an important and difficult question on the necessity of the—active or passive—cooperation of the wrongdoer. This has to do with the second element of forgiveness mentioned above, namely the extension of an attitude of good will towards the wrongdoer as a person. However, this does not mean that the one forgiving does in fact extend this positive attitude to the wrong act. Augustine referred pre-

---

[81] I refer extensively to these points in (Crespo 2002).

[82] This expression was used by the International Theological Commission of the Catholic Church in the document *Memory and Reconciliation: The Church and the Faults of the Past*. "This purification aims at liberating the personal and communal conscience from all forms of resentment and violence that are the legacy of past faults, through a renewed historical and theological evaluation of such events. This should lead—if done correctly—to a corresponding recognition of guilt and should contribute to the path of reconciliation. Such a process can have a significant effect on the present, precisely because the consequences of past faults still make themselves felt and can persist as tensions in the present." (Introduction). "This expression is used in this document, with a theological and in a sociological meaning. Here we use it in a strictly philosophical sense, referring to interpersonal forgiveness" (Introduction).

cisely to this point when he recommended hating the sin, but not the sinner. This attitude underlies the practice of not identifying the wrongdoer with his or her wrong act, i.e., not considering him as "the" wrongdoer, but as a person whose being goes "beyond" the wrong act. This can be explained in positive terms by saying that the forgiver affirms the wrongdoer "as a person." Of course, this does not eliminate the demand for justice. To forgive does not mean that the forgiver enters into some kind of agreement with the evil committed; rather, it acts completely to the contrary. To forgive means recognizing this evil and rejecting it, despite refusing to identify the wrongdoer with the wrong act.

As I have written before, I believe that these two elements of forgiveness, namely, the purification of memory and the attitude of good will towards the wrongdoer, are not in a symmetric relation. What I want to say instead is that this latter positive attitude not only justifies the first element, "the purification of memory," but also goes beyond it. It is superabundant with respect to this purification, precisely because it lies at a deeper level of the human person's moral life. Actually, where the objective evil is inflicted and the moral disvalue of the wrongdoing increases, the positive attitude of affirming the wrongdoer as a person increases all the more. Therefore, forgiving the wrongdoer is much more than telling him that his offense will not be taken into account. This new positive attitude is precisely the ground for not taking the wrong committed into account.

The purification of memory

As I have mentioned, through the deliberated act of inflicting an objective evil, a disharmony arises that gives rise to moral guilt, to what we can call the creation of a "guilt account" between the wrongdoer and his victim. Forgiveness has an element of renunciation, of "closing" this account. To forgive the wrongdoer means to "purify the memory," that is, to let him know: "I will no longer take into account the harm you did me." This "purification" is a process aimed at giving up any form of resentment and any negative feelings. The ground of this process is a new way of taking a stance before the person or the persons who inflicted an objective evil on me.

The purification of memory results in a peaceful relationship with past wrongdoing. This relationship is different, for example, from the relation that a resentful or bitter person would have with that wrongdoing. Vladimir Jankélévitch refers to and carefully distinguishes both kinds of possible relationships to the wrongdoing. The resentful person is, so to speak, "trapped" in the past, rejecting the process of "conversion," while forgiveness "favors" that process. As Jankélévitch rightly points out, forgiveness releases us from a hypertrophy of resentment. Eliminating the old resentment, the person who sincerely forgives is like the traveler who no longer has to carry heavy luggage around with her.

The "closing of the guilt account" which takes place in forgiveness shows its free character. But does this "closing" need some kind of cooperation by the wrongdoer, or is forgiveness an act which the forgiver performs "alone"? Do we need some kind of cooperation of the wrongdoer in order to forgive him? This cooperation can be active or passive. The first consists only in perceiving that his victim has forgiven him. So we could say that forgiveness is fully real when the guilty person perceives that he has been forgiven. This can be explained by saying that forgiving is a social act, as is commanding. Each act of commanding needs to be perceived by its addressee. A commanding which remains in the consciousness of the person who gives it is not a real commanding. The commanding needs not only to be addressed to an addressee, but needs to be perceived by the addressee. However, along with the "active cooperation" of the wrongdoer, we also have the question of the necessity of showing repentance in order to be forgiven. I would like to shed some light on these two points.

As I have just mentioned, the question of the passive cooperation of the addressee has to do with the victim's need to experience some kind of repentance on the part of the wrongdoer. We can formulate the question in negative terms: is it possible to speak of genuine forgiveness when its addressee does not know that he or she has been forgiven? Should we perhaps distinguish between an "inner forgiveness" and an "effective forgiveness," the latter of which needs to be perceived by its addressee? These questions have to do, in the final analysis, with the alleged social character of forgiveness. Lived experiences such as making a decision, asserting something, giving an order, forgiving, etc. do not just belong to the I; rather, the I reveals itself as active in such experiences (cf. Reinach, 1983). It would be insufficient to characterize these experiences as merely intentional. As Reinach wrote:

> *The regret which rises up in me, or the hatred which asserts itself in me, are also intentional in that both refer to some object. Spontaneous acts also have—in addition to their intentionality—their spontaneity, which lies in this, that in them the self shows itself to be the phenomenal originator of the act. (1983, 18)*

Some of these spontaneous acts presuppose "in addition to the performing subject a second subject to whom the act of the first subject is related in a very definitive way" (Reinach, 1983: 19). Reinach calls these experiences—for which "it is essential that the subject to whom they are directed be another person"—"other-directed" (*fremdpersonal*) experiences. This is the case in the act of commanding. I cannot command myself, and I cannot forgive myself. But there is an important difference between the act of commanding and the act of forgiving. Forgiving is not just related to another subject, "it also *addresses* the other (*wendet sich an es*)" (Reinach, 1983, 19). But is it possible that I turn forgivingly to another, that I address him, entirely within myself, without speaking to him? "Commanding, in contrast, announces itself in the act of turning to the other, it penetrates the other, and has by its very nature a tendency *to be heard* (*vernommen*) by the other. The command is, in its essence, *in need of being heard* (*vernehmungsbedürftig*). It can of course happen that commands are given without being heard, thus failing to fulfill their purpose. They are like thrown spears which fall to ground without hitting their target" (Reinach, 1983, 19). Reinach designates as *social acts* those spontaneous acts which are "other-directed" and which need to be heard. My question here is whether forgiving is a social act in this sense, i.e., whether it is a spontaneous other-directed act which needs to be heard. I think it is clear that forgiving is a spontaneous other-directed act. The difficult point here, then, is whether it is an act in need of being heard. Does my act of forgiving need to be heard by its addressee to be a genuine forgiving? Does being heard belong to the essence of forgiving?

A first approach to this question shows that, strictly speaking, forgiving does not need to be heard by the other. I can give expression to my forgiving and tell its addressee: "I forgive you." Nonetheless, it seems that I can forgive my wrongdoer within myself, not letting him know; in this situation he would not "hear" my forgiving. To sum up, in this case forgiveness would not be a social act as Reinach describes it.

Against the alleged non-social character of forgiveness one could raise the objection that there are actually two acts of forgiving: the forgiveness "within" and the act of forgiveness which is in need of being heard. The reasons to defend this position could be the following:

   a) If my wrongdoer asks me for forgiveness, it is not enough to forgive him from within, I have to forgive him in such a way that he hears it.
   b) The "gift" of forgiveness cannot come to be in a simple inner act.

c) Forgiveness has a dialogical structure. Thus, I can forgive the wrongdoer and thereby make his repentance possible.

(a): The fact that the person who has inflicted an objective evil upon me is asking for forgiveness has a special meaning. Of course, I can decide to not forgive the wrongdoer. His asking for forgiveness does not force me to forgive him. Every act of forgiving comes, in the final analysis, from the freedom of its subject. If the wrongdoer is sincerely asking for forgiveness, he is willing to stand at a distance from his wrong act. He does not want to be identified with it and rejects its moral disvalue. Despite the internal relation between asking for forgiveness and standing at a distance from the wrong act, both are quite different acts. Taking distance from a past act is itself an act that must be distinguished from asking for forgiveness. Asking for forgiveness is clearly a social act carried out by the wrongdoer, while internally standing at a distance from the wrong act need not be known by the subject offering forgiveness. On the contrary, to ask for forgiveness is a completely new act which appeals to the victim. The ground of a sincere asking for forgiveness is above all a withdrawal from having inflicted an objective evil. At the same time, the wrongdoer goes beyond these inner acts and addresses his victim. This last act is not just other-directed; it is also social. But we should return to our analysis of forgiving.

Normally we let our forgiveness be known. As a social act, speaking about our forgiveness is directed to another person, who need not be our wrongdoer. The object of my telling is a state of affairs, namely, that I have forgiven my wrongdoer. As Hildebrand points out, this state of affairs is something objective, which I submit for the other's consideration. However, if I tell my wrongdoer "I forgive you," it is not just a communication of my forgiveness: it is a performative act.

In such performative acts we find an organic unity between taking a certain stance and its communication. My forgiveness is not just the object of a communication that I reflect upon; rather, I find myself doing something, namely, forgiving. As Hildebrand has also shown, my forgiveness can only be performed in the presence of my wrongdoer. Strictly speaking, he is the only person to whom I can manifest my forgiveness. One can even say that forgiveness compels us to inform its addressee. So we can talk, again with Hildebrand, of "the dynamic tendency to be expressed" of forgiveness.

However, the fact that forgiving is an other-directed act, that its communication is a social act—and that it compels us to let itself be known—does not necessarily mean that forgiving is a social act. Unlike other acts of taking a stance that are expressed, and which are different from such social acts as commanding and promising, forgiving does not lose its meaning if it is not heard by its addressee. If my forgiveness is neither communicated nor heard, it is still authentic forgiveness. Therefore, forgiving is not a genuinely social act.

(b): We can say something similar regarding the character of "gift" that forgiveness has. Though it is normal that a person who receives a gift will know who the person is that gave this present, I do not think that this knowledge belongs to the essence of forgiveness. In principle, I can give the "present" of my forgiveness without informing my wrongdoer (or any other person).

(c): I do not think that we forgive our wrongdoer in order to obtain his repentance. This would, in my opinion, contradict the character of forgiveness as a "gift." I forgive in a dialogical relation with my wrongdoer in which, ideally, his repenting and his asking for forgiveness go together. I forgive with the hope that the wrongdoer will distance himself from his wrong act and repent for it. Moreover, his asking for forgiveness is not just an interior act, but needs to be heard. Certain moments of forgiveness, such as a new way of "looking" at the other person, the acknowledgement of his value, the disappearance of my angry feelings against him, etc., take place in the context of forgiving, which is an inner act. However, the question asked here is whether such an essential

moment as the closing of the guilt account between the victim and the wrongdoer can take place in an act from within, or if it has to become a social act, a public "yes, I forgive you" which needs to be heard to be effective.

It can also happen that the person who inflicts an objective evil on somebody else both acknowledges her wrong act and asks for forgiveness. So the expression of the forgiveness that has been granted could have a positive effect upon the wrongdoer, and may help to deepen a change of heart already initiated on the victim's side. However, forgiveness is not a "moral strategy," which can be seen in the fact that a person can forgive her wrongdoer even when the latter is already dead, i.e., when forgiveness or its rejection can no longer have any effect on the wrongdoer's character.

To think that moral value of forgiveness consists in the moral improvement of the wrongdoer or that in the forgiver's intention there must be the purpose of achieving such an effect, would give, in my opinion, a certain utilitarian character to forgiveness, a character which is foreign to it. To forgive has—as in the case of love—an element of generosity. If the primary end of forgiveness is the moral change of the wrongdoer, genuine forgiveness would be adulterated.

As I have mentioned before, the active cooperation of the one who is forgiven consists in showing repentance. But is repentance a necessary condition for "purifying memory" and therefore also necessary for forgiveness? Before clarifying this question, I would like to say something on repentance. In his essay *Reue und Widergeburt* Max Scheler analyzes what repentance consists in. He shows that it is a "psyche's form of self-healing," "the only way to the recovery of lost forces."[83] It is neither a psychic burden nor a self-

---

[83] Repentance is neither a spiritual deadweight nor a self-deception, it is neither a mere symptom of mental disharmony nor

deception. Repentance cannot make the wrong acts of which I repent disappear. However, Scheler points out that we do not only have a certain control over our future, but also in some way over our past. The reason is that "our past experience is not closed in regards to its value and sense." To repent means, first of all, to address a part of our past life giving it a new sense, a new value.[84] It thus seems that repentance has three fundamental elements or moments:

---

an absurd attempt on the part of the human soul to cast out what is past and immutable. On the contrary, Repentance, even from the purely ethical aspect, is a form of self-healing of the soul, is in fact its only way of regaining its lost powers. And in religion it is something yet more: it is the natural function with which God endowed the soul, in order that the soul might return to him whenever it strayed from him (Scheler 1960, 39).

[84] We are not the disposes merely of our future; there is also no part of our pat life which (…) might not still be genuinely altered in its *meaning* and *worth*, through entering our life's total significance as a constituent of the self-revision which is always possible (Scheler 1960, 40).

Since, however the total efficacy of an event is, in the texture of life, bound up with its *full* significance and *final* value, every event of our past remains *indeterminate* in significance and incomplete in *value* until it has yielded *all* its potential effects. Only when seen in the whole context of life, only when we are dead (which, however, implies 'never', if we assume an after-life), does such an event take in the completed significance and "unalterability," which render it a fact such as past events in nature are from their inception (Scheler 1960, 40). I grant that everything about the death of Caesar which appertains to the events of nature is as complete and invariable as the eclipse of the sun which Thales prophesied. But whatever belonged on that occasion to "historical reality," whatever is woven of it as meaning and effect into the fabric of man's history, is an incomplete thing, and will not be complete until the end of world-history (Scheler 1960, 41). Repenting is equivalent to re-appraising part of one's past life and shaping for it a mint-new worth and significance. People tell us that Repentance is a senseless attempt to drive out something "unalterable." But nothing in this life is "unalterable" in the sense of this argument. Even this "senseless" attempt alters the "unalterable" and places the regretted conduct or attitude

a) Acknowledging the moral disvalue of a past act;
b) Regretting this act, and;
c) Having the firm intention of not performing this act again.

The integration—in a new way—of the past wrong act in the totality of my life, the emotional rejection of the wrong act, and the relief from guilt, as well as the effort to move it from the center of the person in order to "heal" it, are not sufficient to explain the phenomenon of repentance. As Scheler notes, "there is no repentance which does not include, from the very beginning, the plan of building a 'new heart'. Repentance kills only to create. It eliminates to build." So repentance is different from a bad conscience and from remorse: neither of them includes any wish for "metanoia" (Hildebrand 1975, 30ff); Cf. also (Jankélévitch 1998). Neither bad conscience nor remorse include as essential element the intention of not doing again the wrong act. On the contrary, authentic repentance entails a clear conversion, a rejection of the wrong act. In repentance we find the firm intention of not inflicting an objective evil again (Hildebrand 1975, 33ff). But the central question remains: is the wrongdoer's repentance a necessary condition for granting him or her forgiveness?

---

in a new relation within the totality of one's life (Scheler 1960, 41-42). "For it is the peculiar nature of Repentance that in the very act which is so painfully destructive we gain our first complete insight into the badness of our Self and conduct, and that in the same act which seems rationally comprehensible only from the 'freer' vantage point of the new plane of existence, this very vantage point is attained" (Scheler 1960, 47).

Numerous authors answer this question with a clear "yes." Most of the authors who think that repentance is a necessary condition for forgiveness use the following argument: if forgiveness aims at the restoration of the relationship between two persons, the wrongdoer should repent for his wrong act. If not, the restoration of the past relation would be impossible. According to Margaret Holmgren, there is a different argument for defending the position that repentance is a necessary condition for forgiveness. One can argue that, if we forgive an unrepentant wrongdoer, this means that we were not successful in telling him or her about our respect for morality or for the world of moral values.[85]

---

[85] "It is morally wrong to forgive a wrongdoer unless the wrongdoer has repented of her misdeed. In the absence of repentance, forgiveness betrays a lack of self-respect. Where, however, the wrongdoer repents, forgiving behaviour is morally permissible. It is not morally required. No one has a right to be forgiven, imposing on others a perfect duty to forgive. Notwithstanding, if one never forgave repentant wrongdoers, one would be open to moral criticism. This is because a disposition to forgive when forgiveness is permissible is a virtuous trait and—being a virtue—requires that we ought to forgive on at least some occasions" (Haber, 1991, 103). "Without contrition on the part of the offender, forgiveness is simply a state of mind – a condition that may be emotionally ... meaningful to the one who forgives but has no significance as a social or moral bond, as a medium for restoring civilized relations between the injured and the injurer" (Jacobi, 1983, 347). Holmgren has shown how wrong this argument is: "The person who reaches a state of genuine forgiveness determines that regardless of whether she repents, the wrongdoer is a valuable human being, who has made a mistake and done wrong. He recognizes her intrinsic worth as a person and determines that it is appropriate to extend towards her an attitude of real goodwill. Thus it seems that regardless of whether the wrongdoer repents and regardless of what she has done or suffered, genuine forgiveness is fully compatible with respect for morality. By truly forgiving his offender the victim of wrongdoing does not fail to respect moral standards himself, nor does he fail to communicate respect for these standards to others (Holmgren 1993, 348).

As one can see in this overview, the discussion about the necessity of the wrongdoer's repentance for granting him forgiveness is complex. However, I think one can at least claim the following: first, closing the "guilt account" between the victim and the wrongdoer is a free act of the person who forgives. This act is fully in his hands. It is also an other-directed act, oriented to the addressee of the forgiveness. Secondly, this "guilt account" cannot be totally closed without the wrongdoer's collaboration. This is shown in repentance. In other words, the breaking of the logic of "an eye for an eye"—which takes place through forgiveness and its overcoming by a positive answer to the wrongdoer who asks for that forgiveness—would not reach or "touch" him if he doesn't show any repentance. The benevolent attitude which represents the positive element of forgiveness "touches the wrongdoer's heart," if he does show repentance, while a lack of good will or a lack of repentance restricts the effect of this positive attitude. In this sense, one can say that repentance is a necessary condition for forgiveness. However, this statement has to be nuanced.

The idea of repentance as a necessary condition for forgiving has been all too easily misunderstood. One may have the impression that forgiveness is—in the final analysis—the expression of a kind of utilitarian attitude. Following this line of thought, the forgiver makes some kind of exchange with the wrongdoer: "I grant you my forgiveness, if you first give me your repentance." This would contradict the character of forgiveness as a free gift. Forgiveness would be a "business" between its subject and its addressee.

Forgiveness is not a utilitarian act. It is not a "do ut des," but an invitation to reject the moral disvalue of the act of inflicting an objective evil. The "purification of memory" will be perfect if the addressee of the forgiveness collaborates with his repentance. To sum up, we can say that the fact that forgiveness is not a utilitarian act does not prevent the forgiver from asking, in some way, for an act of repentance on the side of the wrongdoer.

The wrongdoer's repentance is expressed in his asking for forgiveness. Someone asks for forgiveness because he or she has repented of his or her wrongdoing. In this asking for forgiveness there is not just repentance, but also a certain kind of, let us say, "humiliation." In an authentic case of asking for forgiveness, this "humiliation" is accompanied by an *ex professo* assumption of the guilt. One assumes the responsibility for the wrongdoing, but at the same time wishes to distance him or herself from it. The person who asks for forgiveness also asks not to be identified with his wrongdoing. He asks to acknowledge the transcendence of his person beyond his acts. Repentance positions the relation between the person and the wrongdoing in a new way. The person does not "pigeonhole" herself in the past offense, but tries to integrate it, from a new perspective, in the totality of her life.

Asking for forgiveness introduces an element which substantially changes the situation in the relation between two persons. Forgiveness is easier if the wrongdoer asks for forgiveness. He "disarms" us and waits for our answer. If this asking is sincere, if we can "see" authentic repentance in it, then he has something in common with the repentant wrongdoer, namely, both reject the moral disvalue of the offense and the objective evil inflicted by it. If we have "seen" that the wrongdoer is not reducible to his wrongdoing and he himself asks not to be identified with it,[86] we have then good reasons to forgive him.

---

[86] Beatty says, "I am assuming that in asking forgiveness the person affirms that he indeed committed the acts of which he is accused. But he denies – and this is intimately bound to his appeal for forgiveness – that he is in them. For if he were in his acts then an affirmation of his guilt in the acts and his appeal for forgiveness would amount to a denial of himself. He is not sorry for being himself but for having committed certain acts of neglect. The very appeal for forgiveness is a practical demonstration that he transcends his acts and past and is not

The affirmation of the wrongdoer as a person

If somebody has inflicted an evil upon us and we forgive him, we do not merely "purify the memory," or close the "guilt account" between us. There is also a positive, benevolent, attitude of the forgiver towards the wrongdoer. What is this attitude?

Related to this point—in a well-known paper on forgiveness—Auriel Kolnai points out its supposed "logical impossibility." It creates a dilemma, so to speak, a Damocles's sword of forgiveness. This dilemma has to do with the way we conceive the relation between the wrongdoer and his wrongdoing, or in more general terms, how we conceive the relation between agent and action. Kolnai sees only two ways of interpreting this relation: either the relation between agent and actions "breaks" or doesn't. So, a positive attitude with regard to the agent would lead to a non-negative attitude (positive or indifferent) with regard to the action. However, this would mean condoning the evil and thus would not be a genuine occasion of forgiveness. If the relation between the wrongdoer and his wrongdoing "breaks," then it would be morally wrong to judge the wrongdoer on the basis of his

---

identical with them. In seeking the forgiveness of the other, the offender is asserting both that he is and is not the man who committed the offence. For if the offended sees no difference between the man who offended her and the one asking forgiveness, she has no basis upon which to forgive. If she recognizes no difference, then the forgiveness she confers merely amounts to an acceptance of the offender for what he is, viz., an offender. Then, 'forgive me' means 'accept me for what I am' in the offender. Her forgiveness would merely be a confirmation of her masochism, her desire for treatment as an object. In asking forgiveness then, the offender places the offending acts before the offended person and, at the same time, asks her to recognize that he (the offender) transcends his acts" (Beatty 1970, 250).

wrongdoing. A radical form of conceiving the second element of this disjunction rejects the identity between person P, at the time T_1, and person P at the time T_2. In such a case it would not make any sense to consider this person at time T_2 as responsible for having inflicted an objective evil at time T_1. It would not make sense, for example, to judge the Apostle Paul for persecuting Christians before his conversion, because Saul and Paul were "two" different persons. Since, according to Kolnai, one can talk about forgiveness via the frame of this disjunction alone, it would seem that forgiveness is impossible.

I hold that there is a solution to the dilemma described by Kolnai. The starting point for this solution lies in the forgiver's attitude. As I have already said, forgiving a wrongdoer is not merely done to "purify the memory." We also have an attitude which is highly positive. It is not just a matter of saying to the wrongdoer: "I will no longer take into consideration what you did to me." I also acknowledge that the wrongdoer has a greater value that "transcends" the inflicted objective evil and the moral disvalue of the act of inflicting it. To forgive somebody is to see "with new eyes" the indestructible fullness of the value present in every person. Of course, we recognize the moral disvalue of wrongdoing—without that element we cannot talk of forgiveness, but we do not identify the wrongdoer with the wrongdoing in such a way that rejecting the second would lead to rejecting the first. Our new attitude gives us the capacity of rejecting an answer based on the wrongdoing, instead taking a morally noble stance (Hildebrand 1980, 94).

This new positive attitude also gives grounding to the "trust credit" which the forgiver grants to his or her wrongdoer. In a case of authentic forgiveness this attitude overcomes and "defeats" the wrongdoing. It is precisely that which what I have called "the asymmetry of forgiveness" consists in.[87] This positive attitude goes beyond the level of the purification of memory and reaches a new and higher moral level. Where evil increases, the positive attitude towards the wrongdoer abounds all the more.

This points to—and is an important consequence for the metaphysics of the person—a revision of the way of conceiving the relation between an agent and his or her action. There is, certainly, an evident relation between both of them. As Wojtyła pointed out, "action reveals the person and we see the person through her action" (Wojtyla 1979, 12-13). But does this access to the person through her actions authorize us to think that she is just the series of actions which take place between her birth and her death? I don't think so. If this were the case, the judgment of the agent would be strictly determined by the corresponding judgment on the actions, and there would not be place for forgiveness. If the action has to be rejected, one should also reject the agent, since he would be nothing other than his actions. If the action is positively judged, one should also judge the agent positively and forgiveness would make no sense. It is not difficult to see the consequences of such a way of thinking.

I think that Kolnai's dilemmas lies, in the last analysis, in the inability to understand the inner open-mindedness for which forgiveness is asking. One should realize that the agent's evaluation does not depend exclusively on the evaluation of the action. If one reduces the person to her wrong-

---

[87] «Pardonner est un acte limite très difficile, il nécessite générosité et bonté et comporte une dissymétrie essentielle : au lieu du mal pour le mal, je rends le bien pour le mal, alors que la clémence consiste seulement à arrêter le mal et à s'abstenir de châtier. C'est un acte individuel alors que la clémence est souvent un acte politique» (Morin 2000). [Since there is no "official" translation into English of this interview, I prefer to leave it in the original French.]

doing, it is impossible to negatively evaluate only the wrong act and not its subject. Inasmuch as it is possible to separate the wrongdoing from the wrongdoer, it is possible to forgive him or her, without in any way approving the wrongdoing (Murphy, 1982, 508). This does not mean overcoming the profound link between action and agent. Wrongdoers are responsible for their actions, but they cannot be reduced to them. The person who inflicts an objective evil can be distinguished from her action without "damaging" the due respect to the values and the order among them. Repentance is one of the clearest ways of proving that persons who have inflicted evils can fully distance themselves from their wrong act. The sincerely repenting offender accepts his responsibility for his wrong action, but, at the same time, does not wish to be identified with it. With his repentance, he lets the victim know that he rejects his own wrongdoing (Murphy, 1982; Hampton, 1988, 509).

This attitude of the one who forgives does not mean identifying the wrongdoer with his wrongdoing, and as such is the basis of the moral value of forgiveness. It is a "change of heart" on the part of the forgiver, a change which involves acknowledging the guilty person as a person, refusing to consider him as reducible to his wrong act. The forgiver perceives the value of the other (Spaemann 1991, 279). In this sense, forgiveness presupposes that the wrongdoer has not lost his "authentic being" by his wrong act. As Spaemann points out:

> *Of course, I am the person who did this, and will be always so. My personal identity is not something apart from innate or acquired attributes; it is the whole of which my attributes are qualifications. Yet the meaning of these qualifications for the whole—for the Being of the person—is not settled once for all. The person is always more than the sum*

> *of his or her attributes. The person cannot make what has happened into something that has not happened, and must reckon with what he or she has become. But it makes a difference how this reckoning is done. Disowning a deed in repentance is a way of reintegrating what has happened by re-evaluating it. (2006, 232 and 248)*

Therefore, to forgive somebody means not to identify her or him with his or her factual "such being." The identification of act and person would mean "to refuse him as a person, (which is to say, a subject free in respect of all its predicates)" (Ibid., 232).

A possible objection against this way of conceiving the person would consist in claiming that, from this point of view, the disvalue of the act of inflicting an objective evil and the moral disvalues are not taken seriously, that we have a form of value blindness. I do not think, however, that this objection is correct. It is quite clear that forgiveness supposes the disvalue of the wrongdoing and clearly taking a stance against this action. Therefore, forgiveness and *condoning* are completely different.

To assign his wrongdoing to the wrongdoer, to make him responsible for it and, at the same time, to let him know that we acknowledge him as a person, neither contradicts nor excuses the offense and its consequences. With our forgiveness we tell him that, *despite* his wrong act, and inasmuch as he is a person and has a personal dignity, he is *capax remissionis*. As the late Jean Hampton pointed out:

> *The forgiver who previously saw the wrongdoer as someone bad or rotten or morally indecent to some degree has a change of heart when he "washes away" or disregards the*

wrongdoer's immoral actions or character traits in his ultimate moral judgment of her, and comes to see her as still decent, not rotten as a person, and someone with whom he may be able to renew a relationship. This change of heart is the new understanding of the wrongdoer as a person one can be "for" rather than "against." The forgiver trusts that, although he has undergone no rebirth, he is still "good enough" despite what he has done. Forgiveness is thus the decision to see a wrongdoer in a new, more favorable light. (1988, 84)[88]

---

[88]"Forgiveness is thus the decision to see a wrongdoer in a new, more favorable light. This decision is in no way a condoning of a wrong. The forgiver never gives up her opposition to the wrongdoer's action, nor does she even give up her opposition to the wrongdoer's bad character traits. Instead, she revises her judgement of the person himself—where that person is understood to be something other than or more than the character traits of which she does not approve. And she reaches the honest decision that this person does not merit her moral hatred, because he still has value despite his action. She does not condone something bad by forgiving him, because the forgiveness is precisely the decision that he isn't bad (even though his action and the character trait that precipitated it are)" (Hampton 1988, 84–85). Under the sign of forgiveness, the guilty person is to be considered capable of something other than his offenses and his faults. He is held to be restored to his capacity for acting, and action restored to its capacity for continuing. This capacity is signaled in the small acts of consideration in which we recognized the incognito of forgiveness played out on the public stage. And, finally, this restored capacity is enlisted by promising as it projects action toward the future. The formula for this liberating word, reduced to the bareness of its utterance, would be: you are better than your actions (Ricoeur 2004, 493).

More clearly, the message to the addressee of forgiveness is: "As a person you have a value and dignity which make it possible to forgive you. You are a person who, in virtue of your value and quality, can be forgiven".[89] At the same time, we communicate to him that he can be absolved of the guilt we humans cannot remove. The positive attitude of forgiveness sees beyond the wrongdoing suffered, looking in the direction of the inviolable value of the person. If this happens in a sincere manner, the person who is the object of this positive attitude does not feel humiliated, but rather newly found and valued.

Certainly, there are other aspects related to forgiveness which have not been mentioned in this chapter. Here I have mentioned only the two fundamental elements that I believe are present in the moral phenomenon of forgiveness. Moreover, I have claimed that both elements are in an asymmetric relation, inasmuch as the positive attitude is superabundant and surpasses the other element, i.e. the "purification of memory." Therefore, we can say that forgiving our wrongdoer is much more that letting him know that we will not take into account his wrongdoing.

I have also defended the position that forgiveness is possible only if one distinguishes between person and action. I do not mean here the trivial sense that an action is different from its subject. What I mean instead is that if we identify the wrongdoer with his wrongdoing or, in other words, if we think that the wrongdoer's factual such-being is expressed in his wrongdoing, indeed is his authentic being, it would be impossible to forgive him. If we see our wrongdoer just qua

---

[89] In forgiveness the perception of the offender as alien, evil, etc. is abandoned on the basis of considerations of a certain type or types which promote a benevolent perception of the offender (Roberts 1995, 293).

wrongdoer, we are then unable to see that his person goes beyond his acts. This difference between person and action shows, in my opinion, a very important metaphysical point: persons cannot be identified or reduced to the sum of their actions. Every such reduction or identification would ignore the fullness of personal being. To distinguish—in the sense I am discussing here, between person and action—does not at all mean "atomizing" or forgetting the relation between both. Certainly, the person who has slandered me becomes my slanderer. However, to reduce his personal being to his slander is not only incompatible with a sincere forgiveness, but is also the basis for revenge, hatred and other antitheses to forgiveness.

Through an intuition into the full value of the forgiven person, we give her a "credit of trust." We absolve her because of herself and not because of some supposed inner peace we were hoping for in forgiveness. To forgive merely to recover this lost inner peace would mean converting the addressee's forgiveness into an instrument to make us feel better. This makes forgiveness similar to love. Just as in love, the person who forgives is not looking to confirm or prove her own moral goodness. To the contrary, an arrogant forgiveness which seeks to prove the moral superiority of its subject is not forgiveness at all. In the act of forgiving, its subject is fully addressed to its addressee.

This "trust credit" has nothing to do with a kind of naiveté. It does not mean closing one's eyes, suffering a kind of blindness or maintaining an illusory trust in our wrongdoer. As in the case of love, this "credit" goes hand in hand with the awareness of our own fragility. This awareness does not cancel the wrongdoer's responsibility. It can also happen that this credit is not honored, perhaps because the wrongdoer once again commits an objective evil on us. However, this trust credit entails a confidence in the wrongdoer which is different from any kind of acceptance of or complicity with the wrongdoing. It is a hope that the gift of forgiveness will find the right answer in its addressee.

In a beautiful text, Augustine refers in a poetic way to the two elements of forgiveness which are in an asymmetric relation. In the final analysis, this chapter is a series of footnotes to this text:

> *We do not in any way approve the faults which we wish to see corrected, nor do we wish wrong-doing to go unpunished because we take pleasure in it; we pity the man while detesting the deed or crime, and the more the vice displeases us, the less do we want the culprit to die unrepentant. It is easy and simple to hate evil men because they are evil, but uncommon and dutiful to love them because they are men; thus, in one and the same person you disapprove the guilt and approve the nature, and you thereby hate the guilt with a more just reason because by it the nature which you love is defiled. (Augustine 1953)*[90]

---

[90] «Nullo modo ergo culpas, quas corrigi volumus, adprobamus nec, quod perperam committitur, ideo volumus impunitum esse, quia placet; sed hominem miserantes, facimus autem seu flagitum detestantes, quanto magis nobis displicet vitium, tanto minus volumus inemendatum interire vitiosum. Facile est enim atque provlive malos odisse, quia mali sunt, rarum autem et pium eosdem ipsos diligere, quia homines sunt, ut in uno simul et culpam inprobes et naturam probes ac propterea culpam iustius oderis, quod ea foedatur natura, quam diligis» (Augustine 1953b, 335).

References

Augustine. 1953. "Letters." *Augustine, The Fathers of the Church.* Translated by W. Parsons. Washington: Catholic University of America Press.

Beatty, Joseph. 1970. "Forgiveness." *American Philosophical Quarterly* 7.3: 246-252.

Crespo, Mariano. 2002. "Das Verzeihen." *Eine Philosophische Untersuchung.* Heidelberg: Winter Verlag.

———. 2009. "Un capítulo de la crítica de la razón afectiva." *El análisis de las disposiciones de ánimo según Alexander Pfänder.* Pensamiento 65.245: 413-431.

Crosby, John. 1983. "Adolf Reinach's Discovery of Social Acts." *Aletheia* 3: 143-194.

Ferrer, Urbano. 2002. *Desarrollos de ética fenomenológica*, Segunda edición. Albacete: Moralea.

Haber, Joram. 1991. *Forgiveness.* Savage, Maryland: Rowman and Littlefield Publishers.

Hampton, Jean. 1988. "Forgiveness, Resentment and Hatred." *Forgiveness and Mercy.* Edited by Jeffrie Murphy and Jean Hampton. Cambridge: Cambridge University Press.

Hildebrand, Dietrich von. 1975. "Die Umgestaltung in Christus." *Gesammelte Werke*, Volume X. Regensburg: Verlag Josef Habbel.

———. 1975. "Metaphysik der Gemeinschaft." *Gesammelte Werke*, Volume IV. Regensburg: Verlag Josef Habbel.

———. 1980. "Moralia." *Gesammelte Werke*, Volume IX. Regensburg: Verlag Josef Habbel.

Holmgren, Margaret. 1993. "Forgiveness and the Intrinsic Value of Persons." *American Philosophical Quarterly* 30.4: 341-352.

Jacobi, Susan. 1983. *Wild Justice: The Evolution of Revenge.* New York: Harper & Row.

Jankélévitch, Vladimir. 1998. "Le Pardon." *Jankélévitch, Philosophie Morale.* Paris: Flammarion.

———. 1998. "La mauvaise conscience." *Jankélévitch, Philosophie Morale.*

Kolnai, Auriel. 1978. "Forgiveness." *Ethics, Value and Reality.* Edited by Auriel Kolnai and Bernard Williams, and David Wiggins. Indianapolis: Hackett.

Lafitte, Jean. 1995. *Le pardon transfiguré.* Paris: Desclee.

Morin, E. (2000). "Pardonner, c'est résister a la cruauté du monde." *Le Monde des Débats.* Accessed, May 2016: http://www.plusloin.org/plusloin/spip.php?article60.

Murphy, Jeffrie. 1982. "Forgiveness and Resentment." *Midwest Studies in Philosophy* 7.1 503-516.

_____. 1988. "Forgiveness and Resentment." *Forgiveness and Mercy.*

Murphy, Jeffrie and Jean Hampton. 1988. *Forgiveness and Mercy.* Cambridge: Cambridge University Press.Pfänder, Alexander. 1913. *Zur Psychologie der Gesinnungen.* Edited by Edmund Husserl (Halle) and Oskar Becker (Freiburg). Halle a.d.S.: Niemeyer.

Reinach, Adolf. [1913]1983. "The A priori Foundation of the Civil Law." *Aletheia: An International Journal of Philosophy.* 1-142.

_____. 1989. "Die apriorischen Grundlagen des bürgerlichen Reschts." *Sämtliche Werke,* Volumen Teil I: Die Werke, Teil I: Kritische Neuausgabe (1905-1914), and Teil II: Nachgelassene Texte (1906-1917). Edited by K. Schuhmann, & B. Smith. München und Wien: Philosophia Verlag.

Ricoeur, Paul. 2000. *La mémoire, l'histoire, l'oubli.* Paris: Seuil.

Roberts, Robert. 1995. "Forgivingness." *American Philosophical Quarterly* 32.4: 289-306.

Scheler, Max. 1919. "Reue und Wiedergeburt." *Vom Ewigen in Menschen* (Bd. I: Religiöse Erneuerung). Leipzig: Verlag der Neue Geist.

Spaemann, Robert. 1996. *Personen. Versuche über den Unterschied zwischen 'etwas' und 'jemand'.* Stuttgart: Klett-Cotta Verlag.

_____. 2006. *Persons: The Difference Between "Someone" and "Something".* (O. O'Donovan, Trad.) Oxford: Oxford University Press.

Wojtyla, Karol. 1979. *The Acting Person* (Analecta Husserliana, Book 10). D. Reidel.

Zirión, Antonio. 2012. "El resplandor de la afectividad." *Acta Fenomenológica Latinoamericana* (Actas del IV Coloquio Latinoamericano de Fenomenología): 139-153.

Chapter 8

Forgiveness, One's Voice, and the Law

Elisabetta Bertolino

The alternative to forgiveness, but by no means its opposite, is punishment, and both have in common that they attempt to put an end to something that without interference could go on endlessly.

—Hannah Arendt (1958, 241)

Introduction

Drawing from Adriana Cavarero, this chapter will consider the act of forgiveness as an ethical development of the focus on the voice (Cavarero 2005). As Hannah Arendt says in the citation above, both forgiveness and punishment attempt to put a stop to endless violence. However, the act of forgiveness does this differently, by offering newness, unpredictability and the unexpected possibility of speaking in one's unique voice. I argue there is a connection between speaking in one's voice and enacting forgiveness. Enacting forgiveness to end violence, rather than punishment, requires an ontological awareness of life as connection and dependence, rather than as separation and independence. Through speaking in one's voice, a person becomes aware of one's vulnerability and thus connected to oneself and others. This in turn leads to actions that connect one to the community and oneself, breaking with the predictability of resentment and violence.

On the contrary, the ontological subject of resentment is understood as a subject that is cut and disconnected from life. Intolerable and repressive conditions provoke acts of resistance, since the subject wants to break free from those conditions. Resistance can assume various forms, most of them reactive. Yet it is possible also to *respond* rather than *react*. One reacts to violence by reproducing thoughtlessly more violence, following resentment. Whereas one responds to violence by staying with the injury, becoming aware of oneself, and connecting to one's community. Thus, responding means being response-able, able to respond. Howard Caygill explains, for instance, how resistance is often devalued into a simple reaction of retaliation and resentment, because it is based on the logic of resentment found in Hegelian thinking (Caygill 2007, 135). In the Hegelian dialectic, identity formation remains essentially determined by the forces that it opposes, and cannot move beyond the reaction to become itself. Resentment in Hegel is a contradictory attitude that unbounds the self from the other's rights. On the contrary, for Caygill, resistance must avoid being devalued in this logic of retaliation and resentment, because it collapses resistance into mere violence.

In this chapter, I am going to avoid such a mere reaction to intolerable situations by developing a responsive and transformative account focused on "the voice." The voice resists a subject of resentment that reacts to difficult events both by disclosing a unique existent and by affirming an ontology of *natality*, reciprocity, inclination, and thus, of forgiveness.[91]

The voice also opens new possibilities for justice, and supplements some of the reflections on current critical legal theory. For instance, in *Critical Jurisprudence*, critical legal

---

[91] According to Hannah Arendt, natality refers to the fact of beginning a life with birth and to the human capacity to act by beginning something new. Political action is interpreted as rooted ontologically in natality. Natality is for Arendt a central category of political thought.

scholars Costas Douzinas and Adam Gearey criticize law's carrying out of justice that approaches the other as a general other (2005). A person who appears to the law appears in fact to be divested of her singularity and concreteness, by being considered to be the same and equal as all other persons. There is in law the tendency to calculate equally and to make everything symmetrical. Douzinas and Gearey want precisely to disturb the totalizing tendency of the legal system by bringing together the limited calculability and determinacy of law with the infinite openness of ethical alterity. Similarly to what Douzinas and Gearey argue, focusing on the voice brings together both the justice offered by law and the disclosure of one's uniqueness. It opposes the indifference of the equal exchange that operates in law, through resentment and punishment. The voice suspends the judgmental operation of law and resists it by standing outside the typical legal ontology.

The chapter introduces first forgiveness and one's voice; it deals then with the subject of resentment through the insights of Wendy Brown and Gilles Deleuze; it continues to speak of one's voice in relation to forgiveness; it ends with speculating on forgiveness and the law through the theoretical positions of Jacques Derrida , George Bataille, Paul Ricoeur, Hannah Arendt, and Adriana Cavarero.

Forgiveness and one's voice

The Italian philosopher Adriana Cavarero has worked with concept of the voice, and through the voice she finds human categories that help her rethink ontologically the selfhood of women and men in a non-binary schema (Cavarero 2005). The focus on the voice reveals one's uniqueness, corporeality, and vulnerability. Those traits belong both to men and women and cannot be reduced to predictable stereotypes associated to women only. Rather, the traits of the voice make people's actions unpredictable and responsible for the ethical features of wounding or caring. What is at stake with the voice is the potentiality to resist violence without also engaging in violence, because of the awareness of the vulnerable condition exposed by one's voice in the polyphonic community.

Similar to Cavarero's voice, for Arendt, both action and speech (the voice) are deeply related as both reveal someone's uniqueness and thus the actor. Precisely for Arendt, this disclosure of the actor—*who someone is*—leads to a resistance that, instead of repeating violence, affirms actions such as forgiveness that let go of the past and invest in the future; and can thus energize the ability to resist in the present (Arendt 1958). The voice contains precisely the potentiality for an unpredictable response to violence because it implies a selfhood that reconnects to the vulnerabilities of oneself and others and takes into account the possibility of forgiveness. In this framework, forgiveness cannot be refused simply because it has traditionally been associated with the stereotype of the feminine (women have been taught for instance to forgive and accept injustice). Neither should one resent and fight back, in an attempt to re-appropriate the sovereign law of the symbolic order, often construed in terms of masculinity.

A forgiving selfhood corresponds neither to the feminine stereotype, nor to the neutral (in reality masculine) legal subject, but to a type of resistance grounded in one's voice, singularity, and vulnerability. Forgiveness heals, restores and allows speaking and being with oneself and others. On the contrary, those who harm others stand in an unsustainable and illusory position of separation, cutting off from relationality. Peace in the community is broken by their harmful actions. Forgiving is instead an act of newness that allows the possibility of restoring a community and risking exposure despite the wounds of trespasses. Forgiveness does not involve complicity, acquiescence in wrongdoing or forgetting. Rather, it involves an awareness of the unique vulnerability of each of us, coming from one's voice.

Consequently, I maintain that the legal mode of speaking must open way to another ontological perspective; one that is critical of the ontology of blaming and resentment that characterizes the current legal subject and that has the potentiality to transform the legal subject itself. To speak in one's voice means responding and being responsible for *who one is* and one's uniqueness, and implies an awareness that allows one to stay with the unbearable, and to approach life through an ontology of reconnection to oneself and the community. The focus on the voice, as theorised by Cavarero, is precisely grounded on a diverse ontology that begins from oneself and moves beyond stereotypes and the essentialized gender divide and subjectivity (Cavarero with Bertolino 2008).

The subject of resentment

I argue that legal subjectivity is grounded on the fiction of the autonomous individual; a subject thought of as general and abstract, and moreover, in isolation. Consequently, the legal subject is disconnected and cut from oneself and the community of others. Such a disconnection is particularly visible in issues of violence and survival. For the legal subject, surviving violence means becoming aware of the offense of the injury, feeling resentment, pursuing retribution, and then, appreciating that justice has been accomplished when punishment is inflicted on the wrongdoer.

Yet, retribution does not improve the conditions of the victim of violence but only of the subject construed as general. In fact, achieving retribution can be understood as an effect of a cut subject, separated from oneself and the community of others. This is because resentment does not allow movement, but endlessly makes one proceed from wrong to new wrongs. On the contrary, on a singular and vulnerable level, facing violence means speaking in one's voice and reconnecting oneself to oneself and the community of others.

At this point, I would like to reflect a bit more on the mechanism of resentment after an injury. Surviving violence is a difficult process. Violence can have immobilizing effects, in the sense that, we can be damaged so deeply that one's life can stop at the moment of the injury; the injury can continue to send out pain throughout life. A victim of violence can become acted upon by the experience of pain, by internalizing pain and by blaming the object of suffering, trapping one in resentment and desiring vengeance. The point to stress here is that the legal justice system can become a way through which one acts upon one's resentment by pursuing the punishment of the perpetrator. Consequently, justice becomes a manifestation of a subject of resentment, disconnected from the victim's self.

We can therefore say that there are two different levels of conceiving ontologically ourselves in respect to injuries. There is the possibility of speaking in one's voice that discloses an ontology of one as singular, corporeal, and vulnerable; and this exposes the unrepeatable *who-ness* capable of unexpected actions, such as forgiveness. There is also the ontology of the righteous subject, a subject construed as general, which often chooses resentment and needs to restore a balance by punishing the other who has committed the injury. This latter position entails a subject that is cut and separated from one's uniqueness and corporeal vulnerability.

This is not to say that the ontology of law and justice can be replaced *tout court* by the ontology of one's voice. Law remains a necessary place, where one can speak in public what one has suffered. Through law, one can let the other and the community know about the injury. Yet, I think that beyond the legal ontological moment, one's voice shows the constitutive ontology of our human condition of vulnerable beings in the world within a community of others. Such an ontology makes one critical of the fictitious subject of resentment that lies behind the legal justice system, precisely because the voice allows one to become aware of oneself and reconnects the subject's disjunctions.

We can say that a subject of resentment is essentially a person who is unable to stop the pain of injury, and who reacts to wrongdoing with resentment; a sovereign and righteous subject that needs to retaliate through mechanisms of retributive justice, which has the right to speak and decide for others. It is a subject in search of retribution that looks outside itself for someone to blame, and sees the other only for what the other has done and not for who the other is. The emotion of resentment gets directed against the other, for it is the other that is the object of hatred.

A subject of resentment can only repeat the logic of separation from the community, one that is familiar to the subjectivity of violence. A subject of violence, similar to a subject of resentment, is precisely one that chooses to be a resentful victim and embraces a cut and split subjectivity, separating oneself from oneself and one's community in a state of emotional hatred. I think that violence is committed precisely because one is separated from one's vulnerability and voice, and from the vulnerability and voice of others in the community. A resentful action is a violent action and is indicative of splits and cuts from life, because such an action always devalues life. Violent and resentful actions are destined to failure because the relationality with the community and oneself is destroyed, and the position of separation shows to be unsustainable.

Drawing on Friedrich Nietzsche, some scholars have theorized critically on the subject of resentment (Brown 1993, Deleuze 1983, and Cavarero 2013 ab). In her article *Wounded Attachments*, Wendy Brown (1993, 340-410) explains the subject of resentment in relation to liberalism's failure of inclusion. Current liberal identities presume to be universal but in reality exclude many who do not reflect the standard of the liberal bourgeois middle class (Ibid.). Such exclusion leaves an injury in the subject's identity, and creates the desire for recognition, causing resentment. For Brown, on the one hand, liberalism reiterates the terms of a unified and universal subject and its regulatory and normalizing mechanisms, and on the other hand, liberalism's *unemancipatory* language of *unfreedom* in relation to identity recognition results in the logic of the Nietzschean *ressentiment* (Ibid., 399).[92] Brown indicates how *the subject of ressentiment*, situated within power and expressing the impossible tension between freedom, equality in liberalism, and the liberal self-reliant subjectivity, needs to find a reason and justification for this failure within itself through resentment.

For Brown, the cause of resentment consists of the suffering as reaction to the failure of the desire for identity that cannot be met. The subject, that has been wronged, pursues revenge by imposing suffering and revaluing a recognition that is grounded on injury. And yet, Brown makes us reflect on how much subjection and impotence is invested in an identity that seeks to alleviate the suffering via repeating the exclusion and the suffering itself.

Thus, the excluded subject resists the intolerable condition of exclusion by perpetrating the same suffering of liberalism. It continues to exclude others and seeks the punishment of those who commit wrongs. According to Brown, the subject could rather resist by being critical of the structure, reversing the negative terms of liberalism and affirming a positive resistance. Finally, Brown concludes her article by underlining that in claiming recognition and revenge, the liberal subject

---

[92] The French term *Ressentiment* was first introduced as a philosophical/psychological concept by Søren Kierkegaard. Later, Friederich Nietzsche independently expanded the concept in his book *On the Genealogy of Morals*. *Ressentiment* is a re-assignment of the pain that happens when one shifts one's own sense of failure or inferiority to an external scapegoat. According to Nietzsche, the more a person is strong and dynamic, the less place and time is left for contemplating what has been done to one. Gilles Deleuze further develops the concept as discussed by Nietzsche in his work *Nietzsche and Philosophy*.

only reaffirms the same pain and hurt it wants to escape (Brown 1993, 403-6).

Likewise, Gilles Deleuze in his interpretation of Nietzsche offers a critical understanding of the emotion of resentment, introducing in some ways his own position on resentment (Deleuze 1983). Interpreting Nietzsche, Deleuze distinguishes between active and reactive forces. Active forces are creative, whereas reactive forces produce nothing and only lead to *ressentiment* and bad conscience. In his reading of Nietzsche, Deleuze argues for a type of subjectivity that is grounded on the fiction of resentment following an unhealthy mechanism (Ibid., 111). The problem seems to reside in the fact that the subject's reactive unconscious gets defined by mnemonic traces. The subject can never renew his consciousness and is incapable of forgetting the traces. A man of resentment is precisely a man whose consciousness is invaded by mnemonic traces, and his reaction consists both of blaming the object that has caused suffering and a continuous desire to take revenge against it. Such a reaction is permeated by a binary logic of good and evil, and is driven by pain and suffering (Ibid., 119). For Deleuze, Nietzsche exposes the man of resentment as a fictitious subject that multiplies its pain, interiorizes it, and produces what Nietzsche calls "bad conscience." The type of relationship that derives from resentment is the one of the debtor-creditor and requires justice as punishment. But, as Deleuze underlines, punishment does not provoke a sense of guilt in a culprit, since punishment destroys all the fresh energy and makes one *hard* (Ibid.).

The subject of resentment and one's voice

Cavarero also touches indirectly on the theme of the subject of resentment when she focuses on the vertical subject that egoistically becomes powerful precisely when the other is punished, reduced to a horizontal position and dead (Cavarero 2013a, 228; Cavarero 2013b, 118). In particular, she reflects on Elias Canetti for whom a survivor is a subject who stands up right, vertically in front of his rival dead man who lies on the floor horizontally (Canetti 1984, 1979).[93] According to Cavarero, this moment of revenge and victory for Canetti makes the subject feel he has grown taller in his verticality and also has become invulnerable, as opposed to the horizontality and vulnerability of the dead enemy.

The subject survives violence by killing through resentment, following a logic of repeated violence through a vertical posture, as opposed to the horizontal posture of the dead; and the dead man ends up becoming an opportunity for glory in the subject's egoistic verticality and invulnerability (Cavarero 2013b, 118). For Cavarero, what emerges from the subject is *the killability* rather than its *vulnerability*. Yet, the human condition of vulnerability for Cavarero *coincides neither with mortality nor with killability*; it is rather a constitutive and nude exposure to the other. What is missing for Cavarero in such a vertical subject of egoistic autonomy, resentment, and violence is precisely some inclination, some attention to the other.

Consequently, I believe that the legal way of speaking must open way to another ontological perspective, one that is critical of the ontology of blaming and resentment that characterizes the current legal subject, and one that has the potentiality to transform the legal subject itself. To speak in one's voice means being responsible for *who one is* rather than for a construed vertical and righteous subjectivity. *Who one is* expresses uniqueness, vulnerability, relationality and all the aspects of one that are cut off from the legal subjectivity. One's voice allows also one to respond to violence rather than react, because through one's voice one approaches life via an ontology of reconnection to oneself and the commu-

---

[93] Elias Canetti was a modernist, playwright memoirist and non-fiction writer.

nity. As noted above, the focus on the voice, as theorized by Cavarero, is precisely grounded on a diverse ontology that begins from oneself in relationality to others, moving beyond stereotypes and the essentialized gender divide and subjectivity.

The ontology of the voice begins with the experience of a singular body, a being of flesh and blood that can resist the subject of resentment. If, as Cavarero says, we are confronted with the option, either to care or to harm the other, speaking through the voice leads to an opening to oneself and others, to an ethical responsibility towards the vulnerability of others; and as a result, the voice pushes towards care and connection (Cavarero 2009). The awareness of vulnerability that springs from speaking one's voice poses one in front of an ethical responsibility and choice between caring or wounding; it calls for a response of responsibility, a response not a reaction, a response as response-ability, as the ability to respond ethically towards vulnerability.

Although Cavarero has not focused directly on forgiveness in her work, I think that her vocal ontology necessarily emphasizes ethical actions such as forgiveness. An account of forgiveness also relates to her thinking of the subject as being capable of inclination, one that opposes the egoistic, autonomous, and vertical legal subject (Cavarero 2005 and 2013ab). When one speaks in one's voice, one notices the vibration and the sound of one's own body; one experiences one's vulnerability and the vulnerability of other speakers with whom one is communicating. In such an ontological context, the content of communication is not as important as the uniqueness of the one who speaks, beyond any wrong committed. The voice is then linked to vulnerability, inclination, the community, and consequently, to actions of reconnection and thus forgiveness. Such a relation between one's voice and forgiveness shows how Arendt's thought has most inspired the philosophy of Cavarero.

Similar to Cavarero, Arendt spoke of uniqueness and whoness, and theorized a resistance to the current ontology and subjectivity that breaks from vengeance and resentment. Arendt linked uniqueness to natality, action, promise, and forgiveness (Arendt 1958). For Arendt, it is because of our uniqueness that we can act anew bringing natality into the community. Forgiveness is precisely an action that can bring newness and natality. Arendt sees forgiveness as the opposite of vengeance because forgiveness brings newness and unpredictability, whereas vengeance is a repetition of violence and remains predictable.

Forgiveness is unpredictable because it frees the person from the consequence of an act. Enacting forgiveness implies compassion, awareness of human frailty, discovering the wholeness of oneself, being true to oneself, resisting the separations and divisions of the subject, inclining rather than being upright and vertical, becoming aware of one's vulnerability and the vulnerability of others. Thus, forgiveness links a person to one's voice and to the voice of others, because when one speaks in one's voice, one becomes aware that the other is more similar to oneself than what one thinks; the other is vulnerable and in search of connection.

Both one's voice and the action of forgiveness reveal our uniqueness and thus resists the subject of resentment. Forgiving implies also giving away the cut mask of the current legal subjectivity, removing, unveiling such a mask, which is not organically a part of the injured singularity. Both one's voice and forgiveness allow movement towards a new relationality and community between two singularities, the offender and the one injured. Facts cannot be changed, what has happened has happened and remains so. But the meanings of facts can be changed by mechanisms of newness.

Surely, forgiveness requires a time of withdrawal, slowness, reflection, awareness, and gradual release, but only a forgiveness, as linked to our condition of vulnerability and one's voice, can allow the experience of change and newness. Forgiveness changes the influence of the past over the present and the future. In this sense, for Arendt, forgiving and promising are related categories of the political that can bring unpredictability and newness (1958, 243). Through speaking in one's voice, the selfhood does not react through resentment but is able to act in terms of forgiving and promising, to move forward from the past and embrace the future.

In particular, the voice discloses an ontology of the self as unique, one that goes beyond the indifference and the violence of the righteous and autonomous subject, and pays attention instead to *who someone is* and the possibility of unpredictable actions, such as forgiveness. One's voice is a movement of resistance that takes place from a singular, defiant and everyday experience. It should be noted that a forgiving selfhood does not imply a weak subjectivity but a strong one, one that is able to withdraw after the injury, become aware of the experience of the injury, delimit the experience of the injury, face, speak the injury, discern, decide but also let go, tolerate and accept. Whereas, in embracing the subject of resentment as in legal justice, one will continue to blame the external system for one's pain and injuries, and thus will remain trapped in the pain of the past.

On the contrary, in the action of forgiveness there is the Arendtian *miracle of natality*, which reflects in some ways the speaking of one's voice in Cavarero. The birth of a baby gives a glimpse of hope and shows the power of natality in the human condition. As Cavarero says, the newly born is a new life completely exposed to others and vulnerable because it is totally dependent on others for its safety (Cavarero 2009, 29). When one speaks in one's corporeal voice, one's unique vulnerability is necessarily exposed and calls for the necessity to break from the cycles of violence among human beings.

Indeed, when one speaks in one's voice, one breathes and shares air with others, and in doing so, one does not need to struggle with others. Speaking in one's voice is also speaking together with other voices in a polyphonic community. Such a sharing of life allows one to relate to others and be connected. When we speak we expose ourselves to others and we are exposed to others in our vulnerability. Forgiveness becomes a necessary action within a community of sharing air, voices, and vulnerability.

Similar to natality, forgiveness is the power to break away from the cycles of violence by embracing new actions and the ability to respond in human relationships. Vulnerability and natality become intrinsic elements of the maternal that are able to unsettle previous philosophical models of subjectivity. Both one's voice and forgiveness provide such a new maternal path for feminism and women. In particular, forgiveness implies unbinding from the past and binding in a new narrative of freedom, discovering the wholeness of oneself, being true to oneself, escaping the separations and divisions of the self, becoming aware of singularity and vulnerability and being a self that inclines towards others.

Moreover, forgiveness disturbs the distance between self and others. The other is perceived as another singular self that reveals his uniqueness and vulnerability through his actions. In embracing a selfhood that speaks in one's voice, with uniqueness and forgiveness, one could show empathy to what is foreign, fearsome, even repugnant, and would engage, rather than disengage, with the other. This would signify being a subject that does not obligate or morally judge the offender, but transforms relationships and offers compassion for the other's confusion, distortion, and failure. Human action is seen through vulnerability and becomes an ever-present reminder that people will die and that, as Hannah Arendt says, they are not born to die but to begin.

Sadly, we are so used to practices of violence that we conclude they are inevitable and cannot be unlearned, and therefore, that one must continue to use the master's tools. Yet, both Cavarero and Arendt suggest it is necessary to explore whether there are ways to unlearn and break from habits of violence, resist the cycles of violence and vengeance. Action becomes reconnection to oneself and others and a form of newness and natality that ends the cycle of violence. Forgiveness derives from such an awareness of oneself and others, and therefore, forgiveness is viewed here as radically connecting to one's voice.

In line with one's voice, Caygill thinks resistance as being more comparable to a self that is capable of virtue rather than freedom, and is characterized by fortitude and courage (2013, 97-135). In the next section I shall speculate on forgiveness in law and how this differs from a forgiveness that springs from one's voice. I shall explore it through the work of Jacques Derrida, George Bataille, Paul Ricoeur and Hannah Arendt.

Forgiveness: conditionality, unconditionality and circulation

Forgiveness counter-opposes the ontological approach of the subject of resentment. As a result, it has been introduced progressively within law and politics finding its place through restoration, excuses, apologies, amnesty, and prescription. Yet, the forgiveness brought into law and politics differs from a forgiveness that springs from one's voice. I shall focus in particular on the concrete example of forgiveness within law, introduced by restorative justice. Restorative justice shifts the focus of criminal justice from incarcerating offenders to holding them accountable in meaningful ways, showing a concern with the needs of victims and communities (Lerman 1999/2000, 1663-1675). Restorative justice uses tools such as victim-offender conferencing, or dialogue, that allows victims to understand an event and assess it, facilitating the possibility of forgiveness (Ibid.).

There are several positive points in restorative justice. The parties can benefit from a process of the *humanization* of legal justice, where the focus is precisely justice rather than vengeance or punishment. There is also a broadening of the meaning of justice, because the needs of both victims and offenders in the community are taken more seriously into account. There are, however, limits in the application of forgiveness within this framework, since it treats forgiveness as something that can be facilitated, induced within the institution of law and exchanged. This is in conflict with a forgiveness that springs from one's voice and vulnerability.

First, the forgiveness of the victim of restorative justice requires conditions, such as apology, and some form of restitution, reparation, or recompense by the offender. Offenders are asked to repent and take responsibility for their actions, and to repair the harm they have caused through apologizing, community service, or returning stolen property. In restorative justice, punishment is not excluded. Nevertheless, restorative justice is not used for all crimes; rather it is used mainly in cases of less violent, or juvenile crimes (Exeline 2003, 338). Furthermore, some scholars view restorative justice as not being about forgiveness but primarily about reconciliation over retribution (Worthington 1999/2000, 1729).

From what has been said, even though forgiveness has begun to find its place within the legal justice system, there are limits to its application; mainly because of the requirement of repentance, but also because forgiveness cannot be extended to serious crimes. Such conditions contrast with the idea of the inner-forgiveness that springs from one's voice. This latter occurs through the awareness of one's vulnerability and that of others in community. Speaking in one's voice indicates the openness of a desire to get on with one's own life, be centred, respond anew, and leave the past behind. Such an openness is at odds with the closure of wanting repentance, if not punishment and revenge (Bandes 1999/2000, 1599-1606).

There are many questions that emerge around forgiveness and law. For instance, to what extent mainstreaming forgiveness within law is possible; how seeking revenge and applying forgiveness within the limits of law differs from a forgiveness that springs from the voice; and how much can the law translate singular and unique feelings within general, narrow, and technical legal ends? I shall disentangle these questions by examining what forgiveness consists of from Derrida, Bataille, Ricoeur, and Arendt.

The logic theorized by Derrida on forgiveness takes the shape of a contradiction between unconditional forgiveness and conditional forgiveness, that is, between the pure idea of forgiveness and its practical application (Derrida 2001). The result, for Derrida, is that the action of forgiveness presents limitations and necessarily demands compromises. He thus argues for an action of forgiveness that is impossible and that makes our action more of an ethical direction and not something to be reached. For forgiveness to be pure, according to Derrida, it must not succumb to the logic of exchange. Unfortunately, in law and politics, Derrida says, forgiveness is often confused and replaced with calculated actions and often repentance becomes the condition of a forgiveness that can only be conditional.

For Derrida, actions of forgiveness within law, such as excuses and regrets, remain manifestations of forgiveness as an act of comparison, conditional and subjected to exchange. Even though such a proliferation of repentance can be considered an expression of something good, it can be said that it lacks sincerity and may participate in political hypocrisy, calculation and the logic of exchange. Often, then, the language of forgiveness serves various finalities and cannot be said to be pure or disinterested. In addition, in law there are still violent actions, which cannot be forgiven, such as crimes against humanity. Precisely the concept of crimes against humanity shows the conditionality of forgiveness, when it enters law and politics. In law and politics, forgiveness re-establishes what is considered normal.

For Derrida, when forgiveness serves a finality, or attempts to re-establish a normality, then forgiveness is not pure and noble. Derrida thinks that true and pure forgiveness consists of forgiving the unforgivable. If forgiveness forgave only what is forgivable, then it would not be noble, which is required of forgiveness. Forgiveness needs to forgive the unforgivable, which means it is therefore an *impossibility itself.*

According to Derrida, the prescriptability of a crime, or the limiting of the duration of an indictment, cannot be said to share the purity and uncoditionality of forgiveness. According to such juridical acts, forgiveness has meaning in the sense of restoration, salvation, reconciliation, or redemption. But as such forgiveness is still compared to a judgment or punishment; it still rests on the power of the master that says to the other: "I forgive you." For Derrida, those meanings refer to their own closure and the logic of appropriation and exchange. Rather, for Derrida, forgiveness becomes true forgiveness precisely when one is confronted with its impossibility. Forgiveness, Derrida says, is *mad, madness of the impossible* and this can only be foreign to the order of law and politics. Thus, for Derrida, the forgiveness in law and politics is only able to deal with negotiation, conditionality, and calculated transactions, whereas pure forgiveness has nothing to do with judgments or politics; it is *irreducible* to them even though at the same time *indissociable*.

As a possibility of an impossibility, the experience of forgiveness for Derrida remains inaccessible to law, rights and politics because forgiveness is an impossibility that cannot be mainstreamed within institutions. Derrida's forgiveness functions, therefore, as an ideal towards which conditional actions must strive, and he calls for an ethical justice based on the universality of unconditional and pure forgiveness.

A similar approach to forgiveness, even though within a different structure and with different outcomes, is provided by the position of George Bataille. In his book, *Accursed Share*, Bataille explains how the movement of classic economy is only a sub-category of the more general economy of energy that extends as far as the energy of the sun (1989, 58). What is important in his account is that such an energy produces excess. That is, the general economy described by Bataille is explained from the point of view of the excess, rather than from the perspective of scarcity, and such an excess needs to be expended. On a singular level, one can choose to expend the excess energy by way of resentment, aggression, reproducing the cycle of violence, or by forgiving. Therefore, for

Bataille, both, revenge and forgiveness would be only modalities of expenditure of such energy.

For Bataille, the rite of sacrifice represents an expenditure of the excess removed from the game of utility (1989, 58). In the case of sacrifice, people are not dominated by the utility of the restricted economic system, the victim of sacrifice is removed from the utility of the system and consumed profitlessly. Thus, the sacrifice can be understood in terms of a gift, completely beyond the utility system of the restricted economy. And, in turn, the gift resembles also forgiveness as a form of gift that involves a conscious decision to let go or forego bitterness and vengeance, escaping the regime of utility. Therefore, both by giving or for-giving, one engages also with the expenditure of the excess outside the logic of utility.

For Bataille, the gift of the sacrifice is precisely an expression of a new subjectivity and profound freedom, which makes one experience a sacred affirmation and intimacy, as opposed to the appropriation and expenditure of the subject in the restricted economy of exchange. In Bataille, the understanding of giving and forgiving is thus focused on the immediate and the experience of the present, avoiding the planning of rationality. Bataille's theory of the gift escapes then the logic of return, which is part of the logic of exchange behind the gift.

Yet for Marcel Mauss, a gift always expects another gift in return, and its circularity can amount to a form of self-interest, not too different from retribution (1954, 71). At the same time, Mauss underlined how there must be an elapse of time between the gift and the counter-gift, in the sense that, it moves beyond the logic of exchange. If the gift is always returned and thus annihilated by the subsequent gift, what remains is the interval of time between the gift and the counter-gift. Such an interval, when the gift is not yet repaid, is precisely what binds one to another, in a relation either of resentment or cooperation. Going back to Bataille, giving or forgiving consists essentially in an elapse of time that escapes the rational discourse of economic utility, a way to avoid determinism and allow freedom to the subject through the paradox of giving away and expending the excess. However, I think such a conception of forgiveness, in terms of gift sacrifice and freedom from restrictions, cannot find application in law, since the latter functions within the logic of utility and exchange.

Similarly to Derrida and Bataille, Paul Ricoeur has also commented on forgiveness. In his book *Memory, History, Forgetting*, Ricoeur underlines how forgiveness is necessarily linked to the experience of fault and guilt, as *fault constitutes the occasion for forgiveness* (2004, 457). There can be a forgiveness only when we can accuse someone of something. Therefore, forgiveness relates in some way to the experience of punishment. However, Ricoeur's position on forgiveness is linked to memory and the just allotment of it in relation to the past (2004, XV). Forgetting, in Ricoeur, becomes central to achieve forgiveness (Ibid., 455). Forgetting opens an aporia in the representation of the past and breaks with the dialectic of presence and absence, which is essential for the representation of the past. Both forgetting and forgiveness aim at the same horizon of appeasement of the memory. In other words, for forgiveness to happen, we need in same ways to forget the traces of our memory.

For Ricoeur, forgiveness is difficult not only to give but also to be conceived. Similarly to Derrida, Ricoeur is critical of the forgiveness that has been used in the legal justice system. Exceptions such as the imprescriptability of some crimes testify to the difficulty of both giving and conceiving of forgiveness. The imprescriptability of crimes against humanity constitutes the first major test for forgiveness because it shows that forgiveness is difficult to be institutionalized as it underlines how the extreme gravity of the crimes justifies the tracking down of the criminals without any time limit. For Ricoeur, such an exception of the law authorizes the indefinite pursuit of the authors of crimes, shows a deep hatred of the other and indicates how in law unforgivability persists (Ibid., 470).

Imprescriptability shows precisely the condition through which the gift of forgiveness is understood in law. If we intend forgiveness as a gift, which as Mauss noted contains the seeds of a logic of return, forgiveness would operate by balancing people in a sort of horizontal relation of exchange. A gift otherwise, for Ricoeur, would be giving without expecting anything in return, thus requiring the extraordinary. However, even offering love and forgiveness might contain the expectation of transforming the enemy into a friend and therefore some forms of exchange and circularity of the gift.

In order to escape the exchange and the conditionality, Ricoeur proposes then a recovery of the asymmetry in the process of forgiving. He suggests a rethinking of forgiving in terms of giving and receiving rather than giving, receiving, and giving in return. When we give and receive, we focus on the communal dimension of forgiveness and avoid the logic of exchange. On the contrary, for Ricoeur, when forgiveness is institutionalized in the legal discourse, the process of giving and receiving becomes interrupted and gets channelled through the logic of giving, receiving, and giving in return; that is, through conditionality and the logic of exchange.

Going back to the necessity of forgetting, Ricoeur argues that in some ways for forgiveness to be possible it is also necessary to allow the memory to forget. That is, to stop one from being angry with oneself and others, by fixing one's mind on what happened, there is a need to forget the unforgettable and silence the non-forgetting of memory. Forgiving becomes, then, an act of renouncing memory against the will not to forget. By remembering and focusing on past occurrences, we hold ourselves open to the past, we remain concerned about the past, and this might lead us towards concerns for retribution. In this sense, retention of memory means also enduring and remaining the same—sameness, which is predictability of thinking when acting.

On the contrary, speaking in one's voice can make one choose forgetting, preventing the continuation of retribution. From the point of view of both Ricoeur and one's voice, forgetting would then be essentially renouncing knowledge, speculation, and to let the possibility of forgiveness happen. Thus, Ricoeur invites us to develop an *ars oblivionis* together with the *ars memoriea* that has been so much celebrated; to return to the present one must in some ways suspend the links with the past (2004, 68).

Finally, in *The Human Condition*, Arendt stresses the importance of revealing *who one is* in speech and actions (1958, 199). Forgiveness is precisely a special type of action that springs from one's uniqueness and who-ness, which reveals who one is. That is, forgiveness does not come from above in Arendt. It is not a general principle but an action that arises from unique human beings, from knowing *who we are* and what we are doing. Equally for Cavarero, forgiveness would arise from one's unique voice. Forgiveness is, indeed, a new action, one that breaks from the past, from what is normal and requires unexpected thinking and acting. For Arendt, the plurality of our uniqueness entails inevitably weaknesses and wrongdoings. Through acting anew, and thus through forgiveness, it is possible to disrupt the normalizing philosophical and political settlements of violence and trouble the identities of resentment.

> *Without being forgiven, released from the consequences of what we have done, our capacity to act would, as it were, be confined to one single deed from which we could never recover, we would remain the victims of its consequences forever (...) (Arendt 1958, 237).*

For Hannah Arendt, one is not responsible for *what* one is, or what one has been made by history, circumstances. But one might always be responsible for who one is. For Arendt *who one is* gets revealed through words and deeds. When one behaves predictably one is irresponsible, one lets history act for oneself. A woman or a man who enacts violence reacts predictably and only repeats the identities which one is supposed to be. Responding in a different way is being unpredictable, being *who someone is* and thus speaking in one's voice.

In *Eichmann in Jerusalem*, Arendt shows precisely the banality of the evil, in the case of Eichmann, and how easy it is to be a repeater of violence by acting within the constructed identity imposed on us (1994). In the trial, Eichmann appeared as not being fully aware of what he did, was thoughtless, and replied by saying that he only obeyed orders, thus, suggesting the banality of evil. Evil is, for Arendt, this thoughtlessness, the fact that one is not aware of what one is doing. Arendt suggests that to resist such a banality of evil, one needs to know *who one is*, what one is doing and respond through new actions. Thus for Arendt, one needs to counter-oppose the lack of thinking and reflexivity exhibited by Eichmann by speaking in one's voice.

Arendtian forgiveness is an action that fights against thoughtlessness and that requires, on the contrary, awareness. Forgiveness is always of the *who* beyond the *what*; it reflects a self whose *who-ness* is always revealed, despite any injury suffered and any wrong committed. Forgiveness requires a unique self that is able to separate the guilty person from his act, forgiving the guilty person while condemning his wrong actions. The *who-ness* of a person goes beyond any what-ness, any action determined by circumstances. Any language that speaks for our who-ness embraces the speaking in one's voice and an awareness of vulnerability. And such awareness brings us to the Arendtian faculty of interrupting and beginning something anew through action, and it reminds us that although we will die, it is possible for us to begin anew during our lifetime. Birth and natality interrupt violence and resentment, while they disengage from the past and generate renewal, allowing thus openness rather than closure.

To sum up, the positions on forgiveness by Derrida, Bataille, Ricoeur and Arendt complement the focus on the voice. These four philosophers talk of forgiveness as something that touches the dimension of the extraordinary and the unexpected, something that overcomes the normalizing and predictable reaction of violence, retribution, and exchange. For all of them, forgiveness must escape the dimension of exchange, such as repentance and conditionality, a logic that characterizes law and politics. On the contrary, forgiveness is perceived as a gift not purchased by apology, repentance or restitution, as it happens in law.

Arendt most completely shows how the gift of forgiveness comes from within *who one is*, like in the voice that discloses one's uniqueness. This is perhaps the main difference between forgiveness in law and one's voice. The justice system employs forgiveness to deal with wrongs but only in a centrifugal way. With one's voice, on the contrary, one can only act forgiveness in a centripetal way, beginning from oneself and body, producing awareness.

Conclusion

I have argued that within justice in law, we are constructed as subjects of resentment. A subject of resentment seeks to end the pain of the injury by means of retribution, which is essentially a mechanism of exchange, of getting equal and a means for self-interest. The ontological perspective on justice offered by the legal justice system assumes that one is disconnected from oneself and surrounding situations, and thus, one does not feel one's uniqueness and is not aware of one's vulnerability and the vulnerability of the others.

The ontology that comes from one's voice, on the other hand, evokes a new perspective. When one is injured, one stays connected to oneself by speaking in one's voice. Speaking in one's voice discloses one's uniqueness and the awareness of vulnerability, and therefore, the voice leads to potential and ethical possibilities of resisting violence and resentment. When one speaks in one's voice, she is brought to act otherwise, anew, unpredictably, creating a rupture with the cycles of violence. Forgiveness is one such act that springs from one's voice within. I understand forgiveness as an inner-position of awareness of one's uniqueness and vulnerability that leads to openness. In this sense, forgiveness reveals and reconnects the self to herself and the community.

In law, when we perceive an injustice has been done to us, we require that justice is restored through punishment, thus we seek reparations for the costs incurred; often by being righteous in our claims, we repay more than we incurred. However, this means sitting on the same ontological categories of law and its mechanisms of justice. On the contrary, speaking in one's voice teaches us that both voice and action happen in the context of a community and that one's uniqueness is necessarily disclosed. This implies that violence is to be understood as a problem of the community and from the ontological point of a unique selfhood in relationality. This perspective changes the mode of action.

This chapter has also dealt with forgiveness and its possibility within the institutions of law and politics, and has analyzed forgiveness in terms of gift. The perspective on forgiveness by Derrida, Bataille, Ricoeur and Arendt suggests that there remains a problem with the institutionalization of forgiveness. In particular, for Derrida, the forgiveness that can happen within institutions can only be a conditional forgiveness. Whereas, pure forgiveness is unconditional and unexchangeable. Bataille, in his turn, argues for the expenditure of the excess (of energy) as a way to escape the utility and the instrumentalization of the system. The expenditure of excess takes the form of the gift that falls outside the general economy of exchange. Ricoeur suggests a process of forgiving by forgetting the traces of the memory that cause anger and resentment. For Ricoeur, forgiveness happens only in giving and receiving, without giving back and thus breaking with the logic of exchange. Finally, Arendt confirms the forgiveness of one's voice and the possibility of resisting the cycles of violence.

The theoretical speculation throughout this chapter reveals that the subject of law is founded on an ontological violence that paradoxically becomes lawful or legitimate, in so far as it works to posit and preserve the legal framework itself. Therefore, there has been the necessity to think of the voice in terms of one's own voice, to oppose and resist the ontological position of separation and sovereign violence of the general voice of law.

More specifically, Cavarero theorizes the possibility of an awareness of the *who one is* as opposed to the *what* of the subject of identity. The theorization of one's voice remains foreign and non-institutionalizable within the current legal and political subjectivity. Thanks to the dimension of suspension and detachment, *who one is* has the potentiality to speak in one's voice and act unpredictably. The voice inspires unpredictable actions such as forgiveness, in so far as the vocal resistance remains detached and non-accountable to the linguistic frame, and to the extent that one speaks from one's unique voice and becomes aware of the sharing of voices. One's own voice implies awareness of one's own vulnerability, and this can guide and inform our understanding and action. The ontology of the voice leads to acting and speaking in unpredictable ways, because one speaks from within, from one's own awareness. It is precisely this detachment, this suspension in a non-institutionalizable position that makes the vocal resistance strong, centred, and effective.

Voice and forgiveness, interrelated through uniqueness and vulnerability, can offer possibilities of resistance. The voice suggests that the unique awareness of oneself can lead to unpredictable actions, such as forgiveness. Speaking in one's voice means embracing the language of the body with the intention of resisting violence by means of connection to oneself and the community.

References

Arendt, Hannah. [1963] 1994. *Eichmann in Jerusalem: A Banality of Evil.* New York: Penguin Books.

_____. 1958. *The Human Condition.* Chicago: University of Chicago Press.

Bandes, Susan. 1999-2000. "When Victims Seek Closure: Forgiveness, Vengeance and the Role of Government." *Fordham Urban Law Journal* 27: 1599-1606.

Bataille, George. 1992. *The Accursed Share: An Essay On General Economy, Volume I: Consumption.* Translated by Robert Hurtley. New York: Zone Books.

Brown, Wendy. 1993. "Wounded Attachments." *Political Theory* 21.3: 340-410.

Canetti, Elias. 1984. *Crowds and Power.* New York: Farrar, Straus and Giroux.

Cavarero, Adriana. 2013a. "Recritude: Reflections on Postural Ontology." *The Journal of Speculative Philosophy* 27: 220-235.

_____. 2013b. *Inclinazioni: Critica alla Rettitudine.* Milano: Raffaella Cortina Editore.

_____. 2009. *Horrorism: Making Contemporary Violence.* Translated by William McCuaig. New York: Columbia University Press.

_____. 2005. *For More than One Voice: Toward a Philosophy of Vocal Expression.* Translated by Paul Kottman. Stanford: Stanford University Press.

Cavarero, Adriana, with Elisabetta Bertolino. 2008 "Beyond Ontology and Sexual Difference: An Interview with the Italian Feminist Philosopher Adriana Cavarero." *differences, a Journal of Feminist Cultural Studies* 19.1: 128 – 167.

Caygill, Howard. 2013. *On Resistance: A Philosophy of Defiance.* London: Bloomsbury.

Deleuze, Gilles. 1983. "From Ressentiment to the Bad Conscience." *Nietzsche and Philosophy.* Edited by Gilles Deleuze. New York: Columbia University Press.

Derrida, Jacques. 2001. *On Cosmopolitanism and Forgiveness.* Translated by Michael Hughes. London: Routledge.

Douzinas, Costas and Adam Gearey. 2005. *Critical Jurisprudence: The Political Philosophy of Justice.* Oxford: Hart Publishing.

Exeline, Joula J. 2003. "Forgiveness and Justice: A Research Agenda for Social and Personality Psychology." *Personality and Social Psychology Review* 7: 337-348.

Lerman, David M. 1999-2000. "Forgiveness in the Criminal Justice System: If it belongs, then Why is it so Hard to Find?" *Fordham Urban Law Journal* 27: 1663-1675.

Mauss, Marcel. 1954. *The Gift: Forms and Functions of Exchange in Archaic Societies*. Glencoe: The Free Press.

Ricoeur, Paul. 2004. *Memory, History, Forgetting*. Chicago: University of Chicago Press.

Worthinghton, Everett L. 1999-2000. "Is there a Place for Forgiveness in the Justice System?" *Fordham Urban Law Journal* 27: 1721-1732.

Chapter 9

Twixt Mages and Monsters: Arendt on the Dark Art of Forgiveness

Joshua M. Hall

In this chapter, I will offer a strategic new interpretation of Hannah Arendt's conception of forgiveness. In brief, I propose understanding Arendt as suggesting—not that evil is *objectively* banal, or a mere failure of imagination—but instead that it is maximally forgiveness-facilitating to understand the seemingly unforgivable as merely a failure of imagination. In other words, we must expand our imaginative powers (what Arendt terms "enlarged mentality") by creatively imagining others as merely insufficiently unimaginative, all in order to reimagine them as beings whom we are willing and able to forgive. It is in this sense that I understand forgiveness for Arendt as a kind of "magic." That is, forgiveness involves the imaginatively-funded creation of a new reality by merely naming it, like the phenomenon of "magic thinking," wherein one believes one's thoughts or speech are immediately realized in the world. The magic of forgiveness, in other words, is an incantation or performative speech act, based on the forgiver's choice to "make believe," or pretend-into-being, that the forgiven person is forgivable on the grounds that the forgiven person is merely thoughtless.

Before getting into the details, however, I wish to make one acknowledgement regarding my embodiment, and anticipate one objection to the entire chapter. First, especially given the centrality of the Holocaust to Arendt's thought, I feel it is relevant to acknowledge here that I am merely a gentile philosopher, and would not presume to judge on behalf of Jewish people regarding the issue of forgiveness of the perpetrators of the death camps. As will become clearer below, I am actually more interested, as I believe Arendt is herself, in those who were more passively complicit with Nazi totalitarianism, at most including the lowest-level Nazis who never had the occasion to perpetrate acts of violence.

As for the aforementioned objection, some will surely remember Arendt's statement, in *The Human Condition*, that forgiveness is suited only for normal failings, whereas extraordinary acts that deserve the label "evil" are beyond the pale of forgiveness, and belong instead to punishment, or even divine justice. In response to this objection, I suggest thinking of a continuum or spectrum of imaginativeness, at one end of which lies a person so evil, so much a monster, that no one could possibly forgive him/her, and at the other end of which lies a person so superhumanly forgiving that, for such a person, no one would be unforgivable. This could be likened to something like the ends of the medieval Great Chain of Being, with Satan as the nothingness of pure sinful evil, and Jesus as the divine forgiver of sins. My interpretation of this spectrum, however, is that both extremes are fictitious, in that no one (at least not in the human world) is utterly evil, and no one can forgive everything. And yet, for Arendt, the best way to live is to strive to realize (through the use of mental imagery) the image of the maximal forgiver in oneself, and to interpret every offense requiring forgiveness as resulting from a superficiality/lack of depth of thought and imagination.

In support of this conception, the etymology of the word 'monster' means "to show" (or "appear"), such that a pure monster would be a pure appearance or empty show without substance (i.e., a mere appearance without the capacity to observe other appearances, like a television monitor as opposed to a mind). Similarly, I suggest thinking of the perfect forgiver as one with a perfect imagination—a maximally-powerful manipulator of images, or "mage" (i.e., one who can manipulate any image into any other for strategic purposes, in this case to reimagine any offender as forgivable).

Real human life, though it of course always lies between these two extremes (i.e., maximally forgiving mage and minimally-forgivable monster), can nevertheless be intermittently nudged—on my reading of Arendt here—in the direction of greater imaginativeness.

To make my case, in each subsequent section, I will connect forgiveness to: 1) art, 2) magic, 3) imagination, and 4) the world as fantastic theatrical play, respectively. Following Arendt's lead, I have organized these sections around a metaphor—the metaphor of "magic spells." Beginning with forgiveness and art and working through all four sections, each "spell" will bind the elements of these sections together, like "magic thinking" functions to bind heterogeneous elements in the minds of a depressed person, or those in the communities of tribal ancients.

I will begin with a brief investigation into the secondary literature on the role of imagination in Arendt's conception of forgiveness, focusing on essays by Mary Dietz and Marie Luise Knott, both of whom link forgiveness to art and to the miraculous. Second, I will bind this art of forgiveness to the concept of magic, through a rereading of the section on forgiveness in *The Human Condition*, focusing on Arendt's explicit suggestion that forgiveness constitutes a magic beyond even the miraculous in the work of Jesus of Nazareth. Third, I will bind this magical art of forgiveness to imagination, through a consideration of Arendt's account of Nazism in *Eichmann in Jerusalem*, as a failure of imagination. Finally, I will bind the imaginatively magical art of forgiveness to a conception of the world as a fantastic theatrical play. I do this through a reading of Arendt's *The Life of the Mind*, focusing on imagination in its guise of "the common sense" (or, in her more magical synonymous phrase, "sixth sense"), as that which sustains the evolving script of our theater-world.[94] In sum, the best way to live, according to Arendt, is to continuously improvise our performances of community, on the theatrical stage of our world. And the best way to enhance these performances is to increase our power and respect for imagination, through the dark art of forgiveness.

I. Forgiveness as art in Arendt scholarship (Dietz and Knott)

As noted above, the two most important secondary sources on Arendt for this chapter are Marie Luise Knott's *Unlearning with Hannah Arendt* and Mary G. Dietz's chapter from *The Cambridge Companion to Hannah Arendt*, entitled "Arendt and the Holocaust." Ironically for a survey on forgiveness, the first name shared by both of these scholars ('Mary') means "bitterness." More substantially, both interpreters emphasize Arendt's indebtedness, for her concept of forgiveness, to the arts and the miraculous.

Beginning with Dietz, her primary innovation is to read *The Human Condition* as about the Holocaust, more specifically as offering "a grand, optimistic illusion" of the Greek polis as space of egalitarian appearance (2000, 102). The purpose of this illusion, according to Dietz, is to liberate the survivors from their justified hatred, and to liberate the non-Nazi Germans from their complicity, which Arendt termed (in a letter to Jaspers) a "'factual territory' that the Holocaust had

---

[94] For support of the centrality of storytelling, like the plot of a theatrical play, see Melvyn A. Hill, "The Fictions of Mankind and the Stories of Men," in *Hannah Arendt: The Recovery of the Public World*, ed. Melvyn A. Hill (New York: St. Martin's, 1979), 275-300. Hill's thesis is that "the stories that citizens tell are the source and remain the touchstone of political thinking" (277). Toward the end of her essay, Hill introduces the term "political imagination," as that which Arendt's thinking can contribute to action, namely by creating shelters for freedom to emerge (295).

created" for these two groups (1994, 214; quoted in Dietz 2000, 88). The chief difficulty for the survivors in doing so, as Arendt tells Jaspers, is what she terms "the fabrication of corpses" in the camps (1992, 423, quoted in Dietz 2000, 86). This factual territory, Arendt elaborates, "opened up an abyss" within itself, sucking everyone in—and when anyone attempted to pull away from this abyss, it left them in an "empty space" of "individuals" without "nations" or "peoples" (1948, quoted in Dietz 2000, 89). In other words, this abyss is a space empty of human affairs, lacking political appearance in Arendt's sense, in the face of what she terms "the image of hell" (1948 215). Returning to Dietz, on these grounds she reads *The Human Condition* as "a direct and personal effort to offer both Germans and Jews a way back from the abyss" (2000, 91).

More specifically, Dietz for a second time in her essay invokes the phrase "grand, optimistic illusion," which she then reveals to be a quote from Nietzsche on Thucydides's Funeral Oration of Pericles (specifically, from *Human, All Too Human*, Section 474). Nietzsche's main point is that the historical event of Thucydides's speech took place, not only: a) before one of the worst times in Athens' history (including a terrible plague); but b) after those times in the remembrance of Thucydides; and also c) outside of time altogether as an imaginary depiction of what had never been (Dietz 2000, 91). In Nietzsche's metaphor, Thucydides offers an evening glow, in which the evil of the day's events can be forgotten, which Dietz crystallizes with the title of "theorist-as-healer" (Ibid., 92). In other words, Thucydides "creates a contrary world" to "block the human impulse to ruminate upon and incessantly rekindle the perpetual memory of hardship and evil, thereby fanning the flames of desire for retribution and revenge" (Ibid.). Just so, Arendt in *The Human Condition*, according to Dietz, "created a powerful, iridescent image that counters the reality" of the Holocaust (Ibid.). Moreover, the inspiration for this "healing image" comes from the same source, the Funeral Oration as description of pre-philosophical Athenian politics (Ibid., 93).

In her close reading of *The Human Condition*, Dietz claims that the concentration camps are the conspicuously absent heart of the book, which she justifies in part by noting that the extreme forms of labor and work—"labor as routinized deathlessness, and work as the objectified violation of life itself"—have only hitherto come together in the camps (Ibid., 97). So extreme and radically isolating were the camps, in fact, that Arendt claims they "could never be fully embraced by the imagination for the very reason that [this horror stood] outside life and death" (Arendt 1973, 444; quoted in Dietz 2000, 98). And it is this phenomenon, this existential extreme possibility, that Dietz argues is the true purpose of Arendt's concept of "action" as the "space of appearance" (2000, 99). That is, action functions to keep individuals appearing as individuals, through the heroic courage of "self-revelation," rather than becoming again the chattel who are supplied to the camps' "fabrication of corpses" (Ibid., 101).

In sum, Dietz sees Arendt as offering "a disruptive countermemory, attempting to reach over the historical abyss created by Auschwitz, and break the mastery of the Holocaust" (Ibid., 100). With Arendt's "imagistic symbol of the space of appearance," Dietz claims, "there is illuminated a way back from Auschwitz's empty space." In other words, it is a "'recreative escape', a chance to give one's self over to the radiance of light and the 'shining brightness' of the represented world." Finally, in achieving this (and here Dietz anticipates the emphasis of my next section), Arendt performed a kind of "miracle" (Ibid., 102).

On the one hand, I agree with Dietz's characterization of Arendt qua magician, casting a spell over the present in order to heal the future from our totalitarian and genocidal past. But on the other hand, I am concerned about the casual abruptness with which Dietz talks about the undoing of the Holocaust, and the forgetting intended for all parties involved, not to mention Dietz's oversimplified distinction between "Jews" and "Germans" (as if there were no German Jewish people, including Arendt herself, and as if that were not a crucial dimension of the horrors of Nazism). Rather than a forgetting of horrific events, I see Arendt seeking a re-understanding of those events—a throwing of a magical cloak across them—which allow the traumatic memories to remain, without disrupting the individual or community's ability to weave those memories into the fabric of the future.

Turning to my next (etymologically) "bitter" source, Mary Luise Knott organizes her reflections around four themes she finds in Arendt—laughter, translation, forgiveness, and dramatization. Beginning with laughter, Knott affirms Jaspers's linkage of Arendt's laughter to irony, in *Eichmann in Jerusalem*, which constituted "a protection against panic and powerfully aggressive impulses that would only interfere with her ability to judge" (2015, 9). Moreover, Knott adds to Jaspers, it is "a liberating laughter; it creates freedom and connection, gives substantive differences their due and keeps them in flux" (Ibid., 14). Thirdly, this laughter for Knott is the product of Arendt's choice to "allow herself to be touched by what she saw and heard," causing her and her readers to "lose their bearings" (Ibid., 18). Fourth, laughter in the face of such absurdity as Eichmann offers "a pause to catch one's intellectual breath" (Ibid., 19). And finally, since laughter tightens the muscles of the diaphragm, Knott observes that with her laughter, "Arendt allows the show to make her taut rather than slack" (Ibid., 21). Thus, through laughter, and its irony, the literary makes its way to the front of the stage—or, more precisely, Arendt takes her seat in the front row of the audience.

In Knott's discussion of translation, she links translation's etymological "carrying-across" to metaphor and the other literary imaginative powers in language itself, which powers ultimately involve "a celebration of contamination" of a plurality of things and ideas (Ibid., 40). Because of this connectedness, Knott notes, Arendt observes that "the only people who still believe in the world are the poets; they cannot afford to be alienated from it" (Ibid., 41). This latter remark also calls to mind a second uniqueness of the poets, as attributed to the poets by Arendt in *The Human Condition*, namely that only for poets is love "indispensable" (Ibid., 82). This is important for the present chapter in that Arendt claims (as I will discuss below) that love is the private catalyst for forgiveness (as Kantian respect is its public catalyst). Here, a second literary dimension, namely the metaphoric heart of poetry, steps into the spotlight of Arendt's textual stage.

As for forgiveness, Knott emphasizes how Arendt went from: a) condemning the historical version of forgiveness; b) to "unlearning" that version; and then c) affirming Arendt's own modified one. For evidence, Knott cites Arendt's journal from 1950, the *Denktagebuch*, in which she is critical of Christian forgiveness "as a gesture of superiority, a dead end" (namely, because in her view it destroyed the equality between the forgiver and the forgiven) (Ibid., 60 and 66). The motives for this unlearning, Knott claims, were: a) her experience of negotiating post-WWII with former aggressors and survivors; and b) her and her husband's persecution for their earlier views and actions during the McCarthy era (Ibid., 60-1, 67-9). The intellectual catalyst for Arendt's shift toward forgiveness is illustrated, for Knott, in Arendt's claim in the German version of *The Human Condition* (entitled *Vita Activa*) that "the person is forgiven for the sake of humanity" (rather than the sake of the aggressor) (Knott 2015, 80). This catalyst, Knott claims, was the published critique of Arendt's conception of forgiveness by her friend, the poet W. H. Auden. In response, she shifted in order to anchor the concept of friendship in Kantian respect, or "political friendship" (Ibid., 81). In other words, Arendt was able to anchor forgiveness in the imaginative fiction called "humanity." And since this was inspired by a poet, and requires fictive imagination, this also constitutes a third spotlight on the literary in Knott's account of Arendt.

Finally from Knott, her chapter on dramatization focuses on Arendt's metaphor of the world as a stage, which in the modern world requires performing without either marionette strings or a traditional script (Ibid., 93). Like Dietz, Knott emphases the "miracle" nature of these self-revealing performances. Moreover, Knott analyzes Arendt's own texts as each a kind of theater, in which her quotes and citations are the "actors" that spontaneously improvise new and illuminating artistic performances (Ibid., 96-97). Along with these actor-quotes, moreover, Arendt's readers are invited to take the stage as well—to join the political conversation, where "reading becomes a rehearsal for action," and where "readers become (potential) actors in that they achieve self-empowerment" (Ibid., 109 and 111). Here, then, is the final affirmation of the literary in Knott's Arendt, as the play-within-a-play of her thought and texts. To summarize, Knott affirms the centrality of the literary in Arendt through laughing irony, poetic metaphor, fictive imagination, and multi-layered theatricality.

On the one hand, I agree with Knott's claim that Arendt uses artistic strategies to reinterpret the world in the interests of a more flourishing global polis. But on the other hand, I see Arendt's reinterpretations, not as Knott's "unlearning" of knowledge, but rather as acts of forgiving. More precisely, they are acts of forgiving the inadequate conceptions that Arendt takes on from her fellow thinking friends (such as Aristotle and Kant), by making-believe that her own conceptions are merely repetitions of theirs, when they are in reality artful improvisations thereon. And on this improvisatory note, I turn to my own analyses (improvisations?) of Arendt's texts, beginning with forgiveness in *The Human Condition*.

II. The art of forgiveness as magical in
The Human Condition

Having established an intrinsic connection between forgiveness and art/the miraculous, through the interpretations of Dietz and Knott, I will now show how Arendt herself connects this art-of-forgiveness concept to magic in *The Human Condition*. At the beginning of the section on forgiveness,

Arendt introduces forgiveness as a "faculty," a power. More specifically, it is a sub-power, within the power of action, of "redemption" from "the predicament of irreversibility" (Arendt 1988, 237). This sub-power, she elaborates, "serves to undo the deeds of the past," which she compares—apropos of the title of my chapter—to "the magic formula to break the spell" that bound "the sorcerer's apprentice" (Ibid., 237). The limitations on this magic of forgiveness, though, are that one cannot do it to oneself, and that it only works in "the realm of human affairs" (as opposed to "natural science and technology") (Ibid., 237-8).

The creator of human affair-forgiveness, for Arendt, is the most magical Jewish man of all time, Jesus of Nazareth (and the "redeemer" [messiah] to forgiveness as "redemption"). She emphasizes that he transformed forgiveness into a human power (which does not derive from god), and which must be activated among humans before humans ask it of god. In a footnote, she adds that it is this aspect of Jesus's practice, "even more than his performance of miracles, that shocks the people" (Ibid., 239n76). Arendt's reference to Jesus also leads to a new limitation for her on the concept of forgiveness, namely that forgiveness is only intended for unintentional wrongs, and not "crime and willed evil" (Ibid., 239).

Arendt then contrasts forgiveness with revenge, in which context she adds that forgiveness "can never be predicted" as it is "the only reaction which does not merely re-act but acts anew," and thereby frees "from its consequences both the one who forgives and the one who is forgiven." In short, Jesus's forgiveness is "the freedom from vengeance." Arendt elaborates on this, when she adds that "men are unable to forgive what they cannot punish," including that which, "since Kant, we call 'radical evil'" (Ibid., 241). In response to these latter acts, which radically destroy human affairs per se and "the potentialities of human power," Arendt cites Jesus to the effect that capital punishment would, *for the aggressor himself,* be preferable. Finally in this section, Arendt then affirms of Jesus the "recognition" that forgiveness is "an eminently personal (though not necessarily private or individual affair)," in which "*what* was done is forgiven for the sake of *who* did it" (Ibid.). The basis of forgiveness for Jesus, she continues, is love, whereas for the public application she recommends the Kantian concept of "respect" for persons (Ibid., 242-243).

To condense these insights from *The Human Condition*, forgiveness here is a power of action that redeems by undoing, in a way that is magical beyond miracles, but that works only on others, only in the realm of human affairs, and only for non-criminal, unintentional wrongs, as the freedom from revenge, conferred for the sake of the other, and on the basis of respect. One paradoxical aspect of this treatment is that it makes forgiveness both proximal to, and yet barred from, legal and judicial judgment. As I noted above, Arendt claims that forgiveness is not for "crime," but its precedents nevertheless include the Roman principle of sparing the vanquished foe, and the head of state's commuting a death sentence, both of which involve judgments at the border of legality/sovereignty (in Agamben's sense).[95] Moreover, the death of the evil man referenced by Jesus appears to involve some sort of judgment, if only of the man by his own self/conscience. Appropriately, then, I now turn to Arendt's quasi-judicial judgment, in *Eichmann in Jerusalem*, on what she views as the theater of Eichmann's literal trial.

---

[95] Agamben's central example is the ancient Roman law concerning the *homo sacer* ("sacred man"), who both: a) could be killed by anyone without punishment, but also b) could not be sacrificed as part of a ritual (Agamben 1998, 8). His ultimate point, building on Foucault's notion of biopower, is that contemporary sovereignty involves a permanent suspension of the law, leaving all of us in the position of *homo sacer*.

III. The magical art of forgiveness as imaginative in *Eichmann in Jerusalem*

Having shown how Arendt binds the art of forgiveness to magic in *The Human Condition*, I will now bind this magical art of forgiveness to imagination in *Eichmann in Jerusalem*. In brief, Arendt shows us the way to imagine Eichmann such that he could conceivably—though not necessarily, and not deservingly—be forgiven for the horrendous extremes of his mass murdering crimes against humanity. To wit, Arendt paints Eichmann as an extreme case of unimaginative thoughtlessness, in the dual senses of both: a) failing to think carefully and critically, and also b) failing to considerately imagine oneself in another's position. And in light of Eichmann's extreme case, Arendt thereby makes the average, low-ranking Nazis, along with the complicit non-Nazi, non-Jewish Germans of that era, seem much more forgivable as well.

I will attempt this binding of forgiveness to imagining by analyzing a concept I extract from *Eichmann in Jerusalem*, which I will term 'reimagining'. My approach to this concept will be indirect, beginning with Arendt's reflections on thoughtlessness, which I will argue is the result of a lack of reimagining. Arendt defines 'thoughtlessness' in *The Human Condition*—which serves as the text's central concept—as follows: "the heedless recklessness or hopeless confusion or complacent repetition of 'truths' which have become trivial and empty" (1988, 5). Returning to *Eichmann in Jerusalem*, given that Eichmann is her privileged example of thoughtlessness (possessing what Arendt's *Lectures on Kant's Political Philosophy* calls "exemplary validity"), she offers a surprisingly humorous portrait of him. This humorousness is buttressed, moreover, by her reference in *The Life of the Mind* to his "macabre comedy" (Arendt 1981, 4). As this latter phrase suggests, the theatrical is central for Arendt (as already attested above in Dietz and Knott), which foreshadows the connection I will draw (in this chapter's penultimate section) between forgiveness and the world-as-theater.

This theatricality arises at the beginning of *Eichmann in Jerusalem*, where Arendt describes his trial as a theatrical performance (2006, 4). As the book's title suggests, Eichmann's trial took place in the city of Jerusalem in the recently reestablished nation of Israel. The charges leveled against him were referred to as "crimes against humanity," in regard to his actions as a high-level bureaucrat in the Nazi regime during their attempted genocide of the Jewish people. More specifically, Eichmann was in charge of transporting Jewish people from Western Europe to the concentration camps in Eastern Europe. As for her own personal judgment of Eichmann, Arendt concludes that he was—shockingly—too completely "normal," specifically in a horrific Nazi context in which, in her words, "only 'exceptions' could be expected to act 'normally'" (Ibid., 27). Pinpointing the problem, Arendt observes that Eichmann showed an "inability to ever look at things from the other fellow's point of view" (Ibid., 48).

Amazingly, and to return to the macabre comedy of Eichmann's performance at his trial, Arendt somehow manages to find humor in his fatal flaw. She describes the "horrible" phenomenon of his thoughtlessness as "outright funny" (Ibid.). For example, she writes that "officialese," as she terms it, "became his language because he was genuinely incapable of uttering a single sentence that was not a cliché" (Ibid.). As such, Eichmann's role as an actor in the theater of his trial, according to Arendt, is "not a 'monster'," but rather "a clown" (Ibid., 54). Predictably, as a clownish character, Eichmann foreclosed his own mind and judgment, repeatedly comparing himself to Pontius Pilate washing his hands of the murder of the Jewish Jesus. "Who was he," Arendt quotes Eichmann's testimony, "to have [his] own thoughts in this matter" (Ibid., 114)? Finally in regard to Eichmann's thoughtlessness, Arendt notes that "he always thought within the narrow limits of whatever laws and decrees were valid at a given moment" (Ibid., 157). In short, Arendt sees Eichmann as dramatizing the horrendous potential of the clownish thoughtlessness of the average modern person. In support of this interpretation, Richard Bernstein observes, Eichmann's own writings explicitly remark on his thoughtlessness as well.[96]

The opposite of such thoughtlessness, as Arendt writes in her *Lectures on Kant's Political Philosophy*, is a maximally "enlarged mentality" (Arendt 1989, 44). Such a mentality "makes the others present," Arendt explains, "by the force of the imagination (Ibid., 55). By this, Arendt means that reimagining incorporates, in the act of forming a political judgment, indefinitely many other peoples' perspectives. Her analogy for this incorporation is the ideal theatrical spectator, who incorporates various angles on a given performance in order to judge its merits. By this, Arendt means something like an imaginary deliberation staged by every single spectator of a play, in which each spectator voices her/his perspective, the end result being a final judgment maximally informed by a maximal plurality of perspectives.

To return to *Eichmann in Jerusalem*, Arendt also offers, in addition to Eichmann as thoughtless clown, his theatrical counterpoint in the people of Denmark. For Arendt, the Danish were equally theatrical, and in their case the role was heroic. Facilitated by their thoughtful reimagining of their Jewish others as fully human (against the Nazis' racist imagination), the Danes openly defied the Nazis' attempts to forcibly evacuate the Jewish people there (Arendt 2006, 171). And in doing so, Arendt notes, they were "unique among the countries of Europe" (Ibid.). The story of how the Danes ac-

---

[96] Richard J. Bernstein, "Arendt on Thinking," *The Cambridge Companion to Hannah Arendt*, ed. Dana Villa (Cambridge: Cambridge University Press, 2000, 277-292). Bernstein quotes Eichmann's notes as follows: "Now that I look back, I realized that a life predicated on being obedient and taking orders is a very comfortable life indeed. Living in such a way reduces to a minimum one's need to think." Quoted from Cohen 1999.

complished this, she claims, should be "required reading in political science for all students who wish to learn something about the power inherent in non-violent action and in resistance to an opponent possessing vastly superior means of violence" (Ibid.).

The outlines of Denmark's story are as follows. First, Arendt notes that "only the Danes dared speak out on the subject [of "the Jewish question"] to their German masters," whereas all of the other European nations held their tongues, and resisted (if at all) in secret (Ibid.). Second, when the Nazis proposed using the infamous yellow badge to identify Jewish people, the Nazis "were simply told that the King would be the first to wear it" (Ibid.). Third, the Danes argued that "because the stateless refugees [non-Danish Jewish people] were no longer German citizens, the Nazis could not claim them without Danish consent" (Ibid., 172). Fourth (as a consequence which Arendt describes "truly amazing"), "everything went topsy-turvy," as "riots broke out in Danish shipyards, where the dock workers refused to repair German ships and then went on strike" (Ibid.). Fifth, when the Nazis came to kidnap the Jewish people and begin their deportation out of Denmark (and ultimately to the concentration camps), the Danish police only allowed the Nazis to take those Jewish people who were "at home and willing to let them in"—which ended up being a mere 477 out of 7,800 Jewish people there (Ibid., 173). Sixth, the Jewish authorities publicized the impending kidnappings openly in the synagogues, giving the people "just enough time to leave their apartments and go into hiding" among a Danish community in which every citizen welcomed them (Ibid., 173-4). And finally, in regard to the final phase of Denmark's response (namely, secretly evacuating those Jewish people hiding to safety into Sweden) the extensive cost of this effort, Arendt notes, "was paid largely by wealthy Danish citizens" (Ibid., 174).

Even more surprising to Arendt than the actions of the Danish, however, was the fact that their imaginative thoughtfulness proved to be contagious as well, in that "the German officials who had been living in [Denmark] for years were no longer the same" as they had been back in Germany (Ibid., 172). In fact, Arendt elaborates, even "the special S.S. units employed in Denmark frequently objected to 'the measures they were ordered to carry out by the central agencies'" (Ibid., 173). In conclusion, Denmark was "the only case we know if in which the Nazis met with open native resistance," and "the result seems to have been that those exposed to it changed their minds" (Ibid., 175). In other words, the Danish citizens re-imagined themselves in the Jewish peoples' place, and then acted politically on the basis of this reimagining, which managed to inspire even some of the Nazis to reimagine the Jewish people as fully human.

IV. The imaginatively magical forgiving art as script-sustainer in *The Life of the Mind*

Arendt herself makes an explicit connection between: a) what seems like her most concrete/political work (*Eichmann in Jerusalem*), and b) her most abstract/philosophical work (*The Life of the Mind*), on the very first page of the latter. The "immediate impulse" for *The Life of the Mind*, she notes, "came from my attending the Eichmann trial in Jerusalem" (1981, 3). More specifically, she names—and italicizes— Eichmann's "*thoughtlessness*," defined by the fact that "he clearly know no such claim at all" in regard to "the claim on our thinking attention that all events and facts make by virtue of their existence" (Ibid., 4). With Eichmann thus situated at one extreme, or pole, of the thinking spectrum, Arendt asks whether thoughtfulness might "be among the conditions that make men abstain from evil-doing or even actually 'condition' them against it?" (Ibid., 5) If thought does have this ethical power, Arendt elaborates, then "we must be able to 'demand' its exercise from every sane person, no matter how erudite or ignorant, intelligent or stupid he may happen to be" (Ibid., 13). The justification for this universal demand, following Kant, is Arendt's sharp distinction between thinking (as domain of reason) from understanding (as the domain of the same name). While understanding concerns "knowledge," she claims, reason concerns "meaning" (Ibid., 15). Thus, no matter how much or how little a person knows, s/he bears for Arendt an ethical-political obligation to seek meaning.

Arendt then launches into what is arguably the most theatrical metaphysics in Western history. She begins with theatrical rhetoric, in the surprising claim that "Nothing and nobody exists in this world whose very being does not presuppose a *spectator*." And this, in turn, derives from her insistence, going as far back as *The Human Condition*, that "Plurality is the law of the earth" (Arendt 1981, 19). Whereas in her older work, this plurality concerned primarily the human species, here in *The Life of the Mind* she radically extends it to the rest of the animal kingdom, noting "an equally astounding diverseness of sense organs among the animal species," and that the members of each species "lives in a world of its own" (Ibid., 20).

Building on this theatrical rhetoric with a more explicit theatrical metaphor, Arendt goes on to claim that "To be alive means to be possessed by an urge towards self-display," and that "Living things *make their appearance* like actors on a stage set for them" (by previous generations). "The stage is common," Arendt continues, "to all who are alive, but it *seems* different to each species, different also to each individual specimen" (Ibid., 21). The point about the stage is critical, for its concession to objective factuality is what differentiates Arendt from purely social-constructivist metaphysics, and also from totalitarian politics (an issue to which I will return below). Based on this commonness of the objectively-real stage, and despite these indefinitely-many occurrences of seeming, "men and animals" enjoy their "fellow-creatures" of various species "to play with," in what Arendt terms "the play of the world" (Ibid., 21-2).

The only thing unique to humans, for Arendt, is that our "mental activities" not shared by other species all involve "a *withdrawal* from the world as it appears and a bending back toward the self" (Ibid., 22). Interestingly, Arendt follows Aristotle in placing human souls squarely with those of other species, none of which require metaphors to bridge any alleged chasm between soul and world. In fact, souls for Arendt do not even need any verbal language at all. Instead, "the life of our soul in its very intensity is much more adequately expressed in a gland, a sound, a gesture, than in speech" (Ibid., 31).[97] This invocation of gesture is the first indication of the relevance of Arendt's discussion of soul to her theatrical metaphysics. More specifically, we still have a choice, for Arendt, as to which soul-expressions to share with the world, and which to disguise, and when. For example, she claims that a "courageous man" is simply "one who has decided that fear is not what he wants to show," perhaps "because [he wishes] to set an example, that is, to persuade others to be pleased with" what pleases him (Ibid., 36). And thus, "pretense and willful deception on the part of the performer, error and illusion on the part of the spectator are, inevitably, among the inherent possibilities" of appearances in our theatrical world (Ibid.).

Perhaps surprisingly, Arendt draws the inference from this that "the only way to tell pretense and make-believe from reality and truth is the former's failure to endure and remain consistent" (Ibid.). The implication here appears to be that make-believe that is sustainable will eventually become (indistinguishable from) truth. In support of this, Arendt goes

---

[97] Interestingly, Arendt also claims on this topic that "our soul-experiences are body-bound to such an extent that to speak of an 'inner life' of the soul is as unmetaphorical as to speak of an inner sense...of our inner organs" (1981, 32). Additionally, the soul's "passions and emotions" "also "seem to have the same life-sustaining and persevering functions of our inner organs" (Ibid., 35). For the connection to Aristotle, see Aristotle 2001.

on to claim the following, which might be understood as a formula for ethical/legitimate transformation of make-believe into truth:

> *All virtue begins with a compliment I pay to it, by which I express my being pleased with it. The compliment implies a promise to the world, to those to whom I appear, to act in accordance with my pleasure, and it is the breaking of the implied promise that characterizes the hypocrite. (Ibid.)*

Here, Arendt invokes the opposite redeeming power to forgiveness, namely promising. She then summarizes this redemptive power as follows: "The test applying to the hypocrite is indeed the old Socratic '*Be* as you wish to appear', which means appear *always* as you wish to appear to others even if it happens that you are alone and appear to no one but yourself" (Ibid., 37). This point is reinforced in Arendt's next section, where she discusses "true semblances" created by animal perspectival-ness, along with Kant's discussion of "authentic illusions" (including the appearance of "sunrise") (Ibid., 38-9). In other words, at a certain level we cannot get past "semblances" (*doxa*). Thus it is sufficient that we perform our appearances in this world consistently, in order to be virtuous. This includes the etymological sense of the word 'virtuous', namely "power," in this case, to create and recreate our world.

Imagination enters the scene of this theatrical metaphysics shortly after the latter discussion, beginning with Arendt's reference to Aquinas's *"sensus communis,"* which Aquinas himself took from Aristotle's conception of imagination as the power that preserves and combines the images abstracted from sensory-perception images (1981, 50). That is, visual, auditory, tactile, olfactory, and gustatory sensory-perceptions are retroactively coordinated by the imagination, which abstracts them into images in temporal proximity to each other. The "worldly property" of the imagination, the analogue for imagination of visibility for vision, is for Arendt "realness" (Ibid., 50). This realness conferred by the imagination, moreover, is so powerful that she claims that "thinking can neither prove nor destroy" it. She then concludes that "the French, perhaps for this reason, also call" this power "*le bon sens*, the good sense" (Ibid., 52). Thus, Arendt's reader can detect another echo of the ethical within performance (the original sound being that of the courageous man as fear-non-shower, in the above block quote).

It will likely be objected that imagination and common sense are two distinct terms for Arendt. Despite her at times misleading presentation, however, I would argue that these two names refer essentially synonymously to one main power. I find evidence for this synonymy primarily in the way the two terms are deployed in the two most important historical sources for Arendt's conception of them, namely Aristotle and Kant. That is, neither of the latter philosophers makes such a distinction. Consider, for example, Aristotle's discussion in *On the Soul*, or the following passage from Arendt's seminar on Kant's *Critique of Judgment* in 1970:

> *Finally, our sensibility seems to need imagination not only as an aid to knowledge but in order to recognize sameness in the manifold... Without it, there would be neither the objectivity of the world—that it can be known—nor any possibility of communication—that we can talk about it. (Arendt 1989, 79-80)*

Here, Arendt uses the one term, 'imagination' to describe the power to both preserve and improvise on sensory-perception images.

Imagination reappears onstage in *The Life of the Mind* not long after the passage on the *sensus communis*, but this time imagination appears in the guise of "re-presentation" (Arendt 1981, 76). Arendt christens this power "the mind's unique gift," adding that, "since our whole mental terminology is based on metaphors drawn from vision's experience, this gift" is therefore "called *imagination*, defined by Kant as 'the faculty of intuition even without the presence of the object'" (Ibid.). In Arendt's memorable phrase, the imagination works to "*de-sense*" the particulars in the world, leaving images, which in turn can become "thought-objects" (Ibid., 77).

Though Arendt distinguishes images from thought-objects, her reason for doing so is that the initial involuntary images are different from a "deliberately remembered object" (Ibid., 86). On the Aristotelian account of imagination with which Arendt begins, however, the power of memory is merely a sub-power of the imagination. The importance of Aristotle for Arendt's conception is even clearer, moreover, not long after this passage, in her reference to the Aristotelian distinction between "*productive* imagination" and "reproductive imagination" (Ibid.). (The former creates through imagistic combinations, while the latter recalls to mind images as first perceived.)

Arendt's dependence on imagination—or, more precisely, her elevation of imagination—is intensified later in *The Life of the Mind*, when she claims that metaphor is "the only way" that "thinking, can manifest itself," as only a metaphor can transform a thought into "being an appearance among appearances" (Ibid., 103). As Arendt boldly puts it on the next page, "All philosophical terms are metaphors, frozen analogies" (Ibid., 104). More specifically, a metaphor illuminates a truth of the mind by comparing mental phenomena to things in the world.[98] Or, as she clarifies by reference to Kant, metaphor illuminates truth by comparing the relationship between two mental phenomena to an analogous relationship between two worldly phenomena (Ibid.). For example, the (weak) metaphor of "My love for you is like the sun shining on the lilies" illuminates the mental relationship between the lover and the beloved by comparing the love relationship to the physical relationship between the sun and the flowers—rather than by offering a relationship between the lover and the sun as subjects.

This point is significant for Arendt because it illustrates the dependence of mind on world—even when thinking is mostly withdrawn from world—since thought can proceed to itself and its meaning only by recourse to the sensual. "Analogies, metaphors, and emblems," Arendt concludes, "are the threads by which the mind holds on to the world even when, absentmindedly, it has lost direct contact with it, and they guarantee the unity of human experience" (Ibid., 109). Note two things here. First, Arendt's pun indicates that mind, when it forgets the world, ceases to be fully mind (viz. "absentminded"). This "indicates," in her terms, "the absolute primacy of the world of appearances" (Ibid.). Second, the function of metaphor is, as with the "common" or "sixth" sense earlier in the text, the work of the imagination to create a common world. In other words, "the thinking ego obviously never leaves the world of appearances altogether" (Ibdi., 110). In short, the world is only one in imagination, whereas in sensual actuality it is instead an overlapping of different worlds for each member of each species on the earth. That is to say, the first fiction about the world is that there is only

---

[98] Here, perhaps, lies yet another reason for Arendt's idolizing/idealization of Socrates, since he is famous for having described himself primarily in terms of the two metaphors of the gadfly and the midwife.

one. Thus, when we theorize about "the World," including in our political theorizing, the ship of non-fictional truth has already sailed. "There are not two worlds" as in the Platonic theory, nor more than two, for that matter, "because metaphor unites them" (Ibid.). To clarify, this means that, for Arendt, there are many worlds, in practice, on the earth, but imagination makes them one.

Finally on the subject of metaphor, Arendt claims that in the case of thought itself, ironically, "there exists no plausible metaphor." The closest we can get, she claims, is "the sensation of being alive" (Ibid., 123)—thus her title, *The Life of the Mind*. Or, as she puts it in her next section, thinking is a kind of dance, a performance for its own sake, for "the sheer beauty of appearances" (Ibid., 129). And in this dance, "virtue" becomes "what we would call virtuosity" (Ibid., 130-1). Moreover, similar to a common experience in dance, Arendt later compares thought (drawing on Socrates) to the rush of "the wind" (Ibid., 174). Aptly, then, Arendt elsewhere links Socrates to dancing (as does Kierkegaard before her), via the middle term of the "flute-player," as an example of an artist whose performance is an end-in-itself. Socrates, she writes, "*performed* in the marketplace the way the flute-player performed at a banquet" (Arendt 1989, 37). And in dance, one can see another connection to the theatricality of Arendt's metaphysics.

I will now conclude this section on *The Life of the Mind* with a second dance-resonant moment in the text. Arendt suggests two correctives to evil in thought itself, namely in Socrates's claims that it is better to suffer than to do evil, and better to be in conflict with the rest of the world than out of (musical, dancing?) harmony with oneself—in the solitary dance of thought, between the two "partners" and friends, who are both oneself (Arendt 1981, 181, 185, and 188). By contrast, "unthinking men"—like Eichmann—"are like sleepwalkers" (Ibid., 191). Losing the capacity to think, which is dependent on imagination, according to Arendt destroys "the faculty of judgment, which one may call with some reason the most political of man's abilities" (Ibid., 192). With judgment, in the battleground of the present, we must either fall like Eichmann (and Heidegger), or gracefully dance our fight between the opposing forces of past and future (as in the metaphor Arendt invokes from Kafka). In the middle of the "storm," with the infinite "diagonal" of our magical powers of thought, our dances can create our own new imaginative world to share (Ibid., 209).

V. Conclusion: The necessary dark art

Even if the reader is sympathetic to the general drift of my analyses, s/he has perhaps noticed that I have not yet addressed the word "dark" in my title, and wonders about what would make forgiveness—as the imaginatively magical art of theatrical world-sustaining—a dark art. To begin to answers this question, I note that Arendt approvingly cites Kant's claim that the power of the imagination in organizing/creating our reality is a "hidden art in the depths of the human soul" (Kant 1999, A141/B180-1). Forgiveness, too, I would argue, requires a kind of hiddenness, and recourse to psychic depths.

In essence, since forgiveness for Arendt is the "undoing" of action's deeds, and since deeds are above all for her a performance in the proper political sphere of self-revelation, through public appearance, forgiveness would thus seem to involve a magic of disappearing or invisibility—the waters of *Lethe* that drown the *aletheia* of truth as disclosure. More specifically, I wish to suggest that forgiveness involves erasing lines form the script of the world-play, and perhaps especially those lines of dialogue that involve interpretations of tragic and horrific events. In other words, what forgiveness "undoes" are not facts at an objective level, but rather "deeds" conceived as speeches, as well as non-speech actions disclosed in speech. Put still differently, forgiveness creates spaces for freedom of interpretation, rather than trying to pretend that historical events did not occur at all.

This latter point is also important for a reason that connects with scholarly criticisms of postmodern interpretations of Arendt such as the one in this chapter. To wit, forgiveness invisibly undoes lines of the script, rather than visibly uprooting even the boards of the stage. The latter act, by contrast, is instead that of totalitarianism, as it replaces the factual boards with purely fictional ones, forcing falsities into the minds of the people through propaganda. Thus, to follow Arendt, one must instead preserve carefully the theater of world-history, while simultaneously trying to be the most creative and flourishing-enhancing co-playwrights that one can be. Above all, this involves forgiving the inevitable mistakes of one's fellow playwrights, if not for their sakes, then for the sake of the beloved shared world.

References

Agamben, Giorgio. 1998. *Homo Sacer: Sovereign Power and Bare Life*. Translated by Daniel Heller-Roazen. Palo Alto: Stanford University Press.

Arendt, Hannah. 2006. *Eichmann in Jerusalem: A Report on the Banality of Evil*. New York: Penguin.

———. 1992. "Letter to Karl Jaspers, Feb 5, 1961." *Hannah Arendt – Karl Jaspers: Correspondence, 1926-1969*. Edited by L. Kohler and H. Saner. New York: Harcourt Brace Jovanovich.

———. 1989. *Lectures on Kant's Political Philosophy*. Edited by Ronald Beiner. Chicago: University of Chicago Press.

———. 1988. *The Human Condition*, 2nd Ed. Chicago: University of Chicago Press.

———. 1981. *The Life of the Mind*. Edited by Mary McCarthy. New York: Mariner.

———. 1973. *Origins of Totalitarianism* New York: Harcourt, Brace & World.

———. 1948. "Dedication to Karl Jaspers." Hannah Arendt. 1994. *Essays in Understanding, 1930-1945*. Edited by Jerome Kohn. New York: Harcourt, Brace & Co.

Aristotle. 2001. *On the Soul and Memory and Recollection*. Translated by Joe Sachs. Sante Fe: Green Lion Press.

Cohen, Roger. 1999. "Why? New Eichmann Notes Try to Explain," *New York Times*, August 12, 1999: A1, A3.

Dietz, Mary G. 2000. "Arendt and the Holocaust." *The Cambridge Companion to Hannah Arendt*. Edited by Dana Villa. Cambridge: Cambridge University Press, 86-109.

Kant, Immanuel. 1999. *Critique of Pure Reason*. Edited and translated by Paul Guyer and Allen W. Wood. Cambridge: Cambridge University Press.

Knott, Marie Luise. 2015. *Unlearning with Hannah Arendt*. Translated by David Dollenmayer. New York: Other.

Chapter 10

Im/possible Forgiveness: Derrida on Cosmopolitan Hospitality

Adrian Switzer

Please, forgive me: I have forgotten your name. You drove me from the train station at Stoke-on-Trent to the campus of Keele University. I was late for my presentation at the UK Kant Society and I hailed your taxi to get me to the conference site as quickly as possible. Thank you for your help. Thanks to you I made it in time to give my talk on Kant's political progressivism. According to Kant, I argued, we must draw our political principles from the future rather than from the past—otherwise, political sovereignty would be compromised, and with it the order and functioning of civil society would break down. In this way, I connected Kant's idea of cosmopolitanism with the future-orientedness of just political principles through the actuality of sovereign power.

From the actual exercise of future-directed sovereign power, citizens gain civil rights and are assured the realization of their transcendental freedom—assured, that is, as fully as one can be that what is transcendental will appear in the empirical domain. Further, an active sovereign advances a particular citizenry toward a cosmopolitan kingdom of ends: sovereignty exercised toward the future determines the just political state. Transcendental freedom is realized for a citizenry in this promissory, "as if [*als ob*]" manner, and cosmopolitanism becomes a real political end, on the condition that sovereign power is actually exercised. In modal terms, transcendental freedom, which for Kant is necessary, is actualized in practice in being oriented in its exercise toward a possible future-to-come. Perhaps unexpectedly, my presentation that day has quite a lot to do with the forgiveness I am now, here asking of you. Generally—if we can talk about forgiveness "in general"—offering unconditional hospitality toward all persons in a cosmopolitical context is to act on the necessary aporia of im/possible forgiveness; or, so, following Derrida, I will here argue.

As you drove the five miles from the train station to campus you told me about yourself and about your family: where your various brothers and sisters lived and what they did; you told me about your aunts and uncles in Pakistan. You expressed the disappointment you felt in yourself for having completed university but now you were just a taxi driver and how you felt you were wasting your education. Please, forgive me: I have forgotten the names of your brothers and sisters. Please, forgive me: I have forgotten the name of the town in Pakistan where your family emigrated from.

You told me, too, that that day was to be your last as a cab driver. The image of 3-year-old Aylan Kurdi, dead on the shore of Bodrum, Turkey—drowned during his family's attempt to escape Syria for Greece; eventually, to make their way to Canada—had woken you up, you said: it had given direction and purpose to your otherwise disappointing life. You had seen the photograph of Aylan in the news media, as many of us had. You tried to convey to me the heart-sickness and anger you felt in seeing the image. The next day, you said, you were leaving England for Turkey to help the Syrian refugees. You did not know what you could or would do. You explained to me that you had no training in humanitarian aid. But, those images, of young Aylan washed ashore in Turkey, and of the policeman carrying his body from the water's edge: they struck you with the force of a command. Being witness to such an event—seeing the consequences of an unannounced, sudden arrival on the far eastern shores of your Europe—drew you out of your limited sense of self; it reframed your life in the global-political circumstances in which we all now live. You became what you always already were: an un/conditional, forgiving host to strangers in foreign lands. The absolute demand Aylan Kurdi made on you necessitated your response; the transformation you underwent happened with equal necessity.

But please, forgive me: I have forgotten your name. All I can do is address you as "you": you who conveyed me from Stoke-on-Trent to Newcastle-under-Lyme; you who I assured that a life in which we do "nothing" but help train travelers get to their final destination is not a disappointing one. You "ferrier" of foreign lives, you conveyer of persons far from home through unknown lands: you seemed to me that day to be among the best-suited to help Syrians in their journey across Europe. Guest friendship [*xenia*], one of the most ancient of Greek virtues, is often associated with the traveler and messenger god Hermes who transported souls between this world and the Olympian one beyond. In Book V of *The Odyssey*, for example, when Hermes comes to Calypso's island to inform her and Odysseus that the time for his passage home is nigh, Calypso invokes the goddess Xenia in inviting him into her cave (Homer 1999, 155). Hermes is "guest-friend" to Calypso and the first conveyer of Odysseus out onto the open waters of the Mediterranean—"in a raft to cross the ocean's mighty gulfs [...] [s]o vast, so full of danger not even deep-sea ships can make it through" (Homer 1999, 158-159)—precisely in being a traveler between different lands and among different people. As Hermes's message to Calypso and Odysseus, safe and "at home" as they were on their island, so your words to me that day: you felt commanded to go; the next day you would set out onto unknown waters, re-enacting, in a way, the voyage Aylan Kurdi and his family had undertaken.

I can only address you as "you": you who have gone off to receive Aylan Kurdi; you have gone to help him secure safe passage from Syria to Europe and beyond. You who have drawn your political principle from the future that young Aylan would come to no harm in venturing out onto foreign terrain; you who would make of the whole Earth hospitable ground: welcoming of all lives, no matter their contingent point of origin.

What is the form of my address to you? To whom do I address my plea? Borrowing from Derrida to ask this last question: "[I]f the 'you' is not a '*vous*' of respect or distance, as this '*Vous*' [...] is preferable to [...] '*Tu*,' which signifies too much proximity or familiarity" (2015, 147). If the "you" by which I address you is familiar—'*tu*', in French—am I not assuming too much? Have I not assumed a familiarity—a proximity—that renders the asking forgiveness unnecessary? Simultaneously, I have drawn you close enough to address you in the familiar, while also treating you as a stranger to whom my plea must be made explicit. To presume to know you well enough to address you informally and yet to have forgotten your name: please, please forgive me; "pardon me, I am begging you [*pardonnez-moi, je t'en prie*]" (Derrida 2015, 147). But, if the "you" by which I call you is formal—the French '*vous*'—have I not addressed my plea to someone other than you? If "you" is formal, then am I not holding you off at such distance as to ask forgiveness in general rather than to you in your particularity: an indistinct "you" said in the formal "you/*vous*" of "pardon me, I beg you [*pardonnez-moi, je vous prie*]" (Ibid.).

> *If thus the 'you' of 'I beg your pardon,' 'pardon me' is a collective and plural 'you,' the question then becomes one of a collective pardon – collective either because it involves a group of subjects, others, citizens, individuals, and so forth, or because it already involves, and this is even more complicated [...] a multiplicity of agencies or moments, instances or instant, of 'I's' inside the 'I'.* (Ibid.)

Leaving aside, for now, Derrida's suggestion that forgiveness is a "collective pardon" asked of a "plural 'you'," in the first-person singular, the question of 'who "you" are' to whom I address my plea for forgiveness gives rise to the further, related question of 'who "I" am' who makes the address. The "you/I" relation, complex and opaque as it always and ever is, is rendered all the more problematic in the asking for and granting of forgiveness. Moreover, putting forgiveness in these terms might reverse the order of operation. Rather than the "I" being problematized *by* forgiveness, it might be that the subjective referent of the "I" is determined problematically *in* forgiveness.

Julia Kristeva argues that forgiveness constitutes subjectivity in just this manner: the subject emerges in complex form *from* forgiveness rather being brought already constituted *to* forgiveness. Contrary to an Hegelian model of subject-constitution exemplified by the master-slave dialectic in *The Phenomenology of Spirit*, whereby a desire-driven, life-and-death confrontation gives rise to the respective persons who confront one another, Kristeva locates a problematic subjectivity between the asking for and receiving forgiveness. The not-yet-organized drives, the depersonalized impulse to kill or be killed: these are offered up to society in a plea for forgiveness and transformed into one's own oedipalized desires. The want to kill another or to be killed "for one's own sake" *á la* master and slave is transformed—"sublimated," in the psychoanalytic sense of the term—into admitting one's unsociable drives and having them forgiven by society (Kristeva 1992, 216). Generalizing Kristeva's claim, and moving from the specificity of constituting subjectivity to the broader matter of becoming human, Kelly Oliver writes, "[p]hilosophers of forgiveness, Hegel, [...] Derrida and Kristeva, have in various ways made forgiveness a threshold of humanity: To be human is to forgive" (2003, 280).

How problematic is the subject that is constituted, for Kristeva, in and through the act(s) of forgiveness? Might the asking for and receiving forgiveness be so complex an operation as to dissolve subjectivity altogether? Forgiveness, then, might be a question not of "who" but of "what"? In his 1999 essay "*Le Siècle et le pardon*" (hereafter *On Forgiveness*), Derrida puts the same questions as follows: "Who do I forgive?

And whom? What and whom? Something or someone?" (2001b, 38). Do we forgive, Derrida here asks, an action and its consequences—the harm that came from an act, whether foreseen or unforeseen? Or, do we forgive the person or persons who committed the act? Meir Dan-Cohen, for one, suggests that it must be a "what" that is forgiven. Repentance, which is one's condition in pleading for forgiveness, "may be so profound as to count as a change of identity" (2007, 118). To repent—to have a "change of heart"—may not be only a metaphorical change. Perhaps, to repent and to ask forgiveness is to transform oneself so fully and completely as to be other than who one was. Paradoxically, the referent of the "I" to whom forgiveness would be given is then not the same referent of the "I" who asks to be forgiven: in repentantly transforming myself, I have made myself into someone else.

Let us follow what Derrida calls the "syntactic ambiguity" between the "who" and "what" as a guiding thread into the more basic aporia of the im/possibility of forgiveness. Similar as a syntactic ambiguity seems to an aporia, we will find that the latter retains the undecidability of the former while operating in the mode of necessity—different *possibilities* give way in an aporia to a basic *necessity*. No doubt, the everyday language of asking for and receiving forgiveness is telling in ways of its underlying, aporetic logic. Derrida, as much as Kristeva and Oliver, allows language to guide his inquiry. So, Derrida begins "To Forgive: The Unforgivable and the Imprescriptible" (1999) (hereafter "To Forgive") with an extended reflection on the word "*pardon*":

> *'Pardon': 'pardon' is a noun. It can sometimes be preceded (in French) by a definite or indefinite article (le pardon, un pardon) and inscribed, for example as subject, in a constative sentence: forgiveness [le pardon] is this or that, forgiveness [le pardon] has been asked by someone or by an institution, a par-*

don [un pardon] has been granted or refused, and so forth. (Derrida 2015, 146-147)

Derrida goes on in "To Forgive" to consider the linguistic, etymological relation between "*pardon*" and "*don* [gift]" as well, as we have seen, the pronouns '*tu/vous* [you]' and '*moi* [I]' that structure utterances of forgiveness. Similarly, in *On Forgiveness* Derrida maintains that "forgiveness must *announce* itself as impossibility" (2001b, 33): a pronouncement of an im/possible "forgive me" that, if misheard, sounds simply impossible.

Ultimately, a philosophy of the language of forgiveness will not suffice. A linguistic analysis of forgiveness does not expose the complexity—the challenge—of forgiveness in full: it allows the "impossibility" and "possibility" of forgiveness to stand apart as if separate modes of the same act. The language of "*pardon*" does not reveal the strict necessity with which forgiveness functions in its actual exercise. As William Robert describes the problem in reference to another of Derrida's essays on forgiveness from the late 1990s—"*Avouer–l'impossible*" (1998) (hereafter "Avowing – The Impossible")—forgiveness [*grâce*] "precedes and exceeds any grammar for which it remains inexpressible." From this it would follow, were we to continue to pursue the problem of forgiveness strictly in a discursive-linguistic register, that one would have to "invent a new grammar," as Derrida puts it in "Avowing – The Impossible" (2013, 22). A "new grammar" of forgiveness would be one, according to Robert, that is more basic than "ontology, metaphysics, presence, essence"; a "new grammar" of forgiveness that would not operate "by predication in the indicative verbal mood" (2013, 163).

Forgiveness *is* not possible or impossible. Rather, "forgiveness" names, in this other grammar that Derrida and Robert envision, the aporia of the im/possible—marked by the backslash between "im-" and "-possible," which renders the terms inseparable. The differently signifying mark of the im/possible—the inexpressibility of forgiveness, in Robert's above sense—does not relegate us to silence: we are not relieved of the responsibility of pleading for forgiveness by the im/possibility of its actual exercise. No, I *must* ask to be forgiven precisely in and because of the im/possibility of ever actually addressing you with my plea or ever receiving the gift of your forgiveness. As Derrida explains the same idea in *On Forgiveness*, "[I] am disarmed before *what I have to do* so that I have to do it in order [...] to feel freely obligated and bound to respond" (54). Accordingly, I am obliged to ask for your forgiveness in much the same way—because, ultimately, they are rooted in the same im/possible necessity—that you felt obliged to go to Turkey to help Aylan Kurdi.

If we were to name the para-linguistic system in which the other grammar of forgiveness operates, we could call it a politics of difference, or, as Derrida came to refer to the same in his works of the late-1980s into the 1990s, "deconstruction as justice," or, "justice as the undeconstructible": "a justice which ha[s] nothing to do with judicial justice" (2001b, 43). In considering the everyday language of forgiveness, we should not lose sight of the more basic, political landscape across which we are moving. Subsequently, and with reference to Derrida's essay on Kantian cosmopolitanism, we will consider forgiveness in the context of a just, deconstructive politics of difference.

Linguistically speaking, then, who am "I" to ask "you" for forgiveness? Does the syntax of "please, forgive me" not mislead me into assuming a stable self—a re-identifiable referent of "I"—in uttering my plea to "you"? While still allowing the grammar of forgiveness to guide their respective analyses, Kristeva and Oliver problematize the seemingly fixed referents of "I" and "you" by appealing to psychoanalysis. On this approach, as noted above, the self is constituted *through* the act of asking to be and being forgiven rather than being brought, pre-formed, *to* forgiveness. But, it is no simple or direct self- and other-constitution: the scene of forgiveness seen from a psychoanalytic perspective is an unstable, complicated one. The self who comes to be—or, the "becoming-human" that occurs—in and through forgiveness is not, according to what Oliver calls "psychoanalytic forgiveness," a unity: "[T]his forgiveness does not erase or absolve otherness or transgression but rather brings us face-to-face with [...] [an] otherness [to] which we owe our very existence" (2003, 286). Further, even after forgiveness—if there is any sense of an "end" of psychoanalytic forgiveness—you and I are constantly and continually destabilized in our respective selves. As Orna Ophir makes this last point in reference to Kleinian psychoanalysis, "forgiveness can be seen as a lifelong process of an interminable working through" (2015, 110).

Still, we might ask whether the "self" and "other" terms of this shifting psychoanalytic scene are sufficiently far removed from the grammar of what Robert above termed "predication in the indicative verbal mood" to afford insight into its im/possible necessity. Subjectification in Kristeva's sense, or the "becoming human" as Oliver puts it: do such processes in tending toward the formation of self not impart to forgiveness a teleology at odds with its strict im/possibility? Put otherwise, does a psychoanalytic approach to the problem of forgiveness remain too much within a discursive-linguistic framework? Is the syntactic—*not semantic*—ambiguity between the "who" and "what" of forgiveness lost in the utterances of a not-yet-forgiven-subject and not-yet-forgiving-other? For both such reasons, for its implicit teleology and confusion of semantics and syntax, a psychoanalytic approach to forgiveness is unsatisfying. What is needed, and what we will return to below in reference to Kant's cosmopolitanism, is a transcendental forgiveness and a non-teleological account of its actual exercise, i.e., a sense of forgiveness as being always already pleaded for and given.

Interestingly, Oliver also recommends an attentiveness to the unconscious in matters of forgiveness for political reasons: it is "only by accounting for the unconscious" that we can, according to Oliver, "articulate an ethics and/or a politics of difference" (2003, 289). A different "ethics and/or politics" follows from a psychoanalysis of forgiveness in that the latter, by accounting for the unconscious, complicates the forms of subjectivity that bear political rights or that stand under ethical obligation. Here too, as we will see, a psychoanalytic approach to forgiveness is insufficient to describe the political character and circumstances of its exercise.

Further, Oliver recommends attending to the unconscious to correct a mistake, as she sees it, in Derrida's analysis of forgiveness. By "accounting for the unconscious," Oliver thinks we can correct Derrida's mistaken idea of "pure" forgiveness, that is, forgiveness properly so called in being granted only to the unforgivable. The "purity" implied in forgiving the unforgivable corresponds in Derrida, according to Oliver, with the "hyperbolic" ethical claim that forgiveness makes on us. Invoking "purity" in this way risks, Oliver thinks, re-economizing the gift of forgiveness in the very gesture of taking it out of an exchange economy, i.e., as if an exorbitant but still calculable expenditure of pure forgiveness is exchanged with the unforgivable.

At the end of *On Forgiveness*, Derrida presents pure forgiveness as follows: "What I dream of, what I try to think as the 'purity' of a forgiveness worthy of its name, would be a forgiveness without power: unconditional but without sovereignty" (2001b, 59). Notwithstanding the quotation marks in which Derrida here suspends "purity"—similarly, the quotation marks in which Derrida suspends "hyperbolic ethics" a few pages earlier (Derrida 2001b, 51)—we can ask whether a "dream" of pure forgiveness is not something ontologically and essentially other than a philosophical idea thereof. If Oliver's recommendation is to "accoun[t] for the unconscious" in considering forgiveness, and this in order to avoid a too stable, too determinate sense of the self and other who participate in the giving and receiving of forgiveness, has Derrida not done such accounting—the economic metaphorics of Oliver's term, aside—by presenting his idea of pure forgiveness as a *dream* of unconditional power without sovereignty?

Yet, to weigh Derrida in on this point, that is, whether a dream of pure forgiveness is or is not sufficiently accommodating of the unconscious to unsettle the seemingly fixed grammar of "please, forgive me" is to take Derrida's comment out of its specific and general context. As informed as Derrida's work is by Freud and psychoanalysis, and as implicit as his debt to psychoanalysis remains even in those texts where it is not invoked explicitly, my proposal is to read *On Forgiveness* and related essays—"To Forgive" and "Avowing – The Impossible"—politically rather than in terms of intrapsychic subjectivity, i.e., in terms of a psychology of forgiveness. Moving from a psychoanalysis of forgiveness to a politics of the same might be to remain with Freud after all. As Ophir explains, Freud did not think forgiveness worthy of psychoanalytic attention because, "[it] touche[s] upon the interpersonal or social level and less on an intrapsychic one" (2015, 111). Adopting, however unwittingly, Freud's view of forgiveness as a social phenomenon, Derrida treats forgiveness politically. Let us consider textual evidence of this approach; subsequently, I will argue for this same approach on philosophical grounds.

Just before the passage to which Oliver draws our attention, Derrida invokes once more Vladimir Jankélévitch, whose *Le pardon* and "*L'Imprescriptible*" are his occasion and constant points of reference in *On Forgiveness*. Following Jankélévitch, Derrida asks after forgiveness as a matter of history and politics —responding, in so doing, to Jankélévitch's assertion that, "[f]orgiveness is [...] an event that has never occurred in history" (2013, 48). For instance, Derrida considers whether it is possible to forgive the Nazis for their crimes against Jews during the Second World War. Was such forgiveness possible? Further, was the Nuremberg Tribunal fit to exercise it? (Derrida 2001b, 59). With this second question, forgiveness becomes institutionalized: its actual exercise is built, in some sense, into the regular workings of a political office. In this regard, Derrida considers the South African Truth and Reconciliation Commission, which was vested with the power to forgive the persons or history—the "who" the "what"—of apartheid (2001b, 30). Indeed, establishing reconciliation and amnesty commissions on the Occupation and on Algeria became, according to Derrida, "[the] *leitmotiv* of all [...] French" politics after the Second World War (2001b, 40). How the political institutionalization of forgiveness bears on and relates to the more fundamental, im/possible aporia of forgiveness is something that will interest us below. Here, suffice it to note that Derrida in *On Forgiveness* moves between the history of forgiveness and its political practice(s). Derrida follows Jankélévitch in proceeding in this manner; but, he does so to amend Jankélévitch's contradictory claims that on the one hand forgiveness is im/possible while on the other it is simply impossible: "[F]orgiveness died in the death camps," Jankélévitch proclaims in "*L'Imprescriptible*" (Derrida 2001b, 37).

Finally, and again in reference to Jankélévitch, Derrida in *On Forgiveness* discusses the legal designation "*imprescriptible*" as it applies to crimes without statute of limitations. Question of imprescriptible crimes were of the political moment in France when Jankélévitch was writing the two texts around which Derrida structures *On Forgiveness*. The Eichmann trial was conducted in 1961-62 in Jerusalem; the Frankfurt Auschwitz Trial began in 1963; and, the French law designating Nazi crimes against humanity "imprescriptible" took effect in 1964: Jankélévitch's "*L'Imprescriptible*" and *Le Pardon* were published in 1965 and 1967, respectively. In reference to "imprescriptibility," Derrida maintains that "[as a] juridical concept" it is in no way "equivalent to the non-juridical concept of the unforgivable" (2001b, 33); and, in response to Jankélévitch's "*L'Imprescriptible*," Derrida questions the "conditional logic" of criminals needing to "ask [for] forgiveness" in order for it to be granted (2001b, 34). In contrast to this, as already noted, Derrida envisions an unconditional political forgiveness—one, moreover, that operates free of the sovereign positions from which one asks for and receives from another their forgiveness. With this, we return to the immediate context of Derrida's hoped for dream of pure forgiveness at the end of *On Forgiveness*: it is unconditional political power without sovereignty.

Derrida's (Jankélévitchian) attention to the history and politics of forgiveness announces an approach to the topic other than the psychoanalytic one taken by Oliver and Kristeva. Indeed, the way Oliver formulates her position, namely, that attending to the unconscious allows us to articulate a different "ethics and/or politics" of forgiveness, signals the insufficiency of a psychoanalytic approach to political forgiveness. Admittedly, the ethical and political are nowhere easily distinguished; nor do "ethics" and "politics" name separate concerns for Derrida. In *On Forgiveness*, Derrida writes of being "'torn' [...] between" a "'hyperbolic' ethical vision of forgiveness" and a politics of the same: "irreducible" as the one is to the other, an ethics and politics of forgiveness "remain indissociable" (2001b, 51). Accordingly, Dana Hollander compares Derrida's late lectures and essays on forgiveness to his sustained engagement with Kierkegaard in *The Gift of Death*. The command Abraham receives to sacrifice Isaac cuts across ethics and politics: the ethical trespass Abraham is willing to commit in killing his son is equally a threat to the political community of the people of Israel who are to be the progeny of Isaac. Derrida's attempt to "thin[k] together" the im/possibility of forgiveness in *On Forgiveness* is of apiece, Hollander writes, with the im/possible problematics—the im/possible aporiae—with which he is concerned in his other "'ethical-political' writings" (2013, 141).

Oliver's phrase, "ethics and/or politics," and Hollander's "ethical-political" ostensibly allow the ethical and political ambivalently to define and undermine each other across a separating and conjoining hyphen. As we have allowed the grammar of forgiveness to guide our reflections to this point, so let us do the same in attending to the graphism of Oliver and Hollander's "ethical-political" accounts of forgiveness. Indirectly, we also in this way draw attention to a key hyphenated phrase in Derrida's *On Forgiveness*, namely, "juridico-political" as the name of the economy of "negotiations [...] [and] calculated transactions" of political amnesty and reconciliation (2001b, 39)—but also, the name of what exceeds law and calculability in acts of sovereign "forgiveness [*grâce*]" (Derrida 2001b, 46). We will return to this last, difficult—but essential—notion in conclusion.

In *Spurs: Nietzsche's Styles* (1978) (hereafter *Spurs*), Derrida gives us occasion to think about the differing and differentiating function of the hyphen in the syntax of sentences, and he does so in a political context (specifically, the politics of gender identity and sexual difference). By focusing on Nietzsche's various uses of the dash in his writings—to connect two unrelated clauses; to interrupt the coherence of a line of thought; to accent a final word or phrase in a sentence, etc.—Derrida points up the punctuation's plural significance. Further, Derrida argues in *Spurs* that the ambivalence, as it were, of Nietzsche's hyphens and dashes is not an abstraction—they are no mere placeholders on the page over which thought lingers between two equally viable meanings. Nietzsche's hyphens and dashes, as are all marks of the same form, are graphically real and significant as such. At one point in *Spurs*, Derrida borrows the phrase, "granite stratum of spiritual fate" from *Untimely Meditations* to describe the "inscription" of dashes and hyphens into Nietzsche's texts: "irreducible" and "irreducibly plural" marks into the granite-like façade of the page (Derrida 1978, 105). To the extent that we can think significant what seems graphically insignificant, Derrida would have us think hyphens and dashes as really determining marks inscribed into the syntax of a sentence and into the text.

How do these claims from *Spurs* bear on Hollander and Oliver's respective use of the hyphen and backslash in discussing Derrida's "ethical-political" writings on forgiveness? The real graphic significance of these marks leads us, and necessarily so, to position the "ethical" and the "political" along the same level of significance—the dash that separates them effectively draws them together in the same syntactical space of the sentence. This follows from Derrida's assertion that the differentiating and deferring graphic significance of the hyphen is a kind of transcendental condition of the sentence formed from out of its inscription. That is, Derrida would have us treat the hyphenated inscription as significantly basic; the terms of the sentence formed therefrom operate within its inscribed limits:

> *Everywhere operative, and most especially in Nietzsche's text, this [hyphenated] graphic, which inscribes a limit [une limite inscrite] where the control over meaning or code is without recourse, poses the limit the the relevance of the hermeneutic [...] question.*
> (Derrida 1978, 99)

Thus, like the "other grammar" of forgiveness that founds but also operates deconstructively within an ontology of presence and essence, so the real difference marked by the hyphen in "ethical-political" is the transcendental condition of the syntactical interplay of the two terms but also the inscription of that interplay into same plane of significance. This is how we should read Derrida's claim in *On Forgiveness* of being "torn" between a "hyperbolic ethics" and a politics of forgiveness: the "tear" in the later work corresponds with the hyphen as "inscri[bed] mark" in *Spurs*. Read in this way, the "tear" between ethics and politics operates fully within and as the historico-political framework of Derrida's text. Only in this way does the full force of the differentiating and deferring hyphen operate; only in this way does semantic ambiguity become real syntactical difference.

By attending to the graphic conditions of significance, we can reconsider Derrida's hyphenated "juridico-political" from *On Forgiveness*; equally, we are afforded different insight into Derrida's engagement with legal imprescriptibility. At root, "imprescriptible" contains "prescribe" from the Latin "*praescribere*," i.e., to write. By invoking this legal term in the negative, Jankélévitch is implicitly situating certain acts and persons before or outside of the bounds of prescribed law: such acts or persons are "illegible" before the law and as such are unforgivable. By contrast, Derrida would have the im/possibility of forgiveness operate—and necessarily so—within and as the juridico-political domain: the im/possible aporia of forgiveness inscribes and as such is inscribed into the political. In "To Forgive," Derrida makes this point obliquely by invoking Celan's poem "*Todtnauberg*" during his discussion of Jankélévitch's *L'Imprescriptible*. One line of the poem reads, "which in that book [is] inscribed a line of hope [*die in dies Buch geschriebene Zeile von einer Hoffnung*]": a complex, difficult image but one that ties (hope of) forgiveness to inscription—in this case, the inscription of a name [*Namen*] into a book of forgiveness (Derrida 2015, 163).

Applying this same line of thinking to Oliver and Hollander's "ethical-political"/"ethics and/or politics" ambiguity of forgiveness, we must allow the graphic reality of the hyphen and backslash to erase the seeming semantic difference between the two terms—"ethics" and "politics"—and thereby enable difference to operate in its full necessity within and as the syntax of the political. This is no simple matter. To situate forgiveness fully within the political so as to allow the full necessary force of its im/possibility to operate is to de- and reconstruct the political. Borrowing Jankélévitch's phrase, "*pardon fou*," Derrida in *On Forgiveness* explains, "[mad forgiveness] is perhaps the only thing that arrives, that surprises, like a revolution, the ordinary course of history, politics and law" (2001b, 39). There is a madness to the im/possibility of forgiveness, which once situated fully within history and politics radically and revolutionarily unsettles both.

Below, by appealing to Kant's notion of cosmopolitanism and Derrida's reflections thereon, we will return to the question of what "politics" means in the context of im/possible forgiveness. To anticipate this discussion, note that the changed political terrain of im/possible forgiveness is no mere theoretical upheaval; it is not, simply, an occasion to re-think the political. Just as the backslash that signals the difference in "im/possible" is not an abstract ambiguity but a really significant graphic inscription, so the different politics of forgiveness is, Derrida writes, historically and institutionally concrete: "[The] idea of forgiveness and the unforgivable [...] despite its theoretical, speculative, purist, abstract appearance [...] can induce [concrete] processes of transformation – political [and] juridical" (2001b, 53). As we began, in a way, with Kant, so in conclusion we will have to return to him to explain the real "processes of transformation" effected in politics by the im/possibility of forgiveness.

Yet, before concluding in this manner, let us return, briefly, to the above discussion of the "ethics and/or politics" of forgiveness. My claim—announced in the titular "im/possible" of this chapter—is that Derrida's aporetic thinking of forgiveness as an im/possible gift to the unforgivable must be situated fully within the context of a just, deconstructive politics of difference. Only by such means, only by aligning our philosophical approach to the problem of forgiveness along the same level of significance as its actual exercise can I, with Derrida's help, begin to understand what you felt immediately and without question, namely, the strict necessity of responding to Aylan Kurdi's death. A deconstructive, political account of im/possible forgiveness allows us to grasp in full the compulsory necessity with which asking for/giving forgiveness is actually exercised in our shared global, political reality. Derrida's im/possible politics of forgiveness, and Kant's future-oriented cosmopolitanism together enable a philosophy of forgiveness to align with the political experience thereof in all the full weight and bearing of the latter's strict necessity.

What we accomplish by following Derrida and Kant in this way, i.e., recasting the philosophy of forgiveness in a cosmopolitical context, is to reveal that philosophy operates with the same necessity you experienced in seeing the image of Aylan Kurdi. In Kantian terms, we are under no mere hypothetical imperative to think the question of forgiveness philosophically; rather, the imperative to do so is categorical (Derrida 2001b, 39). In this way, the philosophy of forgiveness appears under the same normative force of necessity—that this is the problem philosophy *must* address under contemporary political circumstances—that you experienced and that you acted upon in undertaking the im/possible task of offering guest-friendship and safe passage to Aylan Kurdi as a global-political refugee. In a sense, then, Kristeva is right to locate the question of forgiveness at the heart of philosophical thought in general: *forgiveness is the fundamental philosophical question of our time.* Kristeva is just wrong to frame her meta-philosophical insight in terms of subjectivity. In so doing, Kristeva tempers psychologically the necessity with which this question impacts us philosophically and politically. Rather, cosmopolitically, we *must* take up the necessary task of thinking forgiveness philosophically and politically; with Derrida and Kant, we *must* dream together of an unconditional political forgiveness without sovereignty.

In *Toward Perpetual Peace* (1795) (hereafter *Perpetual Peace*), Kant discusses cosmopolitanism in the context of international law. Against the prevailing political theory of the day—put forward by Pufendorf and Grotius—according to which inter-state war was treated as an executive right, Kant argues that there is no legal-political justification for such an action: "The concept of the right of nations as that of the right to go to war is, strictly speaking, unintelligible" (Kant 1996, Ak. 8:356). It is "unintelligible" to speak of a national "right" to war because absent from the international setting within which wars are waged is the sovereign-based, intra-national foundations of right. Rather, according to Kant, nations that wage war on others hold themselves out in the "lawless [...] savage" Hobbesian state of nature. As Hobbes envisions persons emerging from such a state into the well-defined subjectivity of a citizenry by ceding their autonomy to sovereign rule, so Kant envisions a "savage" warring state ceding some of its authority to a pacifying "league of nations"—thereby gaining international right in an intelligible sense of the word (Kant 1996, 8:357).

The political principle of such an international league of nations is twofold: the future-oriented ideal of no war, i.e., perpetual peace, and "the right of hospitality" extended to strangers in foreign lands. Hospitableness is not simply "philanthropy," i.e.; it is not an exchange of support, monetary, or otherwise, for the welfare and well-being of foreign persons. Hospitality is instead a *right* of a foreigner "not to be treated with hostility" in arriving in new lands (Ibid.). The basis of the right of (foreign) hospitality, Kant continues, is "the right of the possession in common of the Earth's surface" (Ibid., Ak. 8:358). The whole round world belongs to all persons, equally, who inhabit it. We are essentially terrestrial beings; and, without naturalizing the faculty of reason upon which Kant's critical philosophy depends, still, there is no rational justification for our claims on the Earth being limited. That I was born in one nation-state, and you in another: these are empirical contingencies of a different, less significant magnitude than our transcendentally free terrestriality.

Given the unconditional character of Kant's argument for the right of hospitality, it is surprising that he turns in the next paragraph of *Perpetual Peace* to the limits on this right. The hospitality extended by right to a stranger in a foreign land is the right of visitation, not the right of guest-friendship (Ibid.). Whereas the contingency of being from this-or-that different homeland does not compromise the unconditional claim all persons have on the Earth, the geographico-empirical fact that not all lands are habitable, and thus that we must live together in life-supporting areas, does limit foreign hospitality rights to visitation.

As with all of Kant's philosophy, so here the dialectical structure of a transcendentalism realized under empirical conditions—here, specifically, an unconditional right to world inhabitancy exercised under the conditional constraints of the Earth's limited resources—appears as an aporia: foreign hospitality is an un/conditional right. A different articulation of the same cosmopolitical dialectic emerges shortly after Kant's discussion of the right of hospitality. Kant argues that though he is concerned with international politics and law, the right to perpetual peace and foreign hospitality are in fact "supplement[s] to the unwritten code of the right of a state [...] and nation" (Ibid., Ak. 8:360). Intra-statist sovereignty thus remains for Kant the basis of political rights in general—even when the context of those rights is international politics.

Kant seems, then, to subordinate to sovereign nationalism the international political function of a pacific league of nations and the unconditional claim all persons have on equal habitation of the Earth. Kant does so, though, for good modal reasons. As the transcendental conditions of the possibility of (empirical) political freedom, international organizations and cosmopolitan subjectivity are modally necessary. But, the transcendentally necessary, for Kant, is always actually exercised—and, it is so actualized on principle of the possibility of its ultimate realization. Perhaps, under the sway of Hobbes's subject-like image of the nation-state wherein the whole (of the state) is modeled on its parts (the citizenry), Kant locates the modes of actual political exercise and their possible, future-directed principles within the sovereign nation, i.e., the sovereign nation is the subject, as it were, that actually acts in an international setting toward the future possibility of perpetual peace and cosmopolitan citizenship. Questions aside, of the legitimacy of privileging actual sovereignty over cosmopolitical necessity in international politics, the dialectic that appears between unconditional hospitality and the limited right of visitation, as well as between international politics and sovereign intra-nationalism, should be read as different articulations of the modal difference between transcendental necessity and its possible empirical actualization.

Though cast in Kantian terms, these last remarks recall us to the abiding interest of the present essay: the necessity of im/possible political aporiae. Throughout, Kant has informed our reflections; now, finally, the Kantian underpinnings of our work on the politics of forgiveness in a cosmopolitical context can be drawn out. They are seen throughout Derrida's lecture "*Cosmopolites de tous les pays, encore un effort!*" (1997) (hereafter *On Cosmopolitanism*), which occurred around the same time as he presented and published his three major essays on forgiveness.

The occasion for *On Cosmopolitanism* was the 1996 meeting of the International Parliament of Writers—a meeting from which the group issued a call to establish cities of refuge for displaced foreigners. Kant is Derrida's constant point of reference in the lecture. Derrida begins with the rhetorical question from where we, today, received our image of cosmopolitanism—the long history of the idea notwithstanding, "cosmopolitan," in a modern sense, stems directly from Kant (Derrida 2001a, 3). In turn, Derrida concludes the lecture with a discussion of the above-noted aporiae between Kant's sovereign nationalism and his cosmopolitical internationalism. "Kant seems at first to extend the cosmopolitan law to encompass universal hospitality *without limit*"; yet, he does so, Derrida continues, "to expel from [that right] what is *erected, constructed, or what sets itself up above* the soil [of the shared Earth]": the edifices and institutions of the sovereign nation – and even the soil atop which they are built – "must not be unconditionally accessible to all [foreign] comers" (Derrida 2001a, 20-1). Not incidentally, the terms here used to describe the aporia at the heart of Kant's cosmopolitanism repeat the terms Derrida uses to describe his dream in *On Forgiveness* of a different politics of unconditionality without sovereignty. If we read Derrida's concluding dream in *On Forgiveness* as a kind of question, then the answer is given by way of Kant in *On Cosmopolitanism*.

What, then, is unconditional forgiveness without sovereignty? How does Kant's dialectical un/conditional right of foreign hospitality help us think this Derridean idea? In fact, we have answered this question already: above, in citing the "exceptional" status of acts of sovereign *grâce* [forgiveness], we invoked an actual instance of im/possible forgiveness. Let us consider this answer more fully, here, in conclusion. "Sometimes," Derrida writes, "forgiveness [...] must be a gracious [*gracieux*] gift, without exchange and without condition" (2001a, 44). Still, such "unconditional" forgiveness remains "inseparable from what is heterogeneous to it": "the order of conditions, repentance, transformation [...] [which] allow it to inscribe itself in history, law [and] politics" (Ibid.). Further, and this is key, "the unconditional and conditional [...] must remain irreducible to one another"; if one wants— and this want is *necessary*—forgiveness to be historically and politically effective, un/conditionality must remain "*irreconcilable but indissociable*" (Ibid., 44-45).

In terms of Kant's cosmopolitan theory of foreign hospitality—or, what Derrida in *On Cosmopolitanism* refers to as the rights of global refugees (2001a, 12)—what this means is that the unconditional claim all persons have on the Earth is irreconcilably indissociable from the conditions of its actual exercise, which in Kant's account is the inhospitableness of certain ecoregions. Derrida holds to this basic Kantian view. All Derrida does is formalize the point in reference to the sovereign exercise of un/conditional forgiveness. The example Derrida has in mind is the "right of *grâce*" exercisable by a sovereign: the absolute, unconditional right of a sovereign to "pardon [*pardon*; forgive] a criminal" (2001b, 45). This is an exceptional act. Indeed, Derrida claims that the exercise of the sovereign right of forgiveness, "transcends and neutralizes the law"; it is an example of "right [*droit*] beyond law [*droit*]" (2001b, 46). The exceptionalism of this act cuts both ways: it opens the otherwise closed "juridico-political" economy in which repentance is exchanged for amnesty to an aneconomic act, and it introduces conditionality into the otherwise unconditional authority of the sovereign. As Derrida puts this last point in "To Forgive": "[Sovereign right of grace] is [...] what interrupts, in the juridico-political itself, the order of the juridico-political. It is the exception to the juridico-political *within* the juridico-political" (2015, 158).

In actualizing the unconditional right of forgiveness, whether toward a person or event—the ambivalence between the "who" and "what" of forgiveness operates fully here—the sovereign conditions his/her power. Unconditionality is not thereby lost; nor does sovereign unconditionality come to be identified with its conditional exercise. Rather, un/conditionality operates together within and as the juridico-political—the act of forgiveness reveals the full necessity of the aporetic un/conditionality of sovereign power and it allows that necessity to operate juridico-politically. Were this the sum of Derrida's political philosophy of forgiveness, it would be as interesting as it was inconsequential. After all, acts of sovereign *grâce* are rare; the pardoning of criminals is a right infrequently exercised by political leaders. If forgiveness in all of its necessary im/possibility is realized only under the rare circumstances of a sovereign pardon, what Derrida dreams of is the privilege of an exceptional few.

However, Derrida claims in *On Forgiveness* that sovereign acts of *grâce* are both exceptional and exemplary: "What is called the *right of grace* gives an example of [the im/possible aporia of forgiveness], at once an example among others and the exemplary model" (2001b, 45). In Kantian cosmopolitical terms, the "model" exemplarity of sovereign acts of *grâce* can be aligned with the unconditionality of our shared, equal claim on the Earth. In turn, the instantiated example of sovereign *grâce* is like the conditionality with which strangers are welcomed into foreign lands. This last, conditioned exercise of hospitality is not the mistaken juridico-political idea of a refugee "deserving" safe-harbor or being "owed" hospitality because of the dire circumstances under which s/he has been living. No, the condition on unconditional hospitality is that it must *actually* be exercised. With you, whose unnamed forgiveness I have begged throughout, we must *actually* give the gift of guest-friendship though it is always already given in the unconditional claim all persons have on the Earth. Further, in that all persons under present global-political circumstances are unconditionally of the Earth, i.e., we are all cosmopolitical, the always already actual exercise of hospitality is given in our unconditioned political status.

Contrary to Kristeva and Oliver who argue that subjectivity is constituted through forgiveness, in a global political setting we are always already constituted as forgiven: we bear the mark of grace on our global political selves; we instantiate it in our conditioned terrestriality. By being exemplified in this way through the actual exercise of a forgiveness that is always already actual, and by being exercised by persons whose sovereignty is rooted in something outside of themselves, namely, the global-political context within which they act, forgiveness is revealed in all of its unconditionality—and revealed without sovereignty in an empirico-political sense. Here, then, is Derrida's dream of political forgiveness realized: among all persons as refugees, of a sort, in a globalized political setting (2001b, 57-8). Here, then, is the fully necessary im/possible aporia of forgiveness at work: in the un/conditional exercise of the right of hospitality to global refugees. Unfamiliar as it sounds to talk of "forgiveness" in such terms, with Derrida we do well to recall that we have throughout been writing and reading in the other grammar of a just politics of difference—listening in this other language for the mute demand the image of Aylan Kurdi made on you that day as we drove across the English countryside.[99]

---

[99] I want to thank Jessica Borusky in the Art & Art History Department at the University of Missouri Kansas City for her help on previous drafts of the essay. Also, thank you to my fellow panelists at the Derrida Today Conference at Goldsmiths College, University of London: our discussion helped me revise a few of the key points of my argument.

References

Dan-Cohen, Meir. 2007. "Revisiting the Past: On the Metaphysics of Repentance, Forgiveness and Pardon." *Forgiveness, Mercy and Clemency.* Edited by A. Sarat & N. Hussain. Palo Alto, CA: Stanford University Press.

Derrida, Jacques. 2015. "To Forgive: The Unforgivable and the Imprescriptible." *Love and Forgiveness for a More Just World.* Edited by H. de Vries & N.F. Schott. New York: Columbia University Press.

———. 2013. "Avowing – The Impossible: 'Returns,' Repentance and Reconciliation." Translated by G. Anidjar. *Living Together: Jacques Derrida's Communities of Violence and Peace.* Edited by E. Weber. New York: Fordham University Press.

———. 2001a. *On Cosmopolitanism. On Cosmopolitanism and Forgiveness.* Translated by M. Dooley & M. Hughes. New York: Routledge.

———. 2001b. *On Forgiveness. On Cosmopolitanism and Forgiveness.* Translated by M. Dooley & M. Hughes. New York: Routledge.

———. 1978. *Spurs: Nietzsche's Styles.* Translated by B. Harlow. Chicago: University of Chicago Press.

Hollander, Dana. 2013. "Contested Forgiveness: Jankélévitch, Levinas and Derrida at the *Colloque des intellectuels juifs.*" *Living Together: Jacques Derrida's Communities of Violence and Peace.* Edited by E. Weber. New York: Fordham University Press.

Homer. 1999. *The Odyssey.* Translated by R. Fagles. New York: Penguin.

Jankélévitch, Vladimir. 2013. *Forgiveness.* Translated by A. Kelley. Chicago: University of Chicago Press.

Kant, Immanuel. 1996. *Toward Perpetual Peace. The Cambridge Edition of the Works of Immanuel Kant: Practical Philosophy.* Translated by M. Gregor. New York: Cambridge University Press.

Kristeva, Julia. 1992. *Black Sun: Depression and Melancholia.* New York: Columbia University Press.

Oliver, Kelly. 2003. "Forgiveness and Subjectivity." *Philosophy Today* 47.3: 280-292.

Ophir, Orna. 2015. "Looking Evil in the Eye/I: The Interminable Work of Forgiveness." *Love and Forgiveness for a More Just World.* Edited by H. de Vries & N.F. Schott. New York: Columbia University Press.Robert, William. 2013. "To Live, by Grace." *Living Together: Jacques Derrida's Communities of Violence and Peace.* Edited by E. Weber. New York: Fordham University Press.

Chapter 11

Indeterminable Forgiveness: Economic Madness and The Possibility of an Impossible Task

Zachary Thomas Settle

We will ask ourselves if forgiveness does not begin in the place where it appears to end, where it appears im-possible, precisely at the end of the history of forgiveness, of history as the history of forgiveness.

—Jacques Derrida, 1999

Forgiveness is not, it should not be, normal, normative, normalizing. It should remain exceptional and extraordinary, in the face of the impossible: as if it interrupted the ordinary course of historical temporality.

—Jacques Derrida, 2001

Forgiveness is thus mad. It must plunge, but lucidly, into the might of the unintelligable.

—Jacques Derrida, 2001

Introduction

Deconstruction is a rejection of ideals; it is owning-up to the loss of purity and impossibility of definitions of presence inherent to language itself (Deutscher 2005, 3). And as Derrida so forcefully reminds his readers, there is no space of human being outside the text; that is to say that textuality and language characterize the fullness of our being human. Derrida scholar and commentator Penelope Deutscher explains that in deconstruction, Derrida is able to argue that logocentric "hierarchies between the terms natural and unnatural, pure and contaminated, certain and uncertain, are, on closer inspection, unstable" (Ibid., 9). Deconstruction is by no means a mere methodology or tool, but certain characteristics can be applied to it nonetheless (Macey 2001, 86). Deconstruction never leaves the text in the same condition it was found in, but it also changes the reader's understanding of the ideals and ideas he or she has inherited (Deutscher 2005, 23-4). Deconstruction, then, is intervention: it opens new ways of identifying inconsistencies for the sake of heightening the awareness and prejudices of the reader. It is an event; it is something that happens, and it is something that happens from the inside (Derrida and Caputo 1997, 9).

For Jacques Derrida—the late, enigmatic and avante garde French philosopher, perhaps most commonly associated with his work in deconstruction—forgiveness is a fundamental theme. Contrary to the commentators who cleanly divide Derrida's work into epochs of linguistics, politics, and then religion, the deconstructive logic of forgiveness is manifest throughout Derrida's oeuvre. Even when it was not explicitly stated or articulated, the logic of forgiveness—the implicit rules and norms by which it operates and manifests itself—is grounded in Derrida's earliest conception of deconstruction. In light of this connection, an exploration of his understanding of forgiveness helps to frame and shed light on this broader deconstructive project.

Forgiveness, for Derrida, is the possibility of the impossible. Without any possible resolution or end other than the other itself, forgiveness remains a distinct impossibility to which we are essentially responsible. By struggling against such an impossibility, Derrida argues that forgiveness—marked by hospitality and justice—opens itself up to an unforeseen possibility. This is a possibility that remains to come, as forgiveness is a process perpetually underway and never complete. Rather than existing as a single act—a singular possibility of the in-breaking of the infinite—Derrida's articulation of forgiveness sheds light on his broader concerns with subjectivity and ethics as a condition of being marked by anxiety and responsibility. Forgiveness is the most concrete avenue through which an understanding of ethics as a subjective mode can be understood.

(Un)conditional

In typical fashion, Derrida's investigation of forgiveness as both a concept and practice reveals and deals with a set of tensions and problems typically overlooked in the issue. *Cosmopolitanism & Forgiveness* is one of the more lucid articulations of his understanding of forgiveness. In this text, Derrida analyzes the underlying logic of the process of forgiveness as a way of opening up new understandings of the possibilities embedded within forgiveness, and these understandings serve to re-frame our own engagement with forgiveness.

Derrida begins his investigation by distinguishing conditional forms of forgiveness from unconditional forgiveness. Through his employment of that distinction, he points to the logics at work in typical (conditional) articulations and expressions of forgiveness, in which the offender simply asks for forgiveness from the victim and demonstrates a marked change in action in order to receive a pardon. Accordingly, the possibility of conditional forgiveness is grounded in a clearly understood—though regularly un-stated—list of conditions which must be met in order for relations and accounts to be properly squared. There is far more at work in this unstated economy of exchange than typically meets the eye. As Derrida reveals, such an exchange actually adheres to a logic of offense, as the self shirks responsibility and projects its own agenda on to the violated other for the sake of re-establishing its own purity. Is this not a reification of the original violation operating under the guise of "resolution"? Rather than opening up to the other in that moment, and to whatever outcomes such a radical movement might be, such a form of conditional forgiveness only serves to further the victim's experience of alienation and subjection.

In addition to the inter-personal tensions, forgiveness is also riddled with its own linguistic complications. Deconstruction was never just an ambiguous, romantic ethical system by which one might speak of justice and hospitality in nonbinary terms in order to avoid exclusion. Rather, deconstruction is itself grounded in linguistic theory; it is inherently linguistic (Bennington). This is why Derrida ties the notion of *pardon* to the performance of speech as verb (Derrida 2001, 46). The pure, immediate encounter that Derrida highlights as the grounds on which forgiveness unfolds is also troubled by the necessarily linguistic nature of the exchange. Rather than opening up pure, immediate connection with the other, any real knowledge of the other or their motivation only serves to further complicate the process of forgiveness; immediate exchange and clear communication is itself a linguistic impossibility for Derrida. Language is an infinite play of interpretation, and there is no pure encounter with that which is other to the self; it is textuality all the way down the rabbit hole, which constantly features the possibility of slippage in meaning, understanding, and interpretation. Such a linguistic understanding points the radical disjunction between the self and the other, the offender. It is because of the linguistic impossibilities, the responsibility of forgiving without re-inaugurating some sort of manipulative sovereignty—a manipulative sovereignty by which the self subjugates the other in asserting its own logic and agenda onto that other—that forgiving becomes a welcoming of offense, an absorption of violation from the other in which the self simply wills to take on the injustice, to carry it forward in the name of a more perfect union (Smith 2005, 71).

Not everything is deconstructable; Derridean scholar John Caputo contends, "Everything cannot be deconstructable or, better, every *thing* is deconstructable, but justice, if such a 'thing' 'exists,' is not a *thing*" (Ibid., 130). A faithful read of deconstruction, from both critics and advocates alike, must acknowledge that deconstruction is powered by and aims at justice. Derrida grants that, "The condition of possibility of deconstruction is a call for justice" (Derrida and Caputo 1997, 17). Unlike his understanding of the "law," Derrida thinks, "Justice in itself, if such a thing exists, outside or beyond law, is not deconstructable" (Ibid., 945). Derrida's use of 'justice' seems a bit more nuanced than his use of 'law'. Deutscher illuminates, "Derrida associates justice with that which is 'infinite, incalculable, rebellious to rule and foreign to symmetry, heterogeneous and heterotropic.' But we can track a transition in Derrida from his early to his late work based on reference to undecidability" (2005, 95). Derrida remarks that justice must be 'competent': knowledgeable about the plurality and variety of language games in any given context (Ibid.).

Justice, for Derrida, is not calculable; that is, it is not something that can be figured by a computer program or a mathematical equation (Derrida and Caputo 1997, 136). Justice never looks like what is expected upon arrival. Deutscher notes, "Derrida proposes that justice is an experience of the impossible. Many of our impulses—the impulse to criticize a current regime, our attempts to improve it, or the impulse of deconstruction—occur in the name of something we think of as justice" (2005, 96). Justice will always be embedded in singularity, in judgment apart from calculation and formulaic response. In this sense justice cannot be exhausted; it does not arise from the realm of expectation.

It is for this precise reason that Derrida sees such clear correlations between conditional forgiveness and the nature of politics. He knows that the political game functions at a slant, operating in an *interested* manner and employing forgiveness as a tool towards certain beneficial ends. There always remains an essential link—a heterogeneity of sorts—between forgiveness and politics: politics remains calculated, operating according to a particular set of interests (Ibid., 72). Whenever forgiveness comes in the name of something other than itself, it is already interested, with a different purpose or end than forgiveness itself. Forgiveness in the name of maintaining business relations and leveraging a bottom line is a charade, a movement of self-interest couched in altruistic terms. This is one of the distinctive features of conditional forgiveness; as Derrida is so want to remind his readers, forgiveness in the name of reconciliation, after all, is no genuine forgiveness.

A conditional logic of forgiveness is riddled with its own infidelities. The victim may not have the capacity to forgive in their current state. As Penelope Deutscher notes, "For one thing, the forgiving subject is not self-identical to the subject who suffered. A victim may not be in a position to forgive: they may have been deprived of speech, coherence or life" (Ibid., 80). And the perpetrator may not be in the state of mind to ask for forgiveness in the first place; there may simply be no remorse or acknowledgement of any wrongdoing. Such is the reality of aggression—the assertion of the self over against the other—that Derrida highlights as marking unjust actions: it often goes untold, unspoken, never manifesting as more than a trace of a secret. It is precisely into this logic of ambiguity, condition, and difficulty that Derrida inserts his investigation of the nature of forgiveness, as a calculated exchange. Deutscher continues, "To forgive is, in a sense, to assert a sovereignty that rises above the incapacity to forgive. But 'pure forgiveness', Derrida suggests would be forgiveness without such self-appointed sovereignty. Pure forgiveness would involve forgiving what one was unable to forgive" (Ibid.). And the more this exchange takes on the form of calculation, or the prevailing logic of the system or calculated economy, the more possible it seems to become

(Caputo et al. 2001, 4). This conditional form of forgiveness happens quite often; it is manageable, and easy to pull off.

Derrida's engagement with forgiveness revolves around his analysis of the French philosopher Vladimir Jankélévitch. Jankélévitch, in and between the two texts of his own on forgiveness, argues for the unforgivable nature of the Nazi crimes; forgiveness, Jankélévitch argues, died in the death camp (1996, 56). It is precisely this space, this zone of abjection and death leading to the assertion of an absolutizing principle—not too unsimilar to his engagement with the end of history in *Specters of Marx*—that Derrida grounds his deconstructive project. Surprisingly enough, though, he begins his engagement with Jankélévitch by acknowledging that Jankélévitch has properly calculated the costs of the atrocities: it cannot add up, and there's no going back (Caputo et al. 2001, 7). This form of calculation is all too familiar to us, though, and it is this very calculation which serves to prohibit (unconditional) forgiveness in the first place. Such calculations are based in a logic of forgiveness which Derrida insists unconditional forgiveness is no forgiveness at all. The issue he takes with such a form of forgiveness is not one of *mis*calculation. Rather, he is concerned with the nature of the logic as such. In response to Jankélévitch, he writes:

> *Be this as it may, the concept of forgiveness-or the unforgivable—which is often put forward in all of these discourses, and in their commentary, remains heterogeneous to the judiciary or penal dimension that determines both the time of prescription or the imprescriptibility of the crimes. That is, unless the non-juridical dimension of forgiveness, and of the unforgivable—there where it suspends and interrupts the usual order of law—has not in fact come to inscribe itself, inscribe its*

> *interruption in the law itself. This is one of*
> *the difficulties that awaits us. (2001b, 26)*

True forgiveness—of the unconditional sort—is aporetic; it cannot center around a balanced economy of logic in which all the books are squared and the numbers add up one for one. Forgiveness must take place beyond the realm of rational accounting. Religion has typically spelled out the terms of forgiveness as an implied, inter-personal contract, deeming the conditions in which forgiveness between the divine and the human becomes possible (Caputo 2007, 73). Countering this understanding, Derrida writes, "Conditional forgiveness, for example, [is] that forgiveness which is inscribed within a set of conditions of all kinds, psychological, political, juridical above all (since forgiveness is bound up with the judiciary as penal order)" (2001b, 45).

This logic of calculation, interest, and condition, though, flies in the face of the other form of forgiveness at play in Derrida's analysis: unconditional forgiveness. Unconditional forgiveness operates according to an alternative economic logic; it is incalculable and indeterminate, and it always operates according to its own end, as it is that end itself (Smith 2005, 71). True forgiveness—what Derrida wants to refer to as *pure* forgiveness—does not reduce down to a particular form of knowledge, certainty, or recognition (Deutscher 2005, 107).

If we were only ever prepared to forgive venial sins—those deemed by the Catholic institution as minor and not worthy of damnation, as opposed to mortal sins—we would have already done away with the idea of forgiveness itself (Derrida 2001a, 32). Forgiveness should never amount to a calculated therapy of reconciliation (Ibid., 43). He writes, "What I dream of, what I try to think as the 'purity' of a forgiveness worthy of its name, would be a forgiveness without power: *unconditional but without sovereignty* [emphasis original]" (Ibid., 59). Such a shift signifies Derrida's interest in an unconditional form of forgiveness, which ultimately renounces any attentiveness in charging interest, any concern in getting even at all (Caputo 1997, 228). Such a forgiveness defies the logic of conditions (Caputo 2007, 73). Unconditional forgiveness, in contrast to the calculated logic and list of conditions, welcomes offense, absorbing completely the wrongdoings of the other. In this alternative logic of unconditional forgiveness, Derrida finds striking similarities and irreducible relations between forgiveness and the notion of the gift. He aims to articulate forgiveness within such terms rather than those of exchange and debt (2001b, 22). The gift defies logic and calculation; it cannot be anticipated, and it is in no way reciprocal or demanded (Caputo 2007, 73). The gift is no secret sort of calculation by which one indebts the other (Caputo 1997, 178). Rather, true forgiveness is an uneconomic reality, something unconditional and mad—something off the books altogether. Such a relation is characterized by relating to the other on their own terms rather than any self-interested agenda (2005, 71).

"Forgiveness" of the venial—acts which logically entails being forgiven—is no forgiveness at all, and Derrida was surely familiar with Jesus's outright claims of this alternative logic at work in his deconstruction of love (2001b, 30).[100] Derrida is trying to shift away from a *conditional logic of exchange* and point to an alternative logic of madness (2001a, 39). He writes, "If there is something to forgive, it would be what in religious language is called mortal sin, the worst, the unforgiveable crime or harm. Form which comes the aporia, which can be described in its dry and implacable formality, without mercy: forgiveness forgives only the forgivable" (Ibid., 32). Contrary to Jankélévitch's claim that forgiveness died in the death camp, Derrida argues that it is precisely within such spaces of horror, atrocity, and impossibility that for-

---

[100] See, Matthew 5.

giveness finds its actual possibility (Ibid., and Jankélévitch 2013, 567). It's in light of these refusals of calculation that leads Derrida to proclaim that true forgiveness—uncalculated forgiveness—can only forgive that which is truly unforgiveable. The mortal sin—the unforgiveable act—is the very grounding and foundation of unconditional forgiveness (Derrida 2001a, 31-2). He argues, "There is in forgiveness, in the very meaning of forgiveness, a force, a desire, an impetus, a movement, an appeal (call it what you will) that demands that forgiveness be granted, if it can be, even to someone who does not ask for it, who does not repent or confess or improve or redeem himself, beyond, consequently, an entire identificatory, spiritual, whether sublime or not, economy, beyond all expiation even" (2001b, 28). It is precisely in this space that true forgiveness finds its grounding and becomes possible, even in the midst of its own impossibility.

The hyperbolical ethics at play in forgiveness demands of us to forgive when forgiveness has not been requested and is not deserved. It is precisely in these spaces, in the zones where there is no reciprocity and forgiveness is most underserved that forgiveness actually becomes possible (Derrida 2001b, 29). Unconditional, pure forgiveness is, if it is a thing at all, is certainly not concerned with a squaring of the accounts or a balancing of the books. That is, the very condition of forgiveness is its impossibility. If forgiveness is a thing—Derrida constantly reminds us it may not be—then it is impossibility itself; it is the condition of impossibility as such (2001a, 33). On this notion, Caputo, Dooley, and Scanlon argue that "Forgiveness begins by the im-possible, where this 'im-' is not a simple negation by an intensification, driving forgiveness to the most extreme possibility, impelling forgiveness to the possibility of the impossible" (2001, 5). This zone of impossibility, demarcated by the unforgiveable acts of Nazi Germany, is the very grounding and origin of real forgiveness (Derrida 2001b, 30).

That being said, the impossibility of forgiveness does not point to its ontological condition, to the potential of its eruption into time and space. Rather, Derrida aims to articulate the poetic dimensions of forgiveness, the economies and logics by which various forms of the thing are lodged into popular consciousness. The impossiblei is actually the only actualizable form of forgiveness, which is precisely what leads Derrida to argue for the possibility of forgiveness, for the possibility of the impossible *as such*. He writes, "Thus forgiveness, if it is possible, if there is such a thing, is not possible, it does not exist as possible, it only exists by exempting itself from the law of the possible, by impossibilizing itself, so to speak, and in the infinite endurance of the im-possible as impossible" (Ibid., 48).

(Un)characterizable

Commonsense tells us that the victim and the perpetrator should have a common understanding of the crime—an exhaustive list of injuries and consequences unfolding in the wake of the terrible event itself. On this notion, Deutscher writes, "But it is impossible that complete harmony of comprehension and experience could occur, just as it is impossible that any one subject could attain a definitive, self-identical and thoroughly resolved experience, understanding or memory of the event in question (whether they suffered or inflicted it)" (2005, 80). Whatever conditioning or sharing of terms we might be tempted to do would re-establish the sort of sovereign egoism Derrida's entire project is trying to shift away from (Smith 2005, 71). Forgiveness requires an absolute encounter, which is riddled with linguistic impossibilities, dynamics of sovereignty and mastery, and this all falls under the limiting, calculated economic logic that Derrida is so critical of.

Speaking of the juridical order's inability to make sense of unconditional forgiveness, Derrida writes, "In the enigma of the forgiveness of the unforgiveable, there is a sort of 'madness' which the juridico-political cannot approach, much less appropriate" (2001a, 55). Genuine forgiveness—an impossible project—stems from undecidability, from an inability or refusal to land, finish, and determine. On this point, Derrida writes:

> *I shall risk this proposition: each time forgiveness is at the service of a finality, be it noble and spiritual (atonement or redemption, reconciliation, salvation), each time that it aims to re-establish a normality (social, national, political, psychological) by a work of mourning, by some therapy or ecology of memory, then the 'forgiveness' is not pure—nor is its concept. Forgiveness is not, it should not be, normal, normative, normalizing. It should remain exceptional and extraordinary, in the face of the impossible: as if it interrupted the ordinary course of historical temporality. (Ibid., 32)*

This is precisely why Derrida speaks of forgiveness in terms of a perpetually unresolved condition. If forgiveness is to be concerned with justice at all, which Derrida very much thinks it should be, then it must remain unresolved (Caputo et al. 2001, 7). Deutscher explains that, "The impossibility inhabits us with a kind of foreignness, that unsettles and operates as a king of internal critique of the inadequate hospitalities (gifts, pardons) we do accomplish" (2005, 106). Something is not quite right when injustices and forgiveness are squared away too quickly (Ibid.). The unconditional terms have to pass in and through the conditions, the possibilities of determination as we negotiate the most appropriate response to the issue at hand; it remains to come (Caputo et al. 2001, 5).

If we are to say that forgiveness is even possible, we have to own up the possibility that it has not even occurred yet (Deutscher 2005, 79). This unresolved condition with the event itself yet to come, though en route, is the aporia of forgiveness—its condition of indeterminacy and undecidability (Caputo 2007, 73). Forgiveness is an ongoing process, a way of being situated in a certain attempt at justice. On this notion, Derrida writes, "I always betray one for the other, I perjure myself like I breathe. And this is endless, for not only am I always asking forgiveness for a perjury but I always risk perjuring myself by forgiving, of betraying someone else by forgiving, for one is always doomed to forgive (thus abusively) in the name of another" (2001b, 49). Forgiveness can never be final; it's an ongoing act, a condition of being (Derrida 2001a, 52).

(Inter)subjectivity

The anxiety at play in Derrida's notion of forgiveness, riddled with ethical responsibility, points to a condition of being, to a way of positioning the self in relation to others for the sake of fostering justice, of bearing witness to a coming justice that has yet to appear. This notion of forgiveness, marked by anxiety, as an ethical condition stemming from a robust form of subjectivity in the wake of a critique of onto-theology is an obvious point of influence and correlation between Derrida and Emmanuel Levinas. That is, the condition of being Derrida aims to illuminate in his analysis of forgiveness is made all the more lucid in Levinas's notion of subjectivity. Because of Derrida's explicit indebtedness to Levinas's broader project, such assertions seem fairly obvious (Derrida 1993). But a closer look into Levinas's radical inter-subjectivity reveals the deconstructive, unconditional logic of Derridean forgiveness as an ontological, subjective mode of being.

Levinas's chief philosophical task was to describe an ethic relation irreducible to comprehension. For Levinas, ontological relations go hand in hand with the reduction of alterity to sameness, which has essentially characterized the project of Western thought (1996c, 11). This original relation happens in speech, through noncomprehensive, nonsubstantive relations because they deal in the particularities of the one speaking rather than some abstracted universalization. This is primarily an ethical relationship for Levinas. The ethical, though, is not a system of rules for guidance in the mind of Levinas. It is the event of being in an irreducible relation with the other, and this nonsubstantive relation, when we properly approach it, is nothing less than a breach in the horizon (1996b, 10). This relation, this irreducible encounter with the other must be mediated in a certain way so as to make room for the other. Within this encounter relation is itself an entire ethic, and Levinas believes such an ethic to be the foundation of ethics and philosophy as such. We must let the other call us into question; we must discover ourselves put into questioning by the other (Ibid., 4). This ethic is what Levinas refers to as "the problem of comprehension," whereby he means to point to our tendency to seize and assume the other rather than letting him speak for itself. This ethical relation is also characterized by responsibility. We assume responsibility for the other from the very moment of our initial relation to him, which has always already happened (Levinas 1996e, 18). This sort of non-reductionist examination of tactile relations, as they are grounded in encountering the face of the other, stand in stark contrast to the thematizable nature of Being in the work of Heidegger (Ibid., 19).

In Levinas's reflections on his own work in *Ethics & Infinity*, he writes, "In [*Otherwise than Being*] I speak of responsibility as the essential, primary and fundamental mode of subjectivity. For I describe subjectivity in ethical terms. Ethics, here, does not supplement a preceding existential base [as Heidegger would have it]; the very node of the subjective is knotted in ethics understood as responsibility" (1985, 95). This plainly spoken notion is incredibly illuminating. Levinas is essentially surmising that responsibility is the foundational notion of his entire philosophical project. It is the basis of his discussion of alterity, ethics and subjectivity. He continues, "The tie with the other is knotted only as responsibility" (Ibid., 97). Responsibility itself is constitutive of the self's ego; it is that which links the subject to the exterior world, to that which is necessarily other. All sociality is rooted in this ethical responsibility, and such a lucid statement is quite illuminating.

Otherwise Than Being revolves around a beautifully simple, drastically important thesis: ethics precedes ontology. This, being Levinas's central claim of the work, highlights the notion that the ethical relation grounds all being. That is, responsibility both precedes and supersedes all knowledge of being. The other, Levinas argues, interrupts being—in the Heideggarian sense of us being in relation to Being—and calls us beyond Being toward the realm of responsibility to the other. *Otherwise than Being*, then, serves as a radical critique of the history of philosophy up through Heidegger, a history that has posited "First philosophy" as the comprehension of beings. "Being" for Levinas, though, is only relevant in the sense that the self exists in its being for the other.

The ethical relationship to the other is an irreducible reality for Levinas. It is not some part of a systematized reality in which others are able to stand in the place of the self while still maintaining the authenticity of the relationship. Levinas writes, "In the saying of responsibility, which is an exposure to an obligation for which no one could replace me, I am unique" (1998, 138). In a similar sense, the ethical responsibility necessarily implicated by the self's encounter with the other is also irreducible (Ibid., 135). Along these lines, Levinas stresses the ways in which the self is essentially unable to gather itself apart from its inherent responsibility to the other.

It seems that Levinas's notion of subjectivity, or what should actually be referred to as a dramatic *inter*-subjectivity, comes through most clearly on this point (Bergo 2015). For Levinas, the self is not constructed, actualized or realized in relation to Being in general. Rather, the self's essential nature, which is hardly essential at all, is only ever possible in relation to the other. Alterity, then, is the constitutive element of subjectivity. Whereas the thrust of *Totality & Infinity* seems to lie in Levinas's analysis of the other, *Otherwise than Being* sees the analysis turned back toward the self, toward the position and meaning of the subject who meets the other in the ethical encounter (Peperzak, 212). And it is in this ethical encounter that Levinasian inter-subjectivity is most lucidly understood. This ethical inter-subjectivity—ethical responsibility to the infinite other stemming from always-already-previously-established inter-subjective encounter—bears witness the condition of being that Derrida aims to characterize in his investigation of forgiveness, and there can be no doubt that such conceptions of being serve to undergird his broader analysis of forgiveness. This inter-subjectivity is, for Derrida, yet another way of speaking of forgiveness as a mode of being.

(Un)certainty

Derrida remained quite clear throughout his investigations of forgiveness and hospitality that pure acts—pure justice, pure forgiveness, pure love—themselves are impossible and may not have ever actually occurred. They cannot simply appear on their own, though. Much like the phenomenon of pure hospitality—hospitality as such, in its purest form—requires the tangible actor through which to materialize, so it is with forgiveness (Derrida 2001a, 45). Forgiveness in its purest form functions as a sort of relation of references in which the concrete act bears witness to the possibility of the pure thing, a pure thing coming at the least expected time, like a thief in the night (Ibid.). Derrida's analysis, and Derrida himself, remains trapped in a certain anxiety between two dimensions of forgiveness. He's torn between the limit and the limitless, strung out somewhere between that which is and that which could be: between the possible and the impossible. This condition, though, does not lead to despair; rather, it is a calling of sorts, a tension we are responsible to bear in ourselves (Smith 2006, 71).

Forgiveness is not merely a gift, which is to say it is not merely something which comes upon us at unexpected times. Rather, it is an ethical condition and possibility to which we are deeply responsible. As a release from the calculated, foreseeable forms of economic relations, forgiveness is the impossibility to which we are responsible for making possible (Caputo 1997, 227). It is a shift in the relationality, as we no longer encounter one another—each the other—in terms of debt. Forgiveness is the foundation of responsibility (Ibid.). There can be no divorcing his notion of forgiveness from the broader understanding of the ethical/subjective human situation.

Forgiveness is impossibility itself—the condition of impossibility (Derrida 2001a, 33). And in that sense it signifies the larger ethical condition of intersubjectvity that Derrida is so keen to shed light on. Forgiveness remains impossible, and we are responsible to it nonetheless. In its impossibility, in responding with a forgiveness worthy of operating under such a name, we might find new possibilities. Derrida writes:

> *These two poles, the unconditional and the conditional, are absolutely heterogeneous, and must remain irreducible to one another. They are nonetheless indissociable: if one wants, and it is necessary, forgiveness to become effective, concrete, historical; if one wants it to arrive, to happen by changing things, it is necessary that this purity engage itself in a series of conditions of all kinds (psychological, political, etc.). It is between these two poles, irreconcilable but indissociable, that decisions and responsibilities are to be taken. (Ibid.)*

Forgiveness pulls us in two different directions simultaneously. On the one hand, we are called to mobilize it, to make it effective and to bring it out of its entrapment in the logic of condition and calculation so that it can concretize itself in the spheres of injustice that serve to plague humanity—politics, religion, law. At the same time, though, we are confronted by its own force of becoming, by the impossibility of ever enacting forgiveness in its purest form (Caputo et al. 2001, 8). It is these twin tensions, being pulled in these different directions that serve to keep both us and forgiveness—as a condition of being—open to that which has yet to come.

Derridean forgiveness characterizes the essence of the moral struggle as a condition and mode of being human. The only condition for the sort of forgiveness that Derrida is aiming for is through a certain openness of being, an orientation of the spirit as a continual condition—anxiety. This is the sort of anxiety Kierkegaard called for when facing a similar set of contradictory movements. Forgiveness is that to which we are ultimately responsible, but it is also the juridical impossibility which continually eludes our efforts. Forgiveness shows itself only through a certain embrace of the anxiety, which Kierkegaard reminds us essentially characterizes human being, not in a fixed, normative state (1981). On the contrary, it marks the experience to which we must continually attune ourselves. Anxiety is essential to the possibility of forgiveness as it signifies the ethical-political dimensions of human subjectivity.

Conclusion: madness of new economies

Such characterizations are not for the sake of absolutizing forgiveness as a moral standard; rather, this rendition serves to shed light on the force buried within forgiveness itself, the force that disturbs and haunts us, calling us to head toward new moral horizons and possibilities, to alternative economies and more just conceptions of justice itself (Caputo et al 2001, 8). Pure forgiveness—unconditional forgiveness as the possibility of the impossible—is the radical inauguration of a new economy, new possibilities of an alternative order.

There is real possibility in this impossible task. Derrida constantly works to remind his readers that pure gifts are unfolding around us, which we are perpetually missing. What might a shift in our calculated, economically-minded forms of logic do to attune ourselves to that which is unfolding around us? And does the real possibility of this from of forgiveness not free us from these tensions in everyone but our own selves? Is the impetus for genuine forgiveness not on us now? That is a haunting/freeing tension. Such an understanding places unconditional, genuine forgiveness within the realm of the impossible. In Derridean terms, though, this is an impossible task to which we are markedly responsible, and it is in this space that forgiveness actually becomes a reality. For Derrida, the impossible is not a simple logical category. Rather, the tension at work in such a claim as "forgiveness is the possibility of the impossible," marks an opening, an aporia, against which we have to struggle beyond the limits of the foreseeable horizon in order to open up new possibilities not yet in view.

Derrida still haunts us as a specter of sorts, refusing to leave us alone once and for all (2006a). The possibility, the impossible passageway through which we are responsible for passing through, is only found in the midst of a certain destruction, a problematizing of the issue which itself serves as the constructive aspect of de-construction. Only through such a haunting, in light of the new possibilities which it is calling us toward and challenging us to inhabit, can we begin to realize, as Derrida himself argued for so long, that "The madness is perhaps not so mad . . ." (2001a, 60).

References

Bennington, Geoffrey. Accessed March 20, 2016. "Embarrassing Ourselves: On Of Grammatology: The Fortieth Anniversary Edition." *The Los Angeles Review of Books.* https://lareviewofbooks.org/review/embarrassing-ourselves/.

Bergo, Bettina. 2015. "Emmanuel Levinas" *The Stanford Encyclopedia of Philosophy.* Edited by Edward N. Zalta. Accessed Summer 2015. http://plato.stanford.edu/archives/sum2015/entries/levinas/.

Caputo, John D. 2007. *What Would Jesus Deconstruct?: The Good News of Postmodernism for the Church.* Grand Rapids, MI: Baker Academic.

———. 1997. *The Prayers and Tears of Jacques Derrida: Religion Without Religion.* Bloomington, IN: Indiana University Press.

Caputo, John D., Mark Dooley, and Michael J Scanlon. 2001. "Introduction: God Forgive." *Questioning God.* Edited by John D Caputo, Michael J Scanlon, and Mark Dooley. Bloomington: Indiana University Press.

Derrida, Jacques. 2016. *Of Grammatology.* 40th Anniversary Edition. Baltimore: Johns Hopkins University Press.

———. 2006a. *Specters of Marx: The State of the Debt, The Work of Mourning & the New International.* First Edition. New York: Routledge.

———. 2006b *The Politics of Friendship.* Translated by George Collins. London: Verso.

———. 2001a. *On Cosmopolitanism and Forgiveness.* London; New York: Routledge.

———. 2001b. "To Forgive: The Unforgivable and the Imprescriptible." *Questioning God*, Edited by John D Caputo, Michael J Scanlon, and Mark Dooley. Bloomington: Indiana University Press.

———. [1978] 1993. "Violence and Metaphysics: An Essay on the Thought of Emmanuel Levinas." *Writing and Difference*, Reprint. Chicago: University of Chicago Press.

Derrida, Jacques, and John D Caputo. 1997. *Deconstruction in a Nutshell: A Conversation with Jacques Derrida.* New York: Fordham University Press.

Derrida, Jacques, and Richard Kearney. 2001. "On Forgiveness: A Roundtable Discussion with Jacques Derrida." *Questioning God.*

Deutscher, Penelope. 2005. *How to Read Derrida.* New York: W.W. Norton.

Jankélévitch, Vladimir. 2013. *Forgiveness.* Translated by Andrew Kelley. Chicago: University Of Chicago Press.

———. 1996. "Should We Pardon Them?" Translated by Ann Hobart. *Critical Inquiry* 22.3: 552–72.

Kierkegaard, Soren, and Albert B. Anderson. 1981. *The Concept of Anxiety: A Simple Psychologically Orienting Deliberation on the Dogmatic Issue of Hereditary Sin*. Edited by Reidar Thomte. Princeton: Princeton University Press.

Levinas, Emmanuel. 1998. *Otherwise Than Being: Or Beyond Essence*. Pittsburgh: Duquesne University Press.

———. 1996a. "God & Philosophy." *Emannuel Levinas: Basic Philosophical Writings*. Edited by Adriaan Theodoor Peperzak, Simon Critchley, and Robert Bernasconi. Bloomington: Indiana University Press.

———. 1996b. "Is Ontology Fundamental?" *Emannuel Levinas: Basic Philosophical Writings*.

———. 1996c. "Meaning & Sense." *Emannuel Levinas: Basic Philosophical Writings*.

———. 1996d. "Substitution." *Emannuel Levinas: Basic Philosophical Writings*.

———. 1996e. "Transcendence & Height." *Emannuel Levinas: Basic Philosophical Writings*.

———. 1996f. "Transcendence & Intelligibility." *Emannuel Levinas: Basic Philosophical Writings*.

———. 1996g. "Truth of Disclosure and Truth of Testimony." *Emannuel Levinas: Basic Philosophical Writings*.

———. 1985. *Ethics and Infinity: Conversations with Philippe Nemo*. Pittsburgh: Duquesne University Press.

———. 1969. *Totality and Infinity: An Essay on Exteriority*. Pittsburgh: Duquesne University Press.

Macey, David. 2001. "Jacques Derrida." *The Penguin Dictionary of Critical Theory*. New York: Penguin Books.

Mautner, Thomas, and Bernard Harrison (Editors). 2005. "Jacques Derrida." *The Penguin Dictionary of Philosophy*. London; New York: Penguin.

Murphy, Ann V. 2014. "On Forgiveness and the Possibility of Reconciliation." *A Companion to Derrida*. Edited by Zeynep Direk and Leonard Lawlor. Hoboken: Wiley-Blackwell.

Peperzak, Adrian. [1993] 2005. *To the Other: An Introduction to the Philosophy of Emmanuel Levinas*. West Lafayette, IN: Purdue University Press.

Reynolds, Jack. Accessed December 2015. "Derrida, Jacques | Internet Encyclopedia of Philosophy." http://www.iep.utm.edu/derrida/#SH7c.

Smith, James K. A. 2006. *Who's Afraid of Postmodernism?: Taking Derrida, Lyotard, and Foucault to Church*. Grand Rapids, MI: Baker Academic.

———. 2005. *Jacques Derrida: Live Theory*. New York; London: Continuum.

Verdeja, Ernesto. 2004. "Derrida and the Impossibility of Forgiveness." *Contemporary Political Theory* 3.1: 23–47.

Chapter 12

Absolute Forgiveness: Material Intimacy and Recognition in Hegel

Jeff Lambert

take a writer away from his typewriter

and all you have left

is

the sickness

which started him

typing

in the

beginning

—"about the PEN conference," Charles Bukowski

In Hegel's *Phenomenology of Spirit,* the moment of complete recognition[101] is crucial to the full growth of Spirit, and this

---

[101] It should be clarified what the term 'recognition' means for Hegel and how this differs from 'understanding'. To briefly summarize, for Hegel, recognition is the acknowledgement of the other as an equal agent. Understanding, on the other hand, is more generally used in this paper to indicate proper or improper comprehension of a given issue.

complete recognition is realized through the act of forgiveness. However, recognition is not complete, for Hegel, until it is completely universal; that is, recognition must be universal with regard to both Substance and Subject. Thus, forgiveness must feature recognition not only of Subject but also of Substance. It will be argued that this recognition can be understood to be synonymous with a kind of intimacy. When we say 'intimacy', though, we do not simply mean the close relationship established between at least two individuals—if this were the case, then the Subjective recognition which takes the form of forgiveness at the end of the section labeled "Morality" would establish a complete intimacy—rather, we mean a complete intimacy which extends to both Subject and Substance. Such an intimacy recognizes the irrefutable relationship between the Subject who acts *as substantiated* (embodied) as well as the correspondent connection between Substance and the animating Subject. When the movement to Absolute Knowing occurs, it is because this complete intimacy is at play in the forgiveness which takes place after Substance and Subject are recognized in each other. However, it will be argued that even though aspects of Substance may appear throughout "Spirit" and "Religion," the realization of the universality of Substance is inhibited in one way or another in these sections. The reason for the inclusion of the poem by Bukowski is to show that without the recognition of itself as Substance, Spirit will never be free of the "sickness" that prevented it from reaching absolute knowing in the first place.

To show this, we will have to carefully work through various sections from "Spirit," "Religion," and "Absolute Knowing." Additionally, we will have to acknowledge that such a reading conflicts with the readings of Catherine Malabou and John Russon. We will also address points of agreeance and dispute with Rebecca Comay's reading in *Mourning Sickness*. However, both Malabou and Russon clearly agree that a crucial element of forgiveness, for Hegel, is the recognition of Substance. The conflict between the reading offered here and those put forward by Russon and Malabou is that they overemphasize the import of the "Morality" section and claim that substantial recognition does occur in "Morality." Thus, it will be argued that both missed the necessity of the reconciliation through incarnation in "Religion." Our task then, is to show the deficiency of the recognition at the end of "Morality," how this deficiency is corrected in "Religion," and to highlight the material intimacy that Hegel's recognition—and forgiveness—insists upon.

At the end of the "Spirit" section, Hegel shows how forgiveness is the resolution of the moral spirit which culminates in the recognition that occurs due to the realization of the relationship between the two moral actors. Once forgiveness truly takes place, then one is able to realize that the other moral actor *is* oneself in the negative, but more profoundly, one realizes that this negation is itself negated by the universal which unites them. This status is verified by the act of forgiveness. However, the search for recognition of oneself as both universal and singular has been the primary problem throughout the *Phenomenology of Spirit*, so why is this act of forgiveness not the end of the book? Why does one need "Religion" or even "Absolute Knowing" if the resolution of "Spirit" culminates in recognition through the forgiveness which occurs at the end of "Morality"?

It will be argued that the recognition found at the end of "Spirit" is one that *primarily* pertains to Subject rather than Substance. We know from both the Preface and the section on "Absolute Knowing" that recognition of both Subject and Substance must occur, otherwise the recognition of universality and singularity is not total and one cannot understand the way in which all the immediacies are actually still alienated and mediated. This is the act of sublation that one becomes aware of once one becomes an absolute knower. The seeming incommensurability of Subject and Substance is understood in terms of the negative, which works to show how this alienation both is and is not.

It will be shown then that substantial recognition does not begin to happen until the incarnation in the "Religion" section. Moreover, it will be argued that recognition is a type of *intimacy*, and one which is not complete until the substantial aspect has occurred. Thus, absolute, or full and true, forgiveness, does not occur without a recognition of material intimacy.

The (non) presence of Substance in Spirit

In order to prove that Substance is not fully a part of the recognition which occurs in the moment of forgiveness at the end of "Morality," we will argue that whatever substantial or objective element there is in Spirit ends up being subsumed by the subjective side of Spirit. We will start by showing what role Substance does play in Spirit and "Morality."

It would be unwise to argue that Substance is *completely* absent from Spirit. Hegel explicitly writes that Spirit passes back through sense-certainty. As he notes in the second moment of the positive truth of Enlightenment, sense-certainty returns: "Consciousness, which in its very first reality is sense-certainty and mere 'meaning', returns here to this form of the whole course of its experience and is again a knowledge of what is *purely negative of itself*, or of *things of sense*, i.e. of things which *immediately* and indifferently confront its *being-for-self*" (Hegel 1977, par. 558). If sense-certainty—which surely deals with Substance, since sense-certainty is, briefly summarized, the blind assertion of what seems blatantly obvious to the senses[102]—is reappearing

---

[102] Something like the simple pronouncement "I exist!" is the immediate assertion of sense-certainty. Whereas Descartes may be looking for such 'intuitive' knowledge, Hegel is suggesting that any knowledge which is immediately clear to us is not actually immediately clear because the method by which it is clear remains opaque—it all happens too fast.

here, then it becomes difficult to dismiss the idea that Substance is included in the recognition which occurs in forgiveness. This appearance of Substance is made even more apparent when, at the beginning of the subsection on "Morality," Hegel writes:

> *The movement of the world of culture and faith does away with this abstraction of the person, and, through the completed alienation, through ultimate abstraction, Substance becomes for Spirit at first the universal will and finally Spirit's own possession. Here, then, knowledge appears at last to have become completely identical with its truth; for its truth is this very knowledge and any antithesis between the two sides has vanished, vanished not only for us or in itself, but for self-consciousness itself. (Ibid., par. 596)*

Perhaps then, the problem is that even though Substance becomes Spirit's possession, Substance is not wholly Substance in-itself when it is possessed by Spirit's current shape. Like having a car before you have your driver's license; perhaps Spirit possesses Substance in some way but Substance is not yet *active* in Spirit. If this is the case, then when the resolution of forgiveness occurs, Substance is not fully recognized as it is but rather only as Spirit holds it to be in its current shape.

Another obstacle that makes it difficult to accept the possibility that Substance is fully recognized in Spirit at the end of "Morality," comes from Hegel himself in "Absolute Knowing": "This reconciliation of consciousness with self-consciousness thus shows itself as brought about from two sides; on one side, in the religious Spirit, and on the other side, in consciousness itself as such" (Ibid., par. 794). The fact that this reconciliation has two sides, one of which is self-consciousness and the other consciousness, seems to be evidence that "Morality" only deals with part of the problem being resolved through forgiveness. The other side of this comes about within the "Religion" chapter, culminating in the incarnation. Additionally, we should be aware of the way in which intimacy is an integral part of this process and never surpassed, not even once we are absolute knowers.

How is it that Substance, in terms of intimacy, could be more than just the recognition between two embodied subjects? Russon seems to provide some help with regard to this question:

> *This forgiveness... can be adequately effected only by an agency that is capable both of identifying the phenomenon to be understood and identifying it as a phenomenon, and that is capable of seeing it in its integrity as internally unified; it must be able to recognize both the proper extent and the proper intent, and this means the logic of its own comprehension must be adequate to the logic that actually animates the thing... [The agent] must know the object as animated by the same internal dynamic that actually animates it. (Russon 2001, 113)*

It seems then, that the intimacy comes into play through the fact that this realization that the object perceived and the perceiving agent are consistently linked through a commonality which must be continuously upheld. This commonality is Substance and while the same distinct Substance is not the *self* as the individuated Substance one knows to be one's "*self*," this other Substance defines the limits of one's "self" by way of being "*not oneself.*" Thus we are each of us inextricably tied to this other common Substance by way of which we know the boundaries of our "self"—simultaneously this now asserts the Substance we call "self" to truly be an individuated self and not just the Substantial aspect of the total individual Subject. Thus, simply identifying, as Subject, some other manifest thing as Substance and one's self as Substance is not enough, it is not enough to realize some individual Substance as distinct from one's self. We must realize that we are all distinct Substances in a universal way which negate and affirm one another simultaneously. Therefore, we know that to answer our question regarding intimacy and forgiveness with respect to Substance, we will have to show the relationship between how we comprehend Subject and how we comprehend Substance.

I forgive you if you forgive me

The section "Absolute Freedom and Terror" ends with the realization that there must be some universal moral shape of Spirit. Moral duty is understood to be primary to all else, particularly the sensuous. Even though both "pure thought and the sensuous aspect of consciousness, are *in themselves a single consciousness*," this is not clear to the moral consciousness (Hegel 1977, par. 603). In its current shape, "*qua* consciousness," all that is realized is the rejection of what is viewed as "the antithesis of itself"—that is, the "impulses and instincts" of Nature (Ibid., par. 603)—and thus, Reason, or the moral consciousness, is at odds with Nature because it cannot be subject to the whims of impulses and instincts if it is to be moral. This contradiction must be overcome through unification, but Reason is completely against the idea of unifying with Nature; thus, this unification must be one in which Nature is subsumed into Reason. This much is clear when Hegel writes, "Since of the two moments of the antithesis, sensuousness is sheer *otherness*, or the negative, while, on the other hand, the pure thought of duty is the essence, no element of which can be given up, it seems that the resultant unity can only be brought about by getting rid of sensuousness" (Ibid., par. 603). The issue is that sensuousness is *necessary as negative* and as a part of the unity, the unity does not even occur if one part—sensuousness—is simply subtracted from the equation. It is worth highlighting here that Reason's hesitance toward material intimacy in the form of substantial recognition is the main obstacle to achieving unity. Spirit cannot fully mature without acknowledging itself as both Subject (Reason) and Substance (Nature). As an alternative to actually unifying Reason with Nature, a "postulated being" is constructed in which the unity *does* occur. Of course, this postulated being does not ever really occur because the unity does not, and seemingly cannot, occur given the current incommensurability of Reason and Nature. Therefore, in order to avoid the problems that the unity would encounter, the unity is instead infinitely deferred; "this process has to be projected into a future infinitely remote; for if it actually came about, this would do away with the moral consciousness" (Ibid., par. 603). That is, it would "do away with moral consciousness" because the moral consciousness is not yet ready to recognize the necessity of nature/the sensuous.

Now, this deferred unity does in fact occur eventually for the absolute knower. So far, though, it is unclear whether or not this unity is still deferred when forgiveness first comes on the scene. It certainly seems to be the case that if forgiveness truly is the resolution of the moral consciousness in Spirit, then it would have to resolve the tension between Reason and Nature.

Moving somewhat quickly through the "Morality" section, we come to the duplicitous nature of the moral consciousness. As "The moral view of the world" section comes to close, we realize that it is impossible to exist as a perfect moral agent in reality (Ibid., par. 613). The paradox that arises from this, though, is not only that the realization of the perfect moral world is what inhibits the perfect moral existence and thus renders it imperfect, but the imperfect moral existence would also be inhibited if it did not realize the perfect transcendent morality which can only be imagined and never realized (Ibid., par. 614-5).

That leaves us quite a bit of jargon to sort through, but we can imagine that we are children again, excited about the gifts that we will be receiving on our birthday. This suspense of "not-knowing" what gifts we might receive is easily the key part of this excitement. Perhaps the excitement becomes too much and we decide to peek at our gifts so that we can know what we are getting on our birthday. Suppose, though, that after we peek at our gifts, the birthday itself becomes meaningless in terms of the suspense it offers—we already know what we will receive once the day arrives. However, without the occasion of our birthday, there would be no gifts to be excited about. In a similar fashion, we have this perfect moral world, which we are excited to learn more about and to implement. Learning more about the perfect world only discloses that it is impossible and that what we are left with is an imperfect moral world. The perfect moral world still exists, much like our actual birthday will arrive, but the grandeur is diminished since we now realize it to be impossible, just as the grandeur of the suspense of not knowing what gifts we will (or will not) receive is now lost. Nonetheless, neither the receiving of gifts nor the realization of the imperfect moral world would have been possible without what preceded them. To be perfectly moral is impossible, but without realizing the impossibility of perfect morality there can be no imperfect morality which strives toward an unachievable perfection. This, unfortunately, becomes even more complicated as the transition is made to the "Dissemblance or duplicity" section.

The moral view of the world believes itself to be the producer of its object, which is moral duty, and thus perceives there to be no alienation between the moral viewpoint and the object of duty (Ibid., par. 616). As Hegel remarks, all seems well and good at this point, as the moral view should be at peace with this unity. However, "consciousness itself really places the object *outside* itself as a beyond of itself. But this object with an intrinsic being of its own is equally posited as being, not free from self-consciousness, but as existing in the interest of, and by means of, [self-consciousness]" (Ibid., par. 616). Thus, we start to see the ways in which the moral consciousness consistently contradicts itself; by placing its foundational object as a beyond, it has untethered itself from its very foundation. In order for the moral consciousness to be able to act, it is necessary for there to be a supposed harmony between morality/Reason and Nature. However, as we already made clear, this unity is only a pretense which is actually a subsumption of Nature into Reason, but the fact that this is a pretense must be overlooked in the action if the action is to follow from itself—that is, the act of the moral consciousness must follow from the harmony of the moral consciousness *even though this harmony is only a pretense*. If there were no harmony then the moral consciousness would not be unified and properly constituted, thus disabling it in terms of action. The moral consciousness needs to assume, "for the sake of the action, i.e. for the sake of the *actual* harmony of purpose and actuality, this harmony is postulated as *not* actual, as a beyond" (Ibid., par. 618).

Thus we see that the intimacy, recognition or affirmation of relation—whatever we want to call it—between morality and Nature is understood as a *beyond*, as something deferred but possible.[103] Once again, the tension of Subject and Substance, as it is related here, is one in which Substance is de-

---

[103] Rebecca Comay, in her book *Mourning Sickness*, does not appear entirely convinced that "forgiveness," as Hegel understands it, is altogether possible. Comay is especially critical of Hegel's recourse to God and the way he seems to pull the "Religion" section of the text almost out of nowhere after having written himself into a corner as far as the development of Spirit goes (Comay 2010, 118). However, we are taking the stance that the "Religion" section is more than "bland God-talk" and, while perhaps overly theistically dependent, works to illustrate the necessary connection between Substance and Subject in the incarnation.

ferred and understood as incommensurate with the moral consciousness. Because it seems so blatantly obvious that the problem here lies in the recognition of Substance, we must assume that if forgiveness does resolve the issues present in "Morality," then it must do so in a still limited way if this problem is revisited in "Religion."

The moral consciousness, however, quickly starts to realize the inability for it to act since there is no harmony present between morality and Nature; thus, the best and most moral position is one of *non-action*. This results in Hegel's sardonic discussion of the "beautiful soul." The moral view comes to be manifest now as conscience. Having overcome the desire to place the onus of morality on some transcendent being, conscience believes that it can truly understand the right thing to do because conscience has "*immediate certainty* of itself" (Ibid., par. 637). Because this certainty is immediate, the "content of the moral action is the doer's own immediate *individuality*" (Ibid.). A few lines later this is clarified by stating "as conscience, it apprehends its *being-for-self* or its self. The contradiction of the moral consciousness *resolves itself*" (Ibid., par. 638). This resolution, though, only occurs by abandoning the universal morality originally pursued and turning inward. That is, it "runs away into pure negativity; but this precisely is the self, a simple *self* which is both a *pure* knowing and a knowledge of itself as this *individual* consciousness" (Ibid.). What this means is that the inner conscience of the individual has decided it no longer needs to aim toward some higher goal of moral perfection because conscience itself has achieved a perfect understanding of morality. Conscience becomes overly self-confident. The pitfall of this confidence is that conscience does not realize that understanding the best moral perspective for itself is still entirely too narrow a view for Spirit as a whole. While the negative of the universal is clearly understood to be the singular, this is not *recognized* by conscience—individual conscience feels synonymous with the universal without realizing the difference between itself and the universal—and there is no intimacy between the individual and the universal which led to this. Rather, there is a rejection of the universal and a retreat to its negative which is blind to the relation between the two. This individual conscience can thus always justify its actions; "Duty is no longer the universal that stands over against the self... It is now the law that exists for the sake of the self, not the self that exists for the sake of the law" (Ibid., par. 639). One would expect that there is thus no longer any friction, but even if conscience has managed to escape into moral solipsism it is not full solipsism, as it still realizes itself as a "being-for-another" in the community of Spirit. That is, even if conscience judges an action to be appropriate, it still realizes that the rest of the community might disagree with this judgment.

If every individual believes themselves to be able to judge their own moral actions, but also realizes that this capacity for judgment is extended onto all others, then everything comes to a standstill. The potential for inconsistency between one individual's moral appraisal and another's is very real and looms over the relationship of the community as a whole. The relationship between universal consciousness and individual consciousness, then:

> *... is really a relation of complete disparity, as a result of which the consciousness which is explicitly aware of the action finds itself in a state of complete uncertainty about the Spirit which does the action and is certain of itself. The latter acts, it gives being to a specific content; others hold to this being as this Spirit's truth, and are therein certain of this Spirit; it has declared therein what it holds to be duty. But it is free from any specific duty; it is not present at that point where others imagine it actually to be; and this very medium of being, and duty as something pos-*

sessing intrinsic being, counts for it only as a moment. (Ibid., par. 648)

Therefore, if a person were to act upon the moral precedence of their own conscience, others would interpret this as the universal moral action. The problem is, though, that they also realize that this is *not* the universal action since any individual is only acting based on their own conscience at this stage in "Morality." Any action would only be a "moment" of moral Spirit. Luckily, language appears on the scene so that it might be possible for recognition between individuals to occur; "Language is self-consciousness existing *for others*, self-consciousness which *as such* is immediately *present*, and as *this* self-consciousness is universal" (Ibid., par. 652). Language is thus crucial, as it serves as the means to establish the recognition of the universality of the singular and vice-versa. Language serves as the initial medium of intimacy between Subjects. However, as Hegel so elegantly puts it, "Moral consciousness on the other hand, is still *dumb*, shut up with itself within its inner life, for there the self does not as yet have an existence: existence and the self stand as yet only in external relation to each other" (Ibid., par. 653). Thus, even though language is now serving as medium, it is only serving as a medium for expressing the conviction of a given individual's conscience.[104] However,

---

[104] One point where Russon does consider the impact of Hegel's "Religion" section is when he claims that religion establishes the best form of communication for Spirit, writing, "Hegel's phenomenology of religion is essentially the phenomenology of systems of human communication -- systems of language. Religion is precisely the system of discourse according to which we communicate ourselves to ourselves" (Russon 2001, 122). It is unclear why he believes that this refined communication would only be possible in religion, given that he also holds that moral forgiveness is a more total forgiveness than we are willing to concede. It would seem that the forgiveness he believes to be taking place in "Morality" would have

this intimacy between Subjects is still incomplete or vulgarized as each party is only vainly attempting to prove themselves to one another, having realized that each individual is equally morally conscientious and thus capable of validating the moral convictions of each other. At this point, language is being utilized primarily for voicing one's own opinions rather than for understanding the other.

Conscience and the expression of conviction then become less about recognition with the other and more about *distinction from* the other. Conscience is, "its own self divine worship, for its action is the contemplation of its own divinity" (Ibid., par. 655). Even though the divine self-worship is actually simultaneously the worship of Spirit (or community), this simultaneity is only clear to consciousness, not self-consciousness. The universality recognized by conscience is a narcissistic one in which negation is overlooked and the incomplete conscience only affirms *itself* as the universal. Put in this position, conscience now becomes the "beautiful soul" as it "lives in dread of besmirching the splendour of its inner being by action and an existence; and, in order to preserve the purity of its heart, it flees from contact with the actual world" (Ibid., par. 658). Those who still hold firm to duty, though, accuse the beautiful soul that its conscience is being hypocritical in claiming to be moral without ever acting.[105] The univer-

---

to presuppose the system of discourse that he does not believe comes on the scene until "Religion." Russon seems to be arguing that religion as discourse is only possible after the total recognition that occurs in "Morality." However, we are arguing that the moment of forgiveness in 'Morality" is the communication which precipitates total reconciliation of Subject and Substance in "Religion."

[105] Comay brilliantly explains this duplicity of the beautiful soul when she compares it to a literary critic who never attempts to write (Comay 2010, 120). By never acting, the beautiful soul preserves itself but also loses all intimacy with the morality it claims to be slave to.

sal consciousness of duty thus claims that the beautiful soul is in fact evil. Of course, this judgment too is only a subjective judgment based on interpretation of duty.

As we see in the text, though, it is also the individual of action—who equally personifies universal consciousness of duty—who eventually realizes his or her own wickedness and admits this. The individual of action, in realizing this, gives a confession of guilt, believing that the beautiful soul of the judging conscience will also confess his/her own guilt (Ibid., par. 666). What is important to note here is that this first confession on the part of the individual of action, and any subsequent confession, only takes place through language. That is, only by being able to relate intimately to another individual in a way which discloses the attitude of equality between opposites does it become possible for the opportunity of forgiveness to arise. Yet, despite this, the confession by the individual of action does not trigger a confession on the part of the judging beautiful soul. The beautiful soul has become the "hard heart" which "is *for itself*, and which rejects any continuity with the other" (Ibid., par. 667).

Even though the beautiful soul understands that morality is universal and thus has some understanding of the fact that it is one and the same with the individual of action, the beautiful soul still clings to its being-for-self. That is, the beautiful soul denies Spirit as a whole, it denies the community which it knows it is a part of. However, the beautiful soul cannot truly exist apart from the community and this contradiction drives the beautiful soul to insanity and consumption over its inability to maintain this position of denial toward the individual of action (Ibid., par. 668). That is, the beautiful soul is not truly itself if it is not being perceived as the beautiful soul by the rest of the community. By alienating itself from the individual of action it has removed that potential for being perceived by this member of the community. Thus, the only way to achieve the recognition sought after by the beautiful soul is to soften its heart and externalize itself in the act of forgiveness. Both the beautiful soul and the individual of action are now free of their hard heartedness, the latter's heart having been hardened after the former took such pause to acknowledge and reciprocate the act of confession. What breaks the hard heartedness of both is the intimacy of the two, the universality which both recognize in the moments wherein they both negated the other. The intimacy is here taking the form of the undeniable way that each is intagliated with the other: The beautiful soul *needs* to be a member of the same community as the individual of action and likewise the individual of action *needs* for the action to be forgiven so that he or she can once again be welcomed into the community. Both parties then realize that the only way to mend this issue is through forgiveness. When each side recognizes they are each discrete individualities as well as universals (the community), they begin to realize not only the capacity for true recognition but the necessity of it. The mutual rejection of each other is ironically the first step to recognition because they both understand the rejection. Thus, they realize that this recognition arises through negation. When each side realizes that this negation is universal, that this is what allows for the individuality, it is at this point that universality is recognized. As Hegel writes:

> *Both determinatenesses are thus pure conscious Notions, whose determinateness is itself immediately a knowing, or whose relationship and antithesis is the 'I'. Consequently, they are these sheer opposites for one another; it is the completely inner being which thus confronts its own self and enters into outer existence. (Ibid., par. 671)*

This moment must be followed by an act which works to concretize this, however, and this is the act of forgiveness. In this act of reconciliation, both sides acknowledge themselves in the other and renounce the perception that they are completely antithetical to one another. This does not mean that intimacy is complete or that both are completely unified; what this means is that the ever present notion of alienation and negation from the other is recognized as being universal, and as something which must be continuously dealt with and understood.

So why is it being argued that this recognition is one primarily of Subject and not Substance? Part of this is because Hegel claims that "The word of reconciliation is the *objectively* existent Spirit, which beholds the pure knowledge of itself *qua universal* essence, in its opposite, in the pure knowledge of itself *qua* absolutely self-contained and exclusive *individuality*—a reciprocal recognition which is *absolute* Spirit" (Ibid., par. 670). This is all well and good and does nothing to contradict any of the previous statements about the power of forgiveness. However, the fact that this is the recognition of Spirit as "essence" seems to distinguish itself from being truly universal, that is, it still distinguishes itself from Nature. If this distinction holds, then it means that Spirit—as the essence of moral duty—is distinct from the recognition of sensuous universality. The recognition of one's self in the community through negation is different from the recognition of one's self in the substance of the typewriter through negation. The former is a recognition of one's self as a Subject among others, the latter is a recognition of one's self through Substance. Russon claims that the "Spirit" chapter works to elaborate "the self as it exists in a community of selves that support each other's self-certainty through institutionalized structures of recognition" (Russon 2001, 108). On this much we agree with Russon; however, when he claims that the body has been recognized *as* social institutions, we would like to argue that when the body is recognized as social institution, this is not a full recognition of the body or Substance. Russon impels us to realize that, after the moment of forgiveness, we have progressed away from understanding the "body as nature" and have realized the "body as history" (Ibid.). However, we are of the position that the body does not become understood historically until "Religion," when the incarnate God becomes a *part of* history. That is, it is not until Substance is understood to embody Subject *in* history that the intimacy of Subject and Substance is completely established.

Malabou understands forgiveness to work in a similar way, stating, "Forgiveness is 'the work of reconciliation' as the subjectively *and* objectively 'existent Spirit.' The subject of confession opens himself to the substance of community" (Malabou 2011, 25). Thus, like Russon, Malabou seems to hold the position that substantial recognition occurs in the moment when the individual recognizes himself or herself in the community. How is the community closer to the Nature which the moral soul has thus far rejected? Moreover, how is it that the amorphous "community" is here able to stand in for Substance? It would be a very neat and tidy thing indeed for the community to represent the substance needed for a complete moment of forgiveness, but we are incredulous toward this reading. When Hegel shows us how forgiveness is the act of reconciliation between the subjectively and objectively existent Spirit, this is taking place solely in terms of Subject. The subjective Subject (individual of action) must reconcile itself with the objective Subject (the beautiful soul who represents the judgment from the community). This is a powerful moment indeed, but one which is still operating on the assumption of a postulated unity with Nature. Thus, while this act of forgiveness does describe an intimacy between Subjects, it still ignores the sensuous part of ourselves which inhabits, and lives as a part of, history.

Thus, we end with the gesture toward the necessity of "Religion," through which the perfect recognition occurs at the moment when God is made incarnate and facilitates the full reconciliation of Subject and Substance. While it is worth noting that Malabou does insist upon the essentiality of the "Religion" section, this is because, for her, the arrival of the incarnate God affords the individual with the opportunity to have their forgiveness witnessed by the highest authority: "It is God who forgives; it is God who is the witness" (Ibid.).

While God's status as witness is indeed crucial, we are arguing that what is more crucial is understanding God's status as being incarnate *while* witnessing and forgiving. Russon seems to overlook how, in terms of Substantial recognition, the "Religion" section serves a purpose in advancing Spirit. Thus, to summarize our position up to this point: yes, Substance is present in the moment of recognition afforded by the forgiveness at the end of "Morality." However, this recognition is one which operates upon a subsumption of Substance into Subject—that is, Substance is only a part of a posited unity in "Morality." Therefore, the true recognition of Substance has yet to occur. Without the recognition of Substance there is no possibility of a complete forgiveness, as forgiveness is dependent upon identifying fully with the negative and realizing it as negative. Working out how "Religion" works to resolve this lack of material intimacy will be our next task.

The Incarnation

The incarnation serves as the moment when Spirit has progressed to the point wherein it truly acknowledges the sensuous and understands its negation to be the affirmation of universality. There are three revelations which occur in Spirit once God has become incarnate. The first of which directly deals with the fact that Spirit has yet to fully embrace the universality of Spirit and knows itself only as self-consciousness which is distinct from the embodied God. It is perhaps exactly this embodiment which is the problem, as Hegel writes, "Spirit in the immediacy of self-consciousness, is *this individual* self-consciousness, and so in an antithesis to the universal self-consciousness. It is an exclusive One or unit which has the still unresolved form of sensuous 'other' for the consciousness for which it is immediately present" (Hegel 1977, par. 762). The fact that the sensuous is still understood as "other" confirms that it is thus unresolved at this point in Spirit; "This 'other' does not as yet know Spirit as its own i.e. Spirit as an individual Self is not yet equally the universal Self, the Self of everyone" (Ibid., par. 762). Therefore, against Malabou and Russon's readings, the Subjective recognition that occurred when the individual recognized himself in the community is still not a recognition of Substance. However, it is not until after the Subjective recognition in "Morality" that we are able to properly reflect on the incarnation of God. The recognition afforded through God's forgiveness is one which is only possible through being incarnate—moreover, it is the sacrifice of one body which serves as the forgiveness and recognition of sin for all bodies in the biblical narrative. Similarly, Spirit has to recognize itself as unique and universal Substance in order for the recognition afforded by forgiveness to be complete. If God were simply a non-sensuous force or mind, then it might be possible for the individual of action or the beautiful soul (post-forgiveness) to realize their universal relationship to this God. However, the embodiment poses a problem because the recognition which occurred in "Morality" was grounded in the mental rather than the sensuous. Spirit is now ready to be pushed toward a total recognition through recognition of this sensuous incarnation.

The second revelation is precisely the point when "This individual man, then, which absolute Being has revealed itself to be, accomplishes in himself as an individual the movement of sensuous Being. He is the *immediately* present God; consequently his '*being*' passes over into '*having been*'" (Ibid., par. 763). This seems to be where the "body as history" is actually recognized. That is, once God becomes incarnate, God possesses a history and a body that *experiences* history sensuously; "Consciousness, for which God is thus sensuously present, ceases to see and to hear Him; it *has* seen and heard Him; and it is because it only *has* seen and heard Him that it first becomes spiritual consciousness" (Ibid., par. 763). Spirit has to come to the point of realizing both its sensuous and essential universality because the incarnate God is inciting a *historical* notion of Spirit. We are not the atemporal minds that view the world as if from a distance, nor is this—

any longer—an area of our being where God exceeds us. We and God are now alike in being historical Substances, this is the initial window into recognition of Spirit as Substance.

However, these temporal experiences which one is removed from only provide an *immediate* realization and do not fully grasp the mediation and negation at work; "it is merely dipped superficially in the element of Thought, is preserved in it *as* a sensuous mode, and not made one with the nature of Thought itself" (Ibid., par. 764). We are thus currently in a state similar to the postulated unity, except this time it is an immediate unity which lacks reflection. Much like a novice scotch drinker can enjoy the taste of scotch without being able to reflect upon the different types of flavors which comprise the scotch. Similarly, Hegel argues that the immediate realization of the connection between Substance and Subject is understood as "a given." Hegel's term for this unreflective thought is "picture-thinking," or figurative knowledge, where we contemplate the physical from a distance rather than recognize the mediation that is occurring. The "picture" of the connection between Substance and Subject is presented to us, and we *see* it, but we do not actively understand or reflect upon it. The sensuous/essential relationship is perceived as an immediate relationship that has no negation or mediation in picture-thinking. Spirit must move beyond this picture-thinking to the point where it can realize the way in which both Subject and Substance are negating and sublating one another as universal in the incarnate God.

The third revelation occurs when Spirit realizes that it must move past these pictorial representations and see the truth of the relationship. The reason for this realization is that, from the perspective of picture-thinking, the power of the incarnation comes in the fact that it shows God to be completely universal. That is, it shows that God participates in everything, even the "evil" that Nature is susceptible to: "Absolute Being would be but an empty name if in truth there were for it an 'other', if there were a 'fall' from it; on the contrary, the moment of *being-within-self* constitutes the essential moment of the *Self* of Spirit" (Ibid., par. 780). Thus, God had to be incarnate as what is perceived to be its opposite to show that there is no such thing that could be understood as opposite to Absolute Being. In this way God is "reconciled" with "evil"; after all, "If Evil is the same as Goodness, then Evil is just not Evil, nor Goodness Good: on the contrary, both are suspended moments—Evil in general is self-centered being-for-self, and Goodness is what is simple and without a self" (Ibid., par. 780).

The problem with this picture-thinking is that one cannot simply think of Goodness and Evil as being identical nor as incommensurate; "Neither the one nor the other has truth; the truth is just their movement in which simple sameness is an abstraction and hence absolute difference, but this, as difference in itself, is distinguished from itself and is therefore selfsameness" (Ibid., par. 780). Moreover, Hegel claims that this same conundrum holds for the relationship between Being and Nature (Ibid.). Indeed, the problem that is borne out of our picture-thinking's characterization of universality, which leads to the extreme night in which all cows are black, is that we are "clinging to the 'is' and forgetting the thinking of the Notions in which the moments just as much *are* as they *are not*—are only the movement which is Spirit" (Ibid.). Thus, what must be realized is not that Spirit *is* Subject and Substance, nor that one or the other is wrong, but that both perspectives are right and are not, and that it is in this way that they each require the constant negating from the other which leads to the sublimation of Spirit.

This realization, however, does not occur until the incarnate God, who is understood as the Mediator which incites this spiritual unity, dies. The realization that God is dead is the "expression of the innermost simple self-knowledge, the return of consciousness into the depths of night in which 'I=I', a night which no longer distinguishes or knows anything outside of it" (Ibid., par. 785). It would seem as if we were back to dealing with the problems of picture-thinking now that the "I=I" is truly that which perceives nothing to be alien from it. We already know that this is too extreme, for there is no distinction at all, no negation. If the death of God results in the loss of Substance, or rather the subsumption of Substance in Subject once again, then we have not made any real progress. However, Hegel claims that:

> *This feeling is, in fact, the loss of substance and of its appearance over against consciousness; but it is at the same time the pure subjectivity of substance, or the pure certainty of itself which it lacked when it was object, or the immediate, or pure essence. This Knowing is the inbreathing of the Spirit, whereby Substance becomes Subject, by which its abstraction and lifelessness have died, and Substance therefore has become actual and simple and universal Self-consciousness.*
> (Ibid.)

This is where the recognition which happened in part in "Morality" is finally fully present. We finally have the recognition of the universality and negation of Subject and Substance occurring in Spirit. It is not until this knowledge is attained—the knowledge that God has died and universality and negation have been witnessed—that the "inbreathing of Spirit" occurs so that Substance is understood as Subject *through negation*. The fact that Substance becomes actual through the death of its "abstraction and lifelessness" shows that what was needed was for the conception of Substance as *completely* distinct from Subject to be negated.

Absolute Intimacy

Despite this, even the incarnation and the Substantial reconciliation it affords is still not complete. The religious community takes this reconciliation too metaphorically, to use

Hegel's terminology, it remains only a "picture-thought." "This unity of essence and the Self having been *implicitly* achieved, consciousness, too, still has this *picture-thought* of its reconciliation, but as a picture-thought" (Ibid., par. 787). Here we see that it is not even at the end of "Religion" that the reconciliation of Substance and Subject is complete. After all, Hegel clearly states that even the realization of the relationship between Subject and Substance exemplified by the incarnation leaves the religious community lacking complete *actual* recognition, "What enters [the community's] consciousness as the in-itself, or the side of *pure* mediation, is a reconciliation that lies in the beyond: but what enters it as *present*, as the side of *immediacy* and *existence*, is the world which still has to await its transfiguration" (Ibid., par. 787). If Subject and Substance have finally been recognized as universal, then it seems as though the story of the progression of Spirit should be over. Yet the problem remains that this is only an implicit realization achieved through picture-thinking which still defers an actual unity into some distant *beyond*. The intimacy is *felt* but not actualized, and to this extent is still not a complete intimacy. This is similar to being shown the steps to solve a math problem versus actually knowing how to solve the problem. Picture-thinking is the implicit understanding of what has happened, just as we might understand that after the mathematician has completed her calculus she has found a solution. However, what Hegel wants is for this implicit understanding to be an active one, Hegel wants us to understand the calculus of Spirit for ourselves. Absolute Knowing is the final stage when self-consciousness fully and actively recognizes itself as both Subject and Substance.

In "Absolute Knowing" Hegel once again retraces the path of Spirit through its many shapes until finally "The self-knowing spirit knows not only itself but also the negative of itself, or its limit: to know one's limit is to know how to sacrifice oneself. This sacrifice is the externalization in which Spirit displays the process of its becoming Spirit in the form of *free contingent happening*, intuiting its pure Self as Time outside of it, and equally its Being as Space" (Ibid., par. 807). Once Spirit realizes itself through its externalizations it has finally actively realized itself through negation. Thus the intimacy we were pursuing seems complete, we have realized that all happenings, all externalizations, are all affirmations of Spirit through negation. Nature, as externalized Spirit, becomes through its existence "the movement which reinstates the *Subject*" (Ibid.).

Yet this intimacy, once it has become immediately both Subject and Substance, also becomes *History*, because the self-mediation which occurs immediately in the free contingent happenings of Spirit now places the Spirit in *Time* as opposed to in a beyond (Ibid., par. 808). However, in being placed in Time, Spirit now realizes that due to its presence in all free contingent happening, that this kenosis of itself into Time is an externalization which places Spirit in a "gallery of images", each of which is a full externalization—and thus negation/affirmation—of Spirit (Ibid.). Thus the Self now has to move through this History, or gallery, so as to recognize itself; "As its fulfillment consists in perfectly *knowing* what *it is*, in knowing its substance, this knowing is its *withdrawal into itself* in which in abandons its outer existence and gives its existential shape over to recollection" (Ibid.). It is hard to tell if this is a beneficial or detrimental movement for Spirit as it is now clearly most intimate to itself, but this new desire for recollection of itself is also no longer externalized, it is only recounting its previous externalizations. Thus, "Spirit starts afresh and apparently from its own resources to bring itself into maturity," and this "maturity" is the seeking out and revelation of "the depth of Spirit, and this is *the absolute Notion*" (Ibid.). Here, finally, we have the final movement of Spirit, once it has progressed through its history and learned its essence, been truly reconciled with itself, it can finally move on; "This revelation is, therefore, the raising up of its depth, or its *extension*, the negativity of this withdrawn 'I', a negativity which is its externalization or its substance" (Ibid.). At long last, Spirit is able to move forward, yet it does this while always being aware of both itself and the negative of itself, of both its history and its present free contingent happening. The intimacy of Spirit is total and complete because it is never actually complete, or rather, it is both complete and incomplete; the most perfect intimacy is the one which establishes this relationship and recognition through the negative, or the other.

Conclusion

As the result of all this we have hopefully shown that the act of forgiveness is not as complete as it may seem when it first occurs. While the forgiveness was definitely the most crucial development in Spirit, we disagree with Russon about the completeness of this forgiveness. As it occurs at the end of "Morality," forgiveness is the recognition which still subsumes Substance into Subject as a postulated unity rather than letting the negation of each by the other be equally positive. The reconciliation hoped for at the end of "Morality" only becomes implicitly true at the very end of "Religion," once the incarnate God has come and gone for the religious community. This implicit recognition does not become actual until the moment of Absolute Knowing, when Spirit finally realizes its absolute Notion, which is the revelation of the depth of itself as it is throughout its history of free contingent happening. However, simply diagramming the development of Spirit was not the goal of this endeavor. We hoped that by carefully examining the text we could show that "Morality" leaves us with an incomplete forgiveness because it is not yet aware that it lacks a recognition of Substance.

When Bukowski wrote that the "sickness" of the writer is there with or without the typewriter, but that the typewriter *makes the writer a writer,* he perhaps implicitly understood the kind of intimacy between Subject and Substance that we believe Hegel to be putting forth. However, it was Hegel who showed how this intimacy functions and why it is that maybe the sickness of needing Substance is just the condition of being Subject (and vice versa).

References

Bukowski, Charles. 1986. *You Get So Alone at Times that it Just Makes Sense*. Santa Rosa: Black Sparrow Press.

Comay, Rebecca. 2010. *Mourning Sickness: Hegel and the French Revolution*. Stanford: Stanford University Press.

Hegel, G.W. F. 1977. *Phenomenology of Spirit*. Translated by A.V. Miller. Oxford England: Clarendon Press.

Malabou, Catherine. 2011. "Is Confession the Accomplishment of Recognition? Rousseau and the Unthought of Religion in the *Phenomenology of Spirit*." *Hegel & the Infinite: Religion, Politics, and Dialectic*. Edited by Clayton Crockett, Creston Davis, and Slavoj Žižek. New York: Columbia University Press.

Russon, John. 2001. *The Self and its Body in Hegel's Phenomenology of Spirit*. Toronto: University of Toronto Press.

Index

A

action, 16–34, 51–73, 78–136, 152–85, 188–236, 243–67, 287–302
Adams, Marilyn, 69
aesthetic model, 60, 61, 67
aesthetics, viii, x, 52, 63
Agamben, Giorgio, 240
agency, x, 21, 31, 93, 94, 95, 96, 98, 294
Annas, Julia, 69
apology, xi, 67, 68, 73, 74, 75, 76, 77, 79, 81, 83, 84, 117, 202, 210
appropriation, 105, 106, 204, 205
Arendt, Hannah, 213, 240
Aristotle, 51–70, 94–107, 223–40
attitudes, 18–22, 47–71, 109–25, 129–38
Augustine, 162, 183, 184
Austin, J.L., 43

B

Baehr, Jason, 159
Baier, Annette, 159
Bandes, Susan, 213
Bataille, George, 213
BBC News, 109, 139
Beatty, Joseph, 184
Bell, Mcalester, 85
Bennington, Geoffrey, 286
Bentham, Jeremy, 43
Bergo, Bettina, 286
Blustein, Jeffrey, 107
Brown, Wendy, 213
Bukowski, Charles, 315
Butler, Joseph, 69
by proxy, 35, 37, 40

C

calculation, 51, 147, 203, 271, 272, 273, 274, 275, 276, 283
Canetti, Elias, 213
Caputo, John, 286
Cavarero, Adriana, 213
Caygill, Howard, 213
change of heart, 169, 178, 179, 246
character, 38–51, 63–85, 101–18, 129–42, 177–202
Charlie Hebdo, 16
Cohen, Roger, 240
Comay, Rebecca, 315
conditional, 203, 204, 211, 242, 252, 259, 261, 262, 263, 264, 269, 271, 272, 275, 283
congruence, 121, 122, 123, 129, 137
Cosmopolitanism, xiii, 43, 213, 261, 262, 265, 269, 286
credit of trust, 182
Crespo, Mariano, 184
Crosby, John, 184

D

Dan-Cohen, Meir, 265
Darwall, Steven, 43
Davidson, Donald, 43, 139

deconstruction, 248, 268, 270, 271, 275
Deleuze, Gilles, 213
Derrida, Jacques, 43, 213, 265, 286, 287
Deutscher, Penelope, 286
diachronic, 123, 124, 125
Dickey, Walter J., 43
Dietz, Mary, 240
Dillon, Robin, 107
dispositions, xi, 92, 93, 109, 118, 119, 120, 125, 128
disvalue, 156, 157, 163, 167, 171, 173, 174, 176, 179
Dostoevsky, Fyodor, 43
Dougherty, Kathleen Poorman, 107
Douzinas, Costas, 213

E

Eliot, George, 43
emotions, 16, 18, 19, 23, 48, 49, 50, 54, 61, 62, 67, 72, 77, 78, 80, 83, 93, 126, 232
Enright, Robert D., 43
epistemic, ix–xii, 47–51, 130–32, 141–55, 155–58
etiquette, 114
eudaimonia, 51, 53, 54, 59, 60
eunoia, 56, 58, 59, 61
evil, 71–73, 162–84, 195–226, 230–38, 302–10
Exeline, Joula J., 213

F

Feather, N.T, 43
Feinberg, Joel, 43
Ferrer, Urbano, 184
Firth, Roderick, 159
Fitzgibbons, Richard, 43

Flannigan, Beverly, 43
Forgiveness, ix, 241
Forgivingness, 119, 123, 124, 127, 129, 134, 139, 185
Forgivingness economic model of, 115, 116
French, Peter, 107
Frye, Marilyn, 43

G

Garrard, Eve, 69
Gibbard, Allan, 44
gift, 166–83, 205–11, 234–50, 257–83
good will, 57, 109, 162, 163, 173
Green, Jeffrey D, 44
Griswold, Charles L., 44, 139

H

Haber, Joram Graf, 69
Hacking, Ian, 44
Hagberg, Garry L., 44
Hampton, Jean, 85, 184
harm, 28–79, 87–101, 163–202, 238–75
Haslanger, Sally, 44
Hawley, Katherine, 159
Heil, John, 159
Hieronymi, Pamela, 85
Hildebrand, Dietrich von, 184
Hill, Thomas E. Jr., 43
Hollander, Dana, 265
Holmgren, Margaret, 85, 107, 184
Holmstrom, Nancy, 139
Holton, Richard, 159
Homer, 243, 265

Index

hospitality, xiii, xiv, 242, 259, 260, 261, 262, 263, 264, 269, 270, 282
Hughes, Paul M., 107
Hursthouse, Rosalind, 69

I

im/possible, xiii, 242, 247, 249, 252, 253, 256, 258, 260, 262, 263, 264
impossibility, 23–24, 79–176, 203–47, 267–96
impossible, xiii–xiv, 18–24, 80–101, 101–42, 161–82, 193–204, 246–97
interdependence, 118, 123, 125, 126, 129
intimacy, ix–xiii, 141–55, 157–205, 289–304, 304–15
ISIS, 16, 28

J

Jacobi, Susan, 184
Jaeger, Marietta, 43
Jankélévitch, Vladimir, 184, 265, 286
Johansson, Ingvar, 69
Jollimore, Troy, 159
Jones, Karen, 159
justice, vii–xiv, 7–14, 148–63, 188–216, 247–72, 278–85
justification, 77, 113, 121, 151, 152, 155, 157, 194, 230, 258, 259

K

Kahn, Leonard, 44
Kalimtzis, Kostas, 69
kalokagathia, 52, 53, 58, 59, 67, 69

Kant, Immanuel, 240, 265
Keller, Simon, 159
Knott, Marie Luise, 240
Kolnai, Auriel, 184
Konstan, David, 69, 70
Kraut, Richard, 70
Kristeva, Julia, 265

L

Lafitte, Jean, 184
Lander Philosophy, 133, 139
law, vii–viii, 112–14, 188–226, 230–60, 261–300
Leder, Helmut, 70
Lerman, David M., 214
Levy, Neil, 44

M

Macey, David, 287
magic, xiii, 215, 217, 223, 226, 238
Malabou, Catherine, 315
Martin, Adrienne, 85
Mauss, Marcel, 214
Mautner, Thomas, 287
McGeer, Victoria, 159
mercy, 57, 102, 103, 119, 275
Mill, John Stuart, 44
Milliken, John, 70
Morin, E., 184
mortal sin, 275
Moss, Jessica, 70
Murdoch, Iris, 139
Murphy, Ann V., 287
Murphy, Jeffrie G., 44, 139

N

narrative, xiii, 60, 105, 106, 124, 125, 200, 308

O

objective evil, 164, 167, 176
Oliver, Kelly, 265
Ophir, Orna, 265
other, vii–xii, 18–78, 80–151, 155–224, 231–98, 304–14

P

Parfit, Derek, 44
partiality, 146, 147, 148, 149, 150, 151, 152
Peperzak, Adrian, 287
person, 17–78, 81–155, 155–228, 230–301
Petrochilos, George, 70
Pettigrove, Glen, 85
Pfänder, Alexander, 185
phronesis, ix, 54, 56, 60
possibility, ix–xiv, 22–48, 81–132, 187–220, 234–94, 234–94
possible, viii–x, 16–76, 80–152, 163–210, 241–302, 303–8
Proimos, Constantinos V., 70
psychoanalysis, 248, 249, 251
purification of memory, 162, 163, 164, 173, 177, 181

R

Radzick, Linda, 44
reconciliation, 49, 89, 111, 134, 143, 162, 202, 204, 252, 254, 272, 274, 278, 291, 293, 302, 304, 305, 306, 311, 314
Reinach, Adolf, 185
repentance, 74, 75, 84, 164, 165, 167, 168, 169, 171, 172, 173, 174, 178, 179, 202, 203, 210, 262
responsibility, ix–x, 15–16, 74–107, 173–202, 247–83
resentment, 15–79, 79–135, 161–213
Reynolds, Jack, 287
Ricoeur, Paul, 70, 185, 214
Riggs, Wayne, 159
Robert, William, 265
Roberts, Robert, 139, 185
Roberts-Cady, Sarah, 139
Russon, John, 315

S

Scanlon, T.M., 44
Scarre, Geoffrey, 44
Scheler, Max, 185
Searle, John R., 44
self, vii–xii, 39–61, 79–132, 165–225, 231–303, 304–13
self-conception, 96
self-respect, 89, 96
Shakespeare, William, 45
Smith, Angela M., 45
Smith, James K., 288
Smith, Sean, 107
Snow, Nancy, 107
social act, 164, 166, 167, 168, 169
solicitude, 56, 57, 58, 59, 61, 69
Solomon, Robert, 45
sovereignty, 225, 241, 250, 253, 258, 260, 261, 264, 270, 272, 274, 277
Spaemann, Robert, 185
standing to, x, 17, 25, 26, 27, 28, 29, 32, 33, 34, 35, 36, 37, 38, 39
Stich, Stephen, 45

Strawson, Peter, 45
Stroud, Sarah, 159
Swinburne, Richard, 45
Swondon, Paul, 45
synchronic, 123, 124
Szablowinski, Zenon, 107

T

Tännsjö, Torbjörn, 45
third-party, x, 16, 17, 23, 27, 28, 30, 31, 32, 33, 37, 38, 39, 147
Trevor, William, 107
trust, xii, 141, 142, 143, 144, 145, 146, 149, 152, 154, 155, 157, 158, 176, 182
trustworthiness, xii, 141, 142, 152, 157
Tutu, Desmond, 45

U

unconditional, xiii, 59, 65, 84, 142, 203, 204, 211, 242, 250, 252, 258, 259, 260, 261, 262, 263, 269, 273, 274, 276, 277, 278, 279, 283, 284, 285
undecidability, 246, 271, 277, 279
uniqueness, xii, 189, 190, 191, 192, 196, 197, 198, 200, 208, 210, 211, 212, 222
utilitarianism, 91

V

value, 41, 56, 58, 59, 113, 116, 121, 135, 152, 155, 156, 157, 168, 169, 170, 176, 178, 179, 180, 181, 182
Vanhoozer, Kevin, 70
Velleman, J. David, 139
Verdeja, Ernesto, 288
Vetlesen, Arne Johan, 45
Vice, Samantha, 107
virtue ethics, 69
voice, vii–xii, 201–13
vulnerability, xii, 135, 146, 187, 189, 190, 192, 193, 196, 197, 198, 199, 200, 202, 209, 210, 212

W

Warmke, Brandon, 139
Warnock, G.J., 45
Weiler, Ingomar, 70
Wojtyla, Karol, 185
Wood, Robert, 70
wrongdoing, 52–73, 96–138, 163–93

Y

Yandall, Keith E, 45

Z

Zaibert, Leo, 139
Zirión, Antonio, 185

www.ingramcontent.com/pod-product-compliance
Lightning Source LLC
Chambersburg PA
CBHW072121290426
44111CB00012B/1740